D0211312

GET WHAT'S YOURS FOR HEALTH CARE

HOW TO GET THE BEST CARE AT THE RIGHT PRICE

Philip Moeller

SIMON & SCHUSTER

New York   London   Toronto   Sydney   New Delhi

Simon & Schuster
1230 Avenue of the Americas
New York, NY 10020

First Simon & Schuster hardcover edition January 2021

SIMON & SCHUSTER and colophon are registered trademarks
of Simon & Schuster, Inc.

For information about special discounts for bulk purchases,
please contact Simon & Schuster Special Sales at 1-866-506-1949
or business@simonandschuster.com.

The Simon & Schuster Speakers Bureau can bring authors to your
live event. For more information or to book an event, contact the
Simon & Schuster Speakers Bureau at 1-866-248-3049
or visit our website at www.simonspeakers.com.

Manufactured in the United States of America

10 9 8 7 6 5 4 3 2 1

Library of Congress Cataloging-in-Publication Data

ISBN 978-1-9821-3425-9
ISBN 978-1-9821-3428-0 (ebook)

To Cheryl, Kay, Daniel, and Jon—my heroes in all things

CONTENTS

PART THREE: NEW HEALTH CARE CHOICES

PART ONE

HEALTH INSURANCE BASICS

1

GAME ON

In 2019, Donna Ferguson was a poster child for America's out-of-control health care prices and the game-changing ways now emerging to find better and cheaper care. Her meme status stemmed from a story that explained how Ferguson's employer—privately held Ashley Furniture Industries in Wisconsin—had paid for her to fly to Cancun from her home in Mississippi and then put her up in a nearby Sheraton hotel. It flew in a surgeon trained at the Mayo Clinic, and paid him to give her a knee replacement that was free to her.

The quality of the surgery and her care were first-rate. The costs for the procedure at a nice hospital were so much cheaper than in the United States that Ashley, which self-insures its health care coverage, came out ahead—so far ahead that the company cut her a $5,000 check to reward her for her troubles!

In 2020, by sobering contrast, the COVID-19 pandemic took us back decades. There were shortages of critical-care equipment, hospital beds, and caregivers, plus tragic weaknesses in nursing homes. But we also saw what we had been missing in health care.

Dedicated and compassionate healers put their lives on the line. Hospitals, doctors' offices, pharmaceutical and insurance companies, and health care regulators relaxed or waived access and pricing rules so people could get protection and care. Health care heroes were everywhere. This was a health care system we could support.

Beyond the compassionate heroics, what was wrong with U.S. health care in 2019 is not only still wrong today but likely even worse. We have too few caregivers, rising affordability challenges, and a profit-driven system at odds with human needs. However, the pandemic also accelerated positive forces surrounding Ferguson's treatment. They can make health care work for us, not the other way around.

Get What's Yours for Health Care will explain what you can do right now to benefit from these changes. They are elements of a consumer-focused shift in care that is happening now and not waiting for government health reforms.

Self-insured employers like Ashley Furniture are beyond tired of paying out the nose for rising health costs. The tab for employer health insurance is about $700 billion a year and rising at double the rate of general inflation. This does not include the $375 billion in annual premiums and other out-of-pocket health care costs that we as employees pay.

Singly and in growing groups of like-minded organizations, employers are bypassing traditional health pathways. They are contracting directly with hospitals, doctors, and other providers of high-quality care at advantageous prices. These early adapters are proving how to save money—for themselves and their employees—while providing new incentives and decision-making tools that support healthier work forces.

Employer efforts to break the cycle of unsustainable health cost increases are hardly new, of course, so what's changed? The short answer is digitized information and "big data." It has taken hold of health care, just as it has other aspects of our lives.

The ability to capture and analyze massive amounts of health care information has guided existing companies and thousands of venture-backed start-ups to find ways to cut health waste and costs while improving the quality of care.

Within the medical community, this information has created pathways to evidence-based care. What works and what doesn't?

Where are doctors, hospitals, and other medical experts likely to make mistakes in their diagnoses and treatment recommendations? What does health care quality look like, which providers do it the best, and how can you find them?

The organizations and people who pay for health care—that means us!—are learning what care costs and not just what providers charge. Health insurers gather this information as part of their work to process and pay claims. They keep it to themselves, for privacy reasons and because the knowledge generated by their claims information is a competitive asset.

With self-insured plans, the insurers don't always call the shots. They work for employers under administrative service contracts. These employers thus have the opportunity to know the prices their health plans have agreed to pay doctors, hospitals, and other health care providers. Thanks to the enormously detailed coding systems for medical billing that are now standardized, they can get detailed apples-to-apples comparisons of health payments where their employees receive care.

Even without government involvement, health care is already being reformed. Compelling signs that major changes are near a tipping point were provided last spring when hospitals were flooded with COVID-19 victims and closed to routine care, as were doctors' offices.

Virtual health care, also known as telemedicine or telehealth, boomed. A study from management consultants at McKinsey & Company estimated that telehealth services soared in March 2020 from 0.2 percent to 7.5 percent of private health insurance claims. Total spending on telehealth, it projected, could rise to $250 billion a year, or nearly 100 times what had been forecast before the pandemic closed down much of the country.

Health providers "have rapidly scaled offerings and are seeing 50 to 175 times the number of patients via telehealth than they did before," the report said. Ten years of projected growth occurred in sixty days.

Healthcare Bluebook, based in Nashville, Tennessee, was formed in 2008 because cofounders Jeff Rice and Bill Kampine believed they could unlock the secrets of health care pricing, find employers and others willing to pay them for their efforts, and, in the process, create tools to help employees and consumers understand the true cost of health care and how to find care that was less expensive and higher in quality.

They explained their business to me last year in a company conference room. Rice used a black marker to draw a simple word graphic on a well-worn whiteboard. It had only four entries—two across the top and two on the bottom: The top entries were "Patients" and "Employers"; the bottom entries were "Hospitals" and "Insurers." Patients and employers are health care's payers; hospitals, other health providers, and insurers receive our money.

Once upon a time, he explained, employer-funded health insurance paid patients for their health costs, and the patients then paid their health care providers. Over time, the connecting lines between patients and providers and those between patients and insurers began to blur and eventually vanished. Providers and insurers today bypass us. They negotiate in secret with one another over what providers will be paid for care, and then insurers send the agreed-upon amounts directly to providers.

In theory, insurers work for employers and others who pay their premiums. In practice, this has not been the case. "Once insurer payments began going directly to providers, consumers lost control," Rice said. He then drew a new line on his whiteboard—a thick horizontal line separating patients and employers from providers and insurers. "All the money flows from the north to the south" of this line, he explained, and all the information about provider prices and final negotiated health costs stays on the south side of the line.

People pay close attention to their out-of-pocket costs and surveys chart rising health care affordability problems. Out-of-pocket costs, while certainly important, tell only part of the money story. They vastly understate the full costs of U.S. health care, which, as you'll soon see, have largely been hidden from us.

We spent an astronomical $3.6 trillion on health care in 2018, including nearly $3.1 trillion for personal care (the rest went for research and other indirect spending). We will pat ourselves on the back if this total grows by only $100 billion from one year to the next. Health care in this country costs roughly twice as much per person as it does in other developed countries. Imagine for a moment what we could do with an extra $1 trillion or $1.5 trillion *every* year! Education. Infrastructure. Clean energy. Add your spending wish here.

Here's a summary of personal care spending, including major payment sources:

2018 NATIONAL HEALTH SPENDING ($ BILLIONS)

	Total	Out of Pocket	Private Health Ins.	Medicare	Medicaid
Personal Health Care	3,075.0	375.6	1,078.7	697.2	532.8
Hospital Care	1,191.8	34.8	481.1	297.0	196.6
Physician and Clinical Services	725.6	61.2	311.8	170.2	77.4
Other Professional Services	103.9	26.1	35.1	27.2	7.5
Dental Services	135.6	54.9	62.2	1.2	12.8
Other Health, Residential, and Personal Care	191.6	6.8	13.6	4.9	111.1
Home Health Care	102.2	10.2	12.2	40.3	35.9
Nursing Care					
Retirement Communities	168.5	44.8	17.1	38.1	49.9

	Total	Out of Pocket	Private Health Ins.	Medicare	Medicaid
Retail Outlet Sales					
Prescription Drugs	335.0	47.1	134.3	107.2	33.4
Durable Medical Equipment	54.9	25.5	11.3	8.9	8.1
Other Non-Durable Medical	66.4	64.2	-	2.1	-

Source: Centers for Medicare & Medicaid Services

We spend a much smaller percentage of that $3.6 trillion on actual care than in other places, and more dollars on health care coding, billing, administration, and other profit-related work. There is a shortage of doctors in the United States, but this would be a smaller problem if they could spend less time on nonmedical work, as do their peers in other nations.

Do we at least get the best health care in the world for all that money? The answer is a resounding "No." Here are some metrics from the Organisation for Economic Co-operation and Development (OECD), which includes the United States and thirty-five other developed countries, mostly in Europe. In 2018, U.S. health spending totaled 16.9 percent of our economy, nearly double the OECD average of 8.8 percent. In 2017, the infant mortality rate in the United States ranked 31st among OECD members; we ranked 28th in life expectancy.

No other health system is so dominated by for-profit health care providers as is the United States'. They have powerful incentives to charge high and ever-rising prices and the ability to suck profits from the system. Public outrage has failed so far to produce change.

The reason is not a mystery. Reforms threaten health care businesses. They have developed extensive lobbying and public-influence operations to protect themselves. Do not expect them to voluntarily reduce their prices and profits. Instead, expect them to erect time-delaying barriers.

•   •   •

Life expectancy at birth in years, 2017

Japan	84.2
Switzerland	83.6
Australia	82.6
France	82.6
Sweden	82.5
Comparable Country Average	82.3
Canada	82.0
Netherlands	81.8
Austria	81.7
Belgium	81.6
United Kingdom	81.3
Germany	81.1
United States	78.6

Source: KFF analysis of OECD data

Peterson-KFF
Health System Tracker

If the national narrative on health care is so resistant to change and government is not able to act, what are we—consumers and patients—supposed to do? Do we even have it in us to take the fight to health care companies and help create a system that works better? Doing so will be unbelievably difficult because the U.S. health care system is stacked against us.

Study after study points to disappointing results when consumers are given the information and tools to make significant decisions about how they access care, choose providers, and pay them. But health care's current reality, my research found, differs from the rearview mirror view that supported these earlier findings. Using the tools of Healthcare Bluebook and others, companies and consumers can help lower costs—for themselves and other health consumers.

Right now, this effort is being led by those businesses that already are armed with this information and are using it to aggressively shop for health care. They are providing these same tools to their employees and, eventually, this health data will weaponize all consumers to help them get better health outcomes.

The people on the south side of Jeff Rice's Healthcare Bluebook line have worked hard so that you don't think or worry much about the nearly $2.6 trillion in personal care costs that don't come directly out of your pocket. Insurance companies have decided to hide these expenses as part of a codependent relationship with health providers that permits both to feed their money addictions. Look at the chart below and you'll see what a good job they've done.

The incredible shrinking act of out-of-pocket health expenses hardly means we're paying less for care. Just the opposite! *Get What's Yours* can help you even the playing field. Lots of the money health providers collect—easily more than **$1 trillion** a year—rightfully belongs in your pockets, not theirs.

Countless people are proving that consumers can beat the system, that superior care at reasonable prices is possible, and that we don't have to accept the status quo. They are a different breed of health care hero than the caregivers who manned the front lines during the heights of the pandemic. But they are heroes nonetheless.

Total national health expenditures, 1970 and 2018

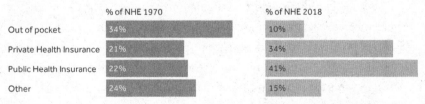

	% of NHE 1970	% of NHE 2018
Out of pocket	34%	10%
Private Health Insurance	21%	34%
Public Health Insurance	22%	41%
Other	24%	15%

Notes: Public insurance in 1970 includes Department of Veterans Affairs, Department of Defense, Medicare, and Medicaid. In 2018, public insurance includes the same categories listed for 1970, with the addition of CHIP. 'Other' includes third party payers and programs like worksite health care, the Indian Health Service, and other state and local programs.

Source: KFF analysis of National Health Expenditure (NHE) data

Peterson-KFF
Health System Tracker

I have found a lot of these people in my research. Many of them, like Rice, work for or even founded "disrupters"—companies trying to upend the system, often with a goal of making lots of money in the process. These entrepreneurs often are motivated by compelling personal health stories.

These heroes also may be found in patient advocate offices. They are the passionate voices heard in social media discussion and support groups. They work in thousands of patient-centric health agencies, nonprofits, and, yes, hospitals, clinics, medical offices, and yes once more, even for what are widely considered the "bad guys" of U.S. health care—insurance, drug, and medical equipment companies.

These heroes shop for the best deal and pore over health quality ratings. They appeal rejections of their insurance claims. They fight the government about which treatments and drugs are approved and the rules for how insurers help pay for them. They don't accept defeat or walk away—they speak up; they kick and scratch; they sue!

Their stories illustrate an evolving movement involving thousands of organizations and millions of engaged patients and consumers. View them not as the end of the transformation story. There will be more heroes and disrupters appearing each day.

As noted, these heroes are mastering data-fueled tools. Once these informational genies have been released, old ways of doing business will change forever.

I'm not suggesting that these tools are enough. Health reform is needed. The point here is that you can use these tools right now to achieve better health outcomes, easier access to care, and lower health care bills. If you do, you will be better off. You will be paying it forward for other health consumers. They will benefit from the changes you spearhead whether they know it or not.

Should we have to do these things to get the care we need? Of course not. *Get What's Yours for Health Care* is based on the system we've got, however, not on the one we'd like. To have the greatest impact, you need to look beyond your self-interest, beyond your own out-of-pocket costs, to the much larger pot of total costs that health providers collect for their services. Failing to do so will help perpetuate a business model that has been harmful to our health for many decades.

Mike Baker's day job has included overseeing the quality of consumer experiences provided to something like 50 million people who are customers of UnitedHealthcare, the largest private health insurer on the planet. Now, you might say, the bar must be set low for his work. We're talking about health insurance, right? Yet of all the people whose views and research are included in *Get What's Yours*, no one stood out as more of a consumer advocate than Baker, ostensibly the fox guarding the henhouse. When he talks about what consumers need from health care—comments I've included in upcoming chapters— Baker is so ardently pro-patient that he sounds like an industry critic. Could this just be an act for my benefit? I don't think so.

What I do think, and what this book is about, is that there are lots of people like Baker in businesses and nonprofits across the country who think people deserve a better deal. Given the daily outrages about the price, quality, and access to care, it is safe to say that these people are not typical. They are outliers in pursuing better outcomes for consumers, and point to better ways of providing and paying for care.

If their ideas and solutions were widely known and used, the fervor for health reform would subside. I am not holding my breath waiting for this to happen. And you don't have to wait, either. These better ways of providing and paying for care are available now, and I will get to them in short order.

Before moving on, I'd like to address another reality of health care. *Everyone* has a health care story, and their view of care—*their* reality—is largely determined by their own experiences. Like the proverbial elephant and the blind man, the part of health care a person touches tends to define all of health care for that individual.

This is as true for doctors and health care experts as it is for us. I have lost count of all the doctors who have expressed "shock and outrage" at injustices inflicted on their loved ones or their patients in the aftermath of disastrous encounters with health care. If even a doctor can come up so short, these stories conclude, what hope is there for the rest of us? The flaw here is the assumption that doctors know how health care insurance, price-setting, hospital billing, and access to care work. For the most part, they do not.

I have tracked anecdotal health care experiences on social media, supported by detailed surveys and studies of millions of American health care consumers. Extrapolating anyone's personal experiences with health care to support broader conclusions is potentially a mistake. Despite this realization and my best efforts, I am likely guilty of making this mistake myself in the following pages. I beg your apology for doing so.

Clearly, the system is broken for many people some of the time. It is not broken for most people most of the time. Where health care tends to break down is at the extremes—serious illnesses, horrendous expenses and bills, seemingly heartless companies that deny and ration care, stories that break our hearts about miracle cures that are tantalizingly out of reach.

Health care costs represent a growing affordability crisis. Families often spend a quarter or more of their incomes on health care. Projections say things will get worse. (A look at health spending for individuals and families is in Appendix 1.)

All of this points back to the 330 million Americans who do not have the luxury of waiting for health reform and must cope with health care as it now exists. Six out of seven Americans need some form of health care each year, according to the government's recent health census.

The number of times we seek care during the year is staggering: a billion visits to doctor's offices, 145 million emergency room visits, and 35 million hospital admissions. Whether you need care now or not, these numbers suggest you will. Fortunately, there are health care heroes who can help you right now. They have found better answers and pathways to provide you access to quality health care at an affordable price. This book is for you and is dedicated to them.

2

HEALTH INSURANCE: FRIEND AND FOE

Health insurers can take your money—lots of it—and then deny you the health coverage you thought you were assured when you laid out all that money. In the process, they make out like bandits, with profits in the billions, accessorized with obscene executive salaries. No wonder hating insurance companies is a national pastime.

I'm not here to pile on or defend health insurers. My task is to explain how they work and how you can work with them. I do happen to think that health insurers play an important role in health care and that we will continue to need them, or at least their skills, regardless of how much we might dislike them and want to reform the system.

By way of disclosure, I once worked for a large health insurance company, and can confirm that many decent human beings worked there. I have been paid money by the biggest health insurer—UnitedHealthcare—to provide online consumer content about Medicare, the subject of a book I wrote a few years ago.

In broad terms, insurance allows a group of people to engage in activities while being protected from potentially ruinous losses. A classic example of insurance, and in fact a primary reason for its invention, involved voyages a long time ago by oceangoing vessels where the risk of losing a ship at sea, along with its valuable cargo, deterred people from setting sail.

Ship owners formed insurance pools and paid money into a common pot. Owners who lost ships received funds to offset their losses.

Such protection encouraged more merchants to enter the maritime trades, creating more opportunities for them and the people who worked on their vessels, provided their cargoes, and bought their wares.

Owners of ships who were not damaged paid owners who did suffer losses. Fast-forward a millennium or two and now take a look at modern consumer insurance markets. Auto insurance is legally required. People who suffer accidents can face big claims, especially for personal injury. Insurance protects them from ruinous expenses, paying their expenses out of premiums from people who don't have accidents.

Safe drivers generally go along with this system and may even get a discount. Bad drivers may get placed in a special risk pool, paying higher premiums. Auto insurers are not running charities and try to make a lot of money. No one squawks too much about their profits, and to support this premise, do you have a clue about how much money your auto insurer makes?

This concept of "pooling" risks—having lots of people share the costs of paying for damages suffered by a small number—has become something we accept if not always understand. If your neighbor's home burns down, you probably don't complain about how much money that claim will cost you personally, or bemoan the profit level of their insurance company.

So it is, or is supposed to be, with health insurance. Here, premiums from healthy people pay for the health expenses of people with health problems. One of the reasons Medicare works, and of course it has many failings, is that it covers more than 60 million people, funded in part by payroll taxes. It has a huge risk pool and even larger payer population.

Because it covers so many people, it has the clout to set relatively low payment rates for the health care that it covers. Even so,

Medicare runs annual deficits approaching half a trillion dollars. They will be headed higher and higher until we figure out how to better manage the system.

Even large risk pools don't support attractive benefits when nearly everyone in the pool regularly needs care. This is why dental insurance benefits tend to be modest, as do benefits for stand-alone hearing and vision plans. Including such benefits in broader employer plans is increasingly common, expanding these risk pools and pointing toward better coverage for those with serious dental, hearing, and vision needs. Shopping for all types of insurance, including these speciality coverages, requires the consumer fact-finding covered in Chapter Thirteen.

The process of managing the care we receive, or even accepting the notion that it should be managed, is at the center of many significant health system challenges. Private insurers are the ones trying to manage our care, and many people would give them a failing grade.

Beyond their profits and rejected claims, the reality is that we love to yell at the refs. That's the role health insurers play and it's been greatly expanded in recent years, leading to rising complaints. Like many problems, this trend originated in a good place.

The 2010 Patient Protection and Affordable Care Act (ACA), for all its endlessly debated benefits and flaws, ushered in a broadened set of health conditions that health insurers are now legally required to cover. The biggest change was the end of restrictions on covering preexisting health conditions. The ACA also expanded coverage of preventive care and encouraged people to stay healthy. Even if the ACA were repealed, few people want to return to the way things were before 2010.

One impact of broader insurance coverage includes the potential for greatly expanded access to and use of care, along with a lot of pressure to raise insurance premiums and health spending. This

consequence threatened to make health care even more unaffordable, and led insurers to ramp up programs to reduce expenses by
managing care.

We don't like being managed, even when it's for our own good.
Of course, insurers' managed care programs often do not seem to be
for anyone's good save their executives and stockholders. In truth,
this is a slippery slope for insurers. Managed care, even when done
correctly, can easily be interpreted as rationed care. This is strongly
associated with rejections of insurance claims and other realities of
being a referee that insurance companies don't like to talk about.

Many studies of managed care programs have shown them to be
effective in reducing care that is not medically effective and encouraging care that has been proven to be effective. This has resulted in
improved health and lower costs—a hard feat to accomplish.

You might think this would earn health insurers some accolades.
Just the opposite has happened, due in no small measure to record
insurer profits in their managed care programs. At the same time,
consumer health prices are rising. People know how to do the math
here.

Right now, managed care is positioned to take on an even more
prominent role in health insurance. There simply is no way to control let alone reduce runaway health spending without some com-
bination of price cuts and reductions in the amount of care. Please
ponder this thought for a few seconds before moving on.

Any meaningful change in health care will require tough gatekeepers to set and manage the rules. Congress could enact laws
giving more or even all of that job to government regulators. If that
day ever comes, there will be valid questions whether government
bureaucrats would manage things any better than, or even as well as,
private insurers.

In the meantime, private insurers are our health care gatekeepers. They exert great influence on health care access, quality, and

affordability. Hate them if you will. Ignore their rules at your peril. This warning is especially true during your plan's annual enrollment period. Do not get locked into a plan that is a bad fit for you and your family.

HEALTH INSURANCE 101

Roughly 300 million Americans are covered by health insurance, with the number of uninsured fluctuating between 20 and 30 million. Many in this last group are only temporarily uninsured and many younger consumers have chosen to go without coverage even though they can afford it.

Here's the breakdown of who has coverage from federal government reports:

PROJECTED U.S. HEALTH INSURANCE COVERAGE IN 2020

Type	Number
Employer group plans	160 million
Medicaid and CHIP (Children's Health Insurance Program)	74 million
Nongroup coverage (incl. ACA)	14 million
Medicare	62 million
Less people with both Medicare and Medicaid	- 9 million
TOTAL INSURED	301 million
Number Uninsured	32 million
TOTAL US POPULATION	333 million

There still are too many cases of people suffering financial and health damage because they lack insurance. Despite these optics, the view from this seat in the peanut gallery is that health care affordability is a greater national problem than access to insurance. Saving you money is a primary goal of this book, so let's move from morality to money.

Beyond health insurance premiums, you need to know industry payment terms. Co-pays and coinsurance, for example, sound interchangeable. They are not. Co-pays are fixed amounts you pay for certain services, such as office visits. Coinsurance is your percentage share of the cost of a service or drug.

The other thing you need to know is your maximum out-of-pocket (MOOP) cost for covered health spending for the year. Some plans, particularly in Medicare, have separate MOOP limits for medical care and drugs.

These money rules are important. Don't expect someone from your insurance company to call you on the phone to tell you about them. The burden is on you to know how your health plan works. In answering thousands of reader health insurance questions over the years, I have found that making assumptions about anything to do with health care may set you up for a bad outcome.

Don't assume. Find out.

HIGH-DEDUCTIBLE HEALTH PLANS

High-deductible health plans reduce employer spending on employee benefits. For 2020, the limits that employers need to follow in setting up high-deductible plans are a minimum annual deductible of $1,400 ($2,800 for a family), and a maximum of $6,750 ($13,500 for a family).

These plans require you or your health providers to submit health expenses to your insurer, thus documenting covered expenses that count toward your annual deductible. It's only when this mark has been reached that your health plan begins paying benefits.

If you buy care on your own without telling your insurer, it won't count toward your deductible. More and more price bargains can be found outside the insurance system, particularly on generic drugs. You need to do the math to figure out if it makes sense to use your insurance here.

Building an annual timeline of predictable health needs can guide these decisions. In some cases, you can defer doctors' appointments and other services until later in the year when you have met your deductible.

Having forked over a bunch of money for health insurance premiums, people are understandably irked about having to pay yet more money for their care before their insurance plan begins to actually provide insurance. I will reserve a virtual spot for you at the bar to nurse a drink and some grudges about this system. Once we sober up, we'll still face the need to pay the money.

Many high-deductible plans include health savings accounts, or HSAs, funded with a mix of employer and employee pretax contributions. These plans are governed by IRS rules, and if you're not already a close friend of IRS Publication 969 (Health Savings Accounts and Other Tax-Favored Health Plans), just wait.

In 2020, HSA plans can be funded with up to $3,550 for individual plans or $7,100 for family plans. People aged 55 or older can contribute an additional $1,000 ($2,000 if a family plan covers two people who meet this age test).

To qualify for tax breaks, a workplace plan must be sponsored by an employer and managed by a financial institution. They can't be set up by employees. Individuals without employer plans, however, can set up their own HSAs if they have individual or family plans, usually found on state ACA marketplaces.

If you're in a plan that covers your spouse, and your spouse is 55 or older, they may need to set up their own HSA to qualify for that extra $1,000 pretax contribution.

Contributions to HSAs need not be limited to your employer, you, or your spouse. Any relative or friend can pitch in, although I've never seen a reliable estimate of how many actually do so. Given the cost of health care, the image of people panhandling for HSA contributions is weirdly plausible.

HSAs have the most attractive tax treatment of any consumer investment account. Contributions to a 401(k) or IRA are tax deductible, but you face a tax hit when you later withdraw these funds. A Roth IRA, by contrast, allows you to invest post-tax funds and later withdraw your proceeds tax free.

HSAs give you a tax-free ride on both ends of the process, so long as your withdrawn funds are spent on approved medical expenses. The definition of such allowable expenses goes beyond what your health insurance covers. For example, payments for genetic tests to 23andMe are approved. IRS Publication 502 (Medical and Dental Expenses (Including the Health Coverage Tax Credit) lists approved expenses.

You can spend HSA funds whenever you like, or you can decide not to spend them at all. These account balances can be invested in mutual funds and are yours to use long after you've retired. They make terrific rainy day health care funds.

Readers approaching eligibility for Medicare or Social Security need to be aware that IRS rules prohibit continued pretax HSA contributions to anyone receiving benefits from either program. More people are continuing to work past the age of 65, and this rule trips up many of them.

In late 2019, President Trump issued an executive order directing Social Security to explore changing its rules so that older workers can collect Social Security and still contribute to workplace HSAs. This would be a game changer for people who continue to work past age 65.

IT'S ALL ABOUT THE NETWORK

A prominent feature of managed care plans is their requirement that people receive care from doctors, hospitals, nursing homes, and other licensed health care professionals in a plan's provider network. Going outside a plan's network can cost a lot more or even result in a denial of coverage, meaning you'd have to pay the full bill yourself.

By agreeing to be in an insurer's network, health providers often accept lower payment rates. These savings are important to insurer profits. Participating providers can, in theory, accept lower rates and still come out ahead because the insurance plan will send more patients their way. In practice, doctors often feel trapped between the two opposing forces that dominate local health markets—insurance companies and area hospitals.

Powerful hospitals often have relationships with so many area doctors that they are in the driver's seat when it comes to insurance plan networks. Alternatively, if an insurer has lots of consumers enrolled in its plan in a local market, it has more clout in convincing doctors, hospitals, and other care providers to join its network and agree to payment terms favorable to the insurer.

I have never met a health care consumer who likes provider networks. Doctors are no fans, either. Networks limit choice, expose people to surprise bills from non-network providers, and lead to many rejected insurance claims from people who innocently violate network rules that probably were never explained to them when they enrolled in the plan. Again, don't assume; find out.

Flaws notwithstanding, networks are here to stay.

Plans with narrow provider networks and small geographic coverage areas are known as HMOs (health maintenance organizations) and provide the cheapest care for insurers and employees. Preferred provider organization (PPO) plans are more expensive, have broader networks and wider coverage boundaries, and give you more control over who provides your care.

Employer plans may include both options. Employers with national workforces may even offer a national PPO that permits employees broad care choices while still achieving favored pricing from providers in the network.

The best way to ensure the accuracy of who your doctors and specialists work with is to ask them and then confirm this with your insurance company. Surveys find that roughly half of provider network listings have at least one mistake. This shouldn't be a surprise. A typical physician practice works with twenty health plans, each with its own information systems, formats, and update requirements.

This is one example of health care's administrative failings. Different technology platforms breed communications and data-transfer problems. More than one-third of U.S. health care spending is on administrative costs—way more than in other countries.

Someday, we will have a common technology platform for provider directory entries and other personal health information. This health care theme park is named "Interoperability" and literally thousands of people are working on blue prints to build it. A physician's office will then be able to enter its information once and it will be shared with all the health plans with which it works. Holy Single Payer, Batman! What a concept! Maybe my heirs will benefit.

WHAT'S COVERED AND WHAT'S NOT

Lauren Bond worked as an emergency room nurse in Southern California for Dignity Health, a big health provider with services in more than twenty states. When she went into the hospital to give birth in the fall of 2018, she thought the insurance provided by Dignity would cover her. Bond's daughter was premature and weighed all of a pound and a half when she was delivered at only twenty-six weeks.

Bond got a bill for $898,984 and learned that Dignity, which self-insures its health coverage, had taken the position that Bond had failed to add the infant to her insurance plan within the thirty-one-day period specified in the fine print of documents she had received when she was hired six years earlier. The company said this requirement was repeated in documents sent to her nine days before her daughter's birth. Bond had already been admitted to the hospital by then.

Bond appealed whenever and wherever she could, to no avail. Dignity repeatedly stuck to its position until Bond took her lament to social media and posted a picture of her enormous bill on Facebook.

ProPublica, a journalism nonprofit that investigates health system abuses, posted a story about her case written by reporter Marshall Allen. He took no prisoners, noting that Dignity's marketing motto was "Hello human kindness" and quoting Bond's Facebook caption that she appended to a photo of her bill: "When Dignity Health (the company I work for) screws you out of your daughter's insurance . . ."

The day after Allen called Dignity to ask about Bond's case, the insurer reversed course and said it would pay her bills.

Bond's story was another in an almost daily stream of media "shaming" stories shining an unflattering light on egregious insurance company practices. With billions of health claims being processed by insurers, stories like hers are statistically rare. The points they so compellingly make are not:

1. Do not assume your health procedure is covered.
2. Do assume you will need prior approval for any serious medical procedure.
3. Call your insurer ahead of time and confirm you are covered and that you have received prior approval if it is required.
4. Get any confirmation and approvals in a written and time-stamped communication.

Getting approvals for procedures that require prior authorization can be a slow process. Make sure you give yourself plenty of time.

Insurance plans often have requirements that must be met before you receive the drug or treatment you and your doctor agree is best for you. This "step therapy" requires people to try less costly approaches first and, if these don't do the job, move on to more expensive treatments and medications.

The burden is on you to comply with a plan's provisions, not to wait for someone from the plan to tell you what's permitted or the steps you need to take.

Step therapy and other insurer denials of care can be overturned. To prevail, do your homework and enlist the help of your doctors' offices. To repeat: these things can take time. Don't wait until the last moment if you know ahead of time that you'll need care or a procedure. And don't give up! Too many people either don't know they can appeal or don't know how to do so. Check out Chapter Fifteen for tips on fighting back.

Different health policies cover pretty much the same things. This is good, because there often is not a lot of choice in the health plans you can pick. The ACA (as noted earlier) and Medicare deserve much of the credit for this standardization.

Although Medicare covers "only" 20 percent of the insured population, its coverage rules set the tone for private health insurers. Once you know how Medicare covers something, you can call different insurers to get more information. Believe me, insurers would much rather you know these things *before* you file a claim. If you have insurance from an employer or other provider, folks at the insurer can help.

Get What's Yours Rx

Private insurers are here to stay, so learn how they work.

Understand insurance deductibles, co-pays, and coinsurance.

Learn what your plan covers and what it doesn't.

Understand high-deductible plans and health savings accounts.

Make sure your doctors are in your plan's provider network.

HEROES I

The Health Navigator

Brian Lehrschall

Brian learned his medical ABCs at a young age. When he was eight, he was diagnosed with ADHD and OCD—attention deficit hyperactivity disorder and obsessive-compulsive disorder. When he was twelve, his immune system betrayed him, leading to a psoriasis diagnosis. By the time he was in middle school, more than 90 percent of his skin was covered with psoriatic eruptions. Just the kind of confidence-building condition a young teen needs, he now jokes. At the age of fifteen, his immune system revolt was complete, and he was diagnosed with arthritis, which is not uncommon in psoriasis sufferers.

"Sufferers" is the correct word, too. Pediatric treatment protocols for children were limited back then, recalled Lehrschall, who was born in November 1981. He could not take biologics, which were just then hitting the market. Instead, he and his mom, with whom he still lives in North Carolina, tried to manage his symptoms with a mix of creams, ultraviolet radiation, vitamin-A derivatives, and anything else they could think of to provide him some relief.

Once he turned eighteen, he could take biologics and other stronger drugs, and he turned to Enbrel. Twenty years ago, he recalled, Enbrel was not available in a convenient self-injection form. It arrived in two parts—a syringe of sterilized water and a vial of the drug in powder form. After carefully mixing the two, he could inject himself.

Lehrschall is among millions of Americans with chronic

health conditions that will accompany them the rest of their lives. They are joined by millions of others with cancers, heart attacks, and strokes, along with others who undergo major surgeries. Long and difficult recuperative journeys are common.

These patients often are forced to fight for their rights in a health system that is not designed or prepared for their needs, makes mistakes in how it treats them, wrongly evaluates their health insurance claims, or simply doesn't make an effort to help them at all. Even the best and well-funded health system would not eliminate these problems and, of course, the U.S. health system is hardly the best or, in some areas, even worthy of a passing grade.

Lehrschall, with his mom's help, has had to navigate this system for more than twenty years. Over that span, he has had to stand up for his rights many times. "I fired many doctors," he said simply. "Once, I had a dermatologist who wouldn't shake my hand. I felt like the guy thought I had leprosy [and] after the second appointment, I didn't go back."

In 2012, Lehrschall was no longer able to perform his job in the North Carolina House of Representatives, where he had been a legislative assistant. With no income to speak of, he was still faced with substantial medical expenses.

"I had to continue seeing my doctor," he recalled. "That was kinda hard, seeing as how I didn't have any money to pay for it." Luckily, Lehrschall's doctor was affiliated with the Duke University medical system. Being treated at a major health and research facility can provide access to superior support services, including financial help.

Lehrschall got access to a "cash-price" program where he could see trained nurses at little cost and see his primary doctor at a reduced rate. Along with pharmacy discount cards, he was able to cope. "I also had my mom," he said. "She was able to help me navigate through this maze of paperwork . . . and all the other things you have to go through to figure this stuff out."

Lehrschall then applied to Social Security for disability benefits and Medicare. Unable to work, he thought his case was pretty good. Wrong. He was denied twice, in large measure because he just didn't know how the system worked. "You have to be rejected twice in order to have an attorney act on your behalf," he said. So he hired an attorney and appealed.

After two years of waiting, due in part to more than a year-long backlog in processing disability claims, Lehrschall found himself in an administrative law judge's courtroom, where he then had to meet with a vocational expert, whose professional evaluation of his condition would be used to determine his ability to work.

The vocational expert is supposed to classify for the judge what kind of job you can do and how much you can make, he said. "And [when] they did mine, they're like, 'Yeah, there's nothing he can do.'"

More delays followed this ruling. In early 2017, Lehrschall got a $20,000 lump-sum payment (about 6 percent of that went to his attorney, per Social Security rules). He began receiving disability benefits of about $1,000 a month and became eligible for Medicare. Because of his continuing low income, he had to apply for Medicaid and was rejected because—wait for it—the North Carolina Medicaid program said he was not disabled. This was resolved by a legal aid attorney and Lehrschall finally prevailed.

Fighting hard for his rights, he said, can sometimes obscure that his most important fight is to have a worthwhile life. Lehrschall is an advocacy volunteer for people with psoriasis and arthritis. He is working to help enact two state laws for people with chronic illnesses.

One would ease restrictions that insurance companies can impose that force people into step therapy. The other measure would require pharmacy benefit managers to include the costs of drug payment assistance when calculating an insurance plan's out-of-pocket maximums. Excluding such costs can sharply increase policyholder payments, thus reducing the effective value of assistance payments.

"I just feel like patients need to learn that they have a voice in the federal and state health care system, and they also have a voice with their doctors," Lehrschall said in describing his advocacy work. "The first time they go to a dermatologist, they have no idea what questions to ask and . . . sometimes get intimidated by what these doctors are telling them."

His arthritis is under control. His psoriasis itches constantly and medication does not help much. "If you've ever had poison ivy, imagine that twenty-four hours a day, 365 days a year. . . . If my feet are itching really bad, I'll put my feet in a bucket of ice water. . . . If I'm having a rough day and I can't walk, it's going to be hard to go in and out of an office."

Lehrschall does not push advice on others. When asked, he said, "The biggest thing is that you've got to find somebody you can trust who can help you get through the process, whether it be an attorney or someone like that. And you've got to have a good support network of folks you can talk with when you're having a bad day and when it's like, 'I can't deal with this crap.' . . .You get a little frustrated now and again, which is understandable."

Lehrschall provides mentoring help to local Boy Scouts and, prior to the pandemic, was able to get occasional telephone work from home helping people make restaurant reservations at busy times of the year. He began mentoring after losing his job. "I like to help people. I'm a trusting sort of person and don't want to become cynical. I might as well do something, and here was something I could do. I hate sitting around doing nothing."

3

EMPLOYERS GET TO WORK
ON HEALTH CARE

Walmart founder Sam Walton continues to cast his shadow on business strategy and the economy nearly thirty years after his death in 1992 at the age of seventy-four. His legacy may not be only his relentless pursuit of lower prices for consumer goods. It just might include health care.

Decades ago, Walton became fed up with how much Walmart was shelling out in health insurance for its soaring workforce, which now numbers 2.2 million worldwide, including 1.5 million in the United States. As recounted in a 2019 *Harvard Business Review* article, here is what the memorably irascible and plain-talking CEO had to say:

> Nearly 30 years ago Walmart founder Sam Walton was taped at a meeting of his senior leadership, excoriating the health care industry for gouging payers like Walmart and, by extension, their employees, himself included. Walton challenged his team to do something about it. "These people are skinnin' us alive," he said. "Not just here in Bentonville but everywhere else, too. . . . They're charging us five and six times what they ought to charge us. . . . So we need to work on a program where we've got hospitals and doctors . . . saving our customers money and our employees money. We haven't even started to do that. And if we don't get it done this year, I'm gonna get real upset. I mean real upset."

Walmart didn't get it done that year, or the next or the next. It did begin the difficult job of building programs to tackle high health care costs while improving the quality of care for its associates. "That impassioned speech is still talked about as a defining moment for the company," the article said—"the point where Walmart turned its formidable procurement capabilities to the challenge of buying affordable, quality health care."

Because of its scale, discipline, and relentless consumer focus, Walmart's achievements figure prominently in the playbooks of other employers who provide private health insurance to 155 million people—roughly half of all insured people in the United States. It also has begun selling health insurance, with an early focus on Medicare Advantage plans.

"In 2019, 61 percent of U.S. workers with employer-sponsored health coverage were enrolled in self-insured plans, including 17 percent in small firms and 80 percent in large firms," researchers said in a 2019 *Health Affairs* piece. The rise of self-insured health plans had so far not changed the role of health insurers. They administer health plans and are controlling gatekeepers of valuable health care use and cost information.

"Instead of sharing useful price information, most insurance carriers provide self-insured employers with monthly summaries of total billed charges, total negotiated allowed amounts, and the 'discount'—the difference between the two," the article said. "The lack of useful pricing knowledge hinders employers' ability to act as active and informed market participants, paving the way for their overpayment for medical services."

Walmart and other like-minded employers who self-insure their employee health care costs have become insurance activists. They require insurers to provide details about individual insurance claims. When they analyze this mountain of data, they can see patterns that differ from what their health insurers used to tell them.

"These insights allow employers to assess whether their negotiated prices are reasonable and how effectively their insurance carriers negotiated with providers," the *Health Affairs* article said, "which further empower employers to apply downward pressure on their insurance carriers to negotiate more effectively."

If you work for one of these companies, you are already benefiting from this shift. You likely have access to better and less expensive care. You may even be able to shop for care from doctors, hospitals, outpatient clinics, and other providers. Your employer knows what they charge for care and how good they are at their jobs, and can guide you to better treatment decisions.

Although consumers will eventually have such choices, progress toward transparent health care is slow. Fortunately, you don't have to wait. *Get What's Yours* will show you how to benefit from this trend now.

Walmart is hardly reinventing the wheel. Employers have found ways over the years to cut health spending in half or even more while providing better care to employees.

Harris Rosen bought his first hotel in 1974 and has since built Rosen Hotels & Resorts into a 6,300-room group of Orlando hotels. In 1991, he started what would become RosenCare, which includes an on-site clinic providing care to the group's six thousand employees and their dependents. Preventive care, exercise, and wellness services are emphasized.

Hourly associates pay about $800 a year for their health coverage—a bit more than half the typical employee share of employer insurance premiums—and have a zero deductible before coverage begins. If they need care, they get time off from work, are provided free transportation, and can get prescription drugs before leaving the clinic.

Because of the emphasis on wellness and reducing unneeded care, employees become and stay healthier, minimizing future costs. Rosen estimates it has saved $400 million in health expenses over the years.

What Rosen does not have, of course, is scale. Walmart *is* scale. Assuming that even only half its 1.5 million U.S. employees had Rosen-like care, cutting annual health costs by $6,000 for those employees would save Walmart $4.5 billion a year.

The problems that Sam Walton bemoaned have hardly gone away, of course. The tendencies of doctors, hospitals, and other medical companies to financially exploit employers and employees have become hardwired into the system.

Paul Starr won a Pulitzer Prize more than thirty years ago for his book *The Social Transformation of American Medicine*, which was updated a few years ago to describe a health care system that had become even more troubled during the intervening decades.

Starr explained the history of private health insurance and the rise during World War II and later of employer health plans. Not surprisingly, major health care providers have tried to control health care since day one. Among the book's vignettes is a description of the behavior of the American Medical Association (AMA), which culminated in a 1943 U.S. Supreme Court ruling that the nation's doctors were guilty of antitrust violations in squelching insurance plans they did not like.

Today, the AMA has lots of company, including well-funded trade groups representing hospitals, health insurers, pharmaceutical companies, and others. Over the years, these groups and the powerful companies and interests they represent have built the system that was illustrated in Chapter One on Jeff Rice's whiteboard at Healthcare Bluebook in Nashville. It has continued to make them fabulously wealthy.

"By deflecting insurance first into the private sector and then away from direct services and lay control," Starr wrote, "the [medical] profession was able to turn the third-party insurer from a potential threat into a source of greatly increased income."

GOING ON OFFENSE

When Haven Healthcare was created in 2019 by Amazon, Berkshire Hathaway, and JPMorgan Chase, there was heightened expectation that it would build a better health care mousetrap, especially after it appointed acclaimed writer and physician Atul Gawande as its CEO. Walmart and a host of related health care innovators—many funded from a seemingly bottomless well of venture capital—didn't wait to see what Haven would do.

"To the best of our knowledge," the *Harvard Business Review* article said, "the data we provide [in the article] is the most thorough and transparent on employer-purchased care ever published. Drawing on this experience and that of other companies and providers, we offer guidance that many employers, even midsize companies, can apply." The *HBR* piece was coauthored by Lisa Woods, a senior director at Walmart who oversees its employee health efforts.

"The article generated enormous attention in health care circles and was covered extensively by the media," an *HBR* spokeswoman said. "It is among the highest performing health care articles *HBR* has published." It made Woods a rock star. Walmart's employee health innovations landed her and company CEO Doug McMillon in tenth place on *Fortune*'s annual list of the world's fifty great leaders.

The potential payoff of these efforts to employers and patients is no longer theoretical. Walmart and others have the numbers. Over time, they have identified hospitals and other care providers as Centers of Excellence (COEs) because they are good at what they do and are willing to perform these procedures at reasonable costs as preferred providers for company health care programs.

Like Donna Ferguson, the medical tourist who traveled to Cancun for top-rate care, Walmart will pay associates who travel to a COE for care, including paying the travel expenses of a caregiver.

Even when the cost of such care is higher than normal, healthier outcomes will still lead to savings over time.

Avoiding invasive care altogether may also be an outcome. When Walmart analyzed the experiences of 2,300 employees referred to one of its spinal COE partners, it found that more than half of those prescribed surgery by their non-COE doctors wound up not needing it at all. Instead, they received nonsurgical therapies that saved money, not to mention forgoing the discomfort and possible complications of surgery.

Those who did require surgery had shorter hospital stays, were able to return to work sooner, and had hospital readmission rates an eye-popping 95 percent lower than non-COE spine surgery patients.

Walmart also tackled the wide cost and quality variations that have long plagued MRI and CT scans. Covera Health, a partner, analyzed 50,000 outpatient procedures around the country and has identified the best machines. (Not all scanners are created equal. Who knew?) It has evaluated the clinicians who do the best jobs of reading and interpreting films and scan results.

Walmart sends employees to the best local testing sites. Over time, as other employers and insured groups follow suit, the best and cheapest providers will get more business, at the expense of lower-quality, more-expensive sites. Sam Walton would be pleased.

There is a lot of other unneeded medical care being prescribed and provided at great expense. Chapter Eleven will help you spot such unneeded care.

Readers without access to such information will be able to get similar help in Chapter Thirteen, courtesy of Healthcare Bluebook and other organizations that are pumping out medical cost and quality information that all consumers can use.

Walmart has partnered with a company named Grand Rounds to develop similar rosters of experts who provide second opinions. And in a logical extension, Grand Rounds has built a database of the nation's best physicians—based on the clinical evidence of their work, not subjective consumer opinions or reputational surveys.

We are "taking the guesswork away from" our associates and "helping them find the best physician in their community," Woods said in fall 2019 at HLTH, a technology trade show. They can use an app on their phones or they can call Grand Rounds, which will make doctor appointments for them. Walmart employees with private health plans can bypass insurers to use this service.

Whether your employer is now using this playbook, the odds are that Walmart's efforts and those of other pioneering employers are going to create the opportunity for more convenient access to higher-quality care. It will first flow to self-insured employees and then out to general consumers.

Health insurers and other major care providers have taken note. They are the powerful incumbents of health care and, based on defensive and business-growth strategies, also are using the playbooks of Walmart and other health care innovators.

The five largest health insurers—Aetna (part of CVS Health), Anthem (BlueCross BlueShield), Cigna, Humana, and UnitedHealthcare—insure upwards of 150 million people directly. Their reach approaches 250 million people if you include wholly owned pharmacy operations and growing networks of health providers, hospitals, and clinics.

If you are insured by one of them, expect to be guided to care provided by their affiliates. Such vertical consolidation is one way the insurers can manage cost and quality to hold down your annual insurance cost increases while still pleasing their investors with fat profit margins.

Entrepreneurs trying to provide people with better health solutions often partner with these incumbents. They are tapping into big customer bases to quickly achieve scale and profitability. We'll see more of these "disrupters" in Chapter Sixteen.

The jury is out on how long it will take these new approaches to improve health outcomes or on whether they will lead to lower health costs. So far, the results have not been encouraging.

"Self-insured and fully insured companies are equally bad at controlling health care costs," Kaiser Family Foundation CEO Drew Altman wrote in early 2020. In 2019, the average annual insurance premium at employers with external health insurance was $20,627. For large, self-insured firms, it was $20,739.

"There hasn't been a meaningful difference for the past 20 years," Altman said. The ability of self-insured employers to find better deals for care are, as noted, being used by other employers, "and they buy insurance from the same companies that administer self-insured plans."

Even if overall costs remain high, however, your costs can decline if you take advantage of the pricing and quality tools presented in *Get What's Yours*.

To repeat the experts' mantra, voiced with the certainty of rearview mirror studies, people have hated to shop for health insurance, did not know how to shop for health care, and often didn't even know they could.

I have seen no credible research that informed and motivated consumers who do shop don't benefit from doing so. Just the opposite.

Here's a summary of major changes. Later chapters will help you take advantage of them.

IT'S ALL ABOUT THE DOCTOR

THE TREND: Access to high-quality doctors and hospitals identified by new tools that can evaluate the outcomes of literally billions of medical procedures.

"Doctors in the United States are responsible for driving most of the medical spend, most of the medical decisions," said Owen Tripp, cofounder and head of Grand Rounds. "They may draw only about 17 percent of the overall cost buy, but they're directing the remaining 83 percent."

Over time, that 83 percent figure will drop. Patients will become more active retail health consumers, seek cheaper medications, and go to clinics and the growing array of retail health outlets—online and in an explosion of brick-and-mortar retail locations.

Walmart has employees everywhere, so Grand Rounds' use of external measures of individual provider quality needed to be done on a national scale. With data on a million-plus doctors, it can provide Walmart with provider quality rankings in every county in the nation.

Since 2016, Tripp said, the percentage of Walmart associates seeing the lowest-quality doctors has dropped to 29 percent from 60 percent. The implications of the shift are enormous, Tripp said, using the example of opiate prescriptions. "The lowest decile of providers," he said, "are six times more likely to prescribe opiates than the top decile."

THE TREND: A heightened focus on stronger patient-doctor relationships, often with expanded physician practices that include behavioral health, physical therapists, financial counselors, and others. Chapter Nine will drill down into the growing importance of finding a good primary care practice.

Comcast NBC Universal insures more than 200,000 employees scattered across the United States, often in small clusters of only a few cable installers in a local community. Its strategy began with the belief that the primary care doctor is the linchpin in the nation's health system, explained chief medical officer Dr. Tanya Benenson.

Right now, this linchpin often fails and the system doesn't work for patients. On average, it takes 29 days to see a primary physician.

"When you finally get there, the experience may not be great," Benenson said, with physicians having only enough time to focus on the health problem that brought the patient into their office "They only can focus on sick care, not on keeping people healthy."

Many communities don't even have enough physicians to provide this inadequate quality of care, leading to higher emergency room use and more health care problems that could have been avoided with better ongoing care. "If you have good primary care, you can prevent a lot of this downstream stuff," she said.

Based on this assessment, the company's goal was to figure out how to deliver such quality care to all of its employees, including its many small groups of service employees scattered across the country. Before tackling this issue, Benenson said the company wanted to develop the "ideal primary care setting" and began trying to do so through clinics at some larger office sites.

"Primary care to us is not just that one-on-one interaction with your PCP [primary care physician]," she said. "Primary care is the whole taking care of you. It is physical therapy, it is behavioral health, health coaching, and nutrition coaching. And it's team-based." This is the model the company introduced.

More than half of all employees at the sites used the clinics and, more impressively, three-fourths of them decided to make them their primary providers of medical care. So far, so good. "How do we extend this beyond the walls of our clinics?" Benenson asked. "How do we get to all of our sites across the country?"

The answer for Comcast is the creation of virtual care teams. Partnering with Crossover Health, Comcast has started rolling out what Crossover CEO Dr. Scott Shreeve calls a "connected system of health."

Comcast can see fewer than 10 percent of its far-flung employees in its clinics, he noted, "So you have to use a digital-first approach. You have to find people and meet them where they are."

Crossover's teams—all employees—include a physician, nurse, behavioral health specialist, a physical therapist, and in some locations a health coach. The teams work at the clinics Crossover is setting up for Comcast. They focus on remote care, connecting to employees with smartphone apps.

Unlike typical doctor-patient relationships, Shreeve told me, Crossover's teams know the details of Comcast's benefit programs plus the history of insurance claims involving employees and the private health insurers who are still administering Comcast's self-insured health programs.

Beyond the numbers, Shreeve said the big difference in Crossover's approach is that "we are not incented to perform more medicine but incented to improve health." This leads to less care and better outcomes, saving Comcast about 20 to 30 percent on short-term medical expenses and leading to further long-term savings because healthier employees will require less care in the future.

Eventually, Shreeve said he wants to expand his care model. He first has to make it work for employers. After speaking with me, Crossover took a big step in that direction in an agreement with Amazon that will include building twenty health centers near Amazon fulfillment facilities.

"If we can solve this for the employer," he said, "how do I now make this available for everyone? Because we agree if all we do is provide great health care to these elite employers—for people who are well off enough to have a job like that—we haven't really moved the needle."

CENTERS OF EXCELLENCE

THE TREND: Programs that bypass commercial insurers to negotiate A-to-Z bundled care packages with top-rated and, wherever possible, lower-cost providers. These are often provided under the umbrella of Centers of Excellence (COE) programs. Be careful here, as this term has become so attractive that it's being pirated by providers who don't always apply the same standards as Walmart and other leaders.

In its annual outlook for 2020 employer insurance plans, the Business Group on Health said more than one in four large employers will expand their COE programs. The group is composed of big employers funding health insurance for more than 60 million people. "Nearly half of large employers will have COEs for musculoskeletal conditions in place for 2020. In addition, a growing number of employers are turning to COE models for fertility and maternity programs."

(The list of sixteen Walmart COE providers and their specialty care areas as of mid-2019 is in Appendix 2.)

ON-DEMAND, 24x7, AND BUILT FOR CONSUMERS

THE TREND: Smartphone tools that tell you where to find the best and cheapest care based on your health condition and your specific health insurance policy. Increasingly, these tools include online appointments.

Health care's complexities and attendant frustrations are linked to poor health care decisions that can raise costs, lead to incorrect care, or even to no care at all.

By the time you read these words, the odds are good that your smartphone will have health tools tailored to you. It will be loaded with the details of your health insurance coverage. Your co-pays and deductibles plus your prescription drugs would be in your app. So would a full rundown of what was covered and what wasn't. Information on your available doctors and hospitals would be there, plus recommendations on preferred sources of care determined by price and quality. If your insurer is on the ball, your health records will be there, too.

Optum, the massive health services unit of even more massive UnitedHealth Group, thought such a tool would be a powerful ally of beleaguered employer health plans, helping the plans save money and contributing to improved employee health and satisfaction.

So it built one, called Rally, which is now available on more than 30 million smartphones. During the pandemic, Rally use quintupled, accelerating widespread acceptance of digital health.

Other health insurers have built their own tools or are busy working on them. Big tech companies—think Apple, Amazon, Google, Microsoft—are investing heavily to turn your smartphone into a mobile storehouse of personalized health information that can monitor your health and automatically connect you to designated caregivers if something goes wrong.

"In some ways, the system is starting to tilt back to the future," said Karl Ulfers, CEO of Rally Health. The growth of high-deductible employer health plans has meant that "more and more, the individual patient, the consumer, is the one that is paying the first dollar of expense." Of course, this was the way things used to be when consumers paid their health bills directly to doctors and hospitals.

"There is similar growth in terms of consumers wanting to get information about the cost of care." Ulfers said during a 2019 interview in his downtown Minneapolis office. "Once somebody looks at a single price," he said, Rally data show "they tend to look at roughly three other doctors" providing the same service.

Ulfers compared the evolutions of shopping for health care and automobiles. A trigger decades ago for auto shopping was the emergence of *Consumer Reports*, *Money*, and *Kelley Blue Book* (clearly a model for the founders of Healthcare Bluebook). They educated consumers about auto prices and helped them negotiate better deals.

To get an accurate handle on consumers, Ulfers said, "we do everything from going into people's homes and actually seeing how they deal with the health care system" to aggressively mining how people search the Internet and the information that's important to them.

"We're looking for clustering of what people are searching for in terms of care," he explained. "Consumer reviews are by far the most searched-for variable online," he said, "followed by price and then quality." Studying online search patterns, he added, it appears that consumers struggle with how to define quality and evaluate quality rankings.

Employer benefits experts at Mercer, a large employee benefits and consulting company, said consumer-centric health care apps are booming. "With a laser focus on convenience, they are making services available 24/7 through the palm of your hand—like Anthem's AI-powered Sydney app, or Aetna's Attain app," the firm said.

"The thinking is that engaging people as consumers will help them to be better patients when the time comes. . . . [M]any employees are already willing to use new digital solutions that make healthcare more convenient and affordable."

Mercer and Oliver Wyman (both owned by Marsh & McLennan) took a close look at digital health care in 2020 and concluded that workers and employers alike think its time has come.

Support and interest in digital health aligned with respondents' ages, with millennials and other younger persons topping the list. The survey clustered people into four groups, which it labelled in order of interest:

1. Sign Me Up (37 percent of all respondents)—Tech savvy, dominated by millennials (born between 1981 and 1996).
2. Impress Me (19 percent)—Educated workers not loyal to their employers.

3. Get Me Comfortable (40 percent)—Lower-skilled workers, dominated by Generation X (born between 1966 and 1980).

4. Not for Me (5 percent)—Older persons skeptical about technology.

THE DIGITAL DOCTOR
WILL SEE YOU NOW

THE TREND: Virtual care, known as telehealth or telemedicine, went mainstream during the coronavirus pandemic and has become a major way people get all sorts of physical and behavioral care. Some of these services are available at low cash prices to people who either don't have health insurance or, often for privacy reasons, aren't comfortable using their employer's insurance platform to disclose sensitive information.

"Most employers will provide employees with additional virtual care services beyond those traditionally offered through telehealth to help improve access and enhance the employee experience," the Business Group on Health said in its outlook report.

"More than three-quarters (82 percent) will provide mental health services to employees virtually; and 60 percent will provide weight management programs virtually. Digital solutions for musculoskeletal care management, prenatal care and coaching, sleep management, diabetes management, prenatal care, and cardiac care management show the greatest potential for growth over the next several years."

Tips on types of telehealth and how to find quality virtual care are in Chapter Ten, while Chapter Sixteen includes a look at a company focused on modestly priced, on-demand virtual care.

GET YOUR CARE—WIN A PRIZE

THE TREND: Financial rewards for using program services plus penalties for not using them when they are available. Not surprisingly, employers prefer carrots to sticks.

Efforts to get employees to engage in healthy behaviors have spawned a multibillion-dollar system of employer awards programs. Ulfers calls rewards "a behemoth of a business for us." If it can be measured, if it saves employers money, and if it is associated with better health outcomes, there's likely to be an app for that, and a rewards program.

How many steps are you walking each day? Are you getting the recommended doctor exams and other preventive care tests and services? Are you looking up available cost estimates for the care you may need?

Anna D. Sinaiko, a health policy economist at Harvard, studies consumer health behaviors. Simpler incentive programs work better, she said, and Ulfers echoes this. Consumers are not used to finding health care information. In using Rally's online tools, he said, "they know so little about health care they get intimidated by the search box [on the site] and don't know what to type in."

Simplicity rules here. For example, a tool might group doctors with price and quality "scores" above average, average, and below average. Picking someone from the top group merits a reward; picking a provider from the bottom group may trigger a cautionary email or perhaps the loss of a discount on a related employee benefit.

Reference-based pricing compares projected health costs of your decision—a specific procedure, the doctor providing it, and the facility where it will be performed—with the costs of comparable care choices.

Tying rewards programs to reference pricing intelligence can be an effective way to change consumer behavior, Sinaiko said. Variables here include price and whether a provider is in or out of a plan's provider network. Reward programs that provide employees with actual cash rewards are not widely used at present, she added. This, too, is changing.

Talking to analysts earlier this year, UnitedHealthcare CEO Dirk McMahon said, "For the nearly one-half million people enrolled in our Motion [wellness] program, we offer incentives for increased individual mobility. People can earn more than $1,000 a year when they achieve defined walking frequency and intensity targets."

PRICE AND QUALITY TRANSPARENCY

THE TREND: Powerful tools that can tell you, down to the county and ZIP code, who charges the least and most, and who provides the worst and best health outcomes.

Health insurers, large self-insured employers, entrepreneurs (like Healthcare Bluebook), nonprofits (like the Health Care Cost Institute), and the federal and state governments have developed databases with literally billions of health insurance claims payments to identify low-cost and high-quality health providers. This knowledge is then programmed into decision-making tools that guide consumers to high-quality, cost-effective care.

Right now, these tools are only available to consumers with health insurance. Over time, this employer-led effort will provide price and quality information to all consumers.

Get What's Yours Rx

Employer insurance plans are leading the charge to find cheaper and better health care.

Getting regular care from a primary care physician improves health and reduces future spending.

There are new tools and apps that identify the best care and how much it costs.

You can shop for on-demand retail health care.

4

THE AFFORDABLE CARE ACT
AND OTHER HEALTH PLANS

The verdict is *not* in on the Patient Protection and Affordable Care Act (ACA). Legal oddsmakers say the U.S. Supreme Court will sustain the law in its third review—a decision not rendered when these words were set in type. If the ACA is toast by the time you read this, turn the page. If, as I suspect, it is still with us, let me explain how it works.

This chapter draws upon the Kaiser Family Foundation's 2020 ACA primer. Kaiser updates its studies regularly, so check for new developments. Annual enrollment for ACA plans runs from November 1 through December 15 each year. People can enroll anytime under certain circumstances.

ACA plans, as noted, protect people with preexisting health conditions from being denied coverage or having their premiums increased because of such conditions. This is the way Medicare coverage works; it was not the way private coverage worked prior to the law. When the ACA went into effect, its rules on preexisting conditions were widely adopted by new ACA plans and by other insurance plans that cover employees.

According to rules posted on Healthcare.gov, there are six health conditions that all ACA plans must cover.

- Preventive health services
- Coverage for preexisting conditions

- Dental coverage in the marketplace
- Birth control benefits
- Breastfeeding benefits
- Mental health and substance abuse coverage

Across these categories, the law defines "10 essential benefits":

1. Ambulatory patient services (outpatient care you get without being admitted to a hospital)
2. Emergency services
3. Hospitalizations
4. Pregnancy, maternity, and newborn care (before and after birth)
5. Mental health and substance use disorder services, including behavioral health treatment
6. Prescription drugs
7. Rehabilitative and habilitative services and devices
8. Laboratory services
9. Preventive and wellness services and chronic disease management
10. Pediatric services, including oral and vision care (adult dental and vision coverage aren't considered essential health benefits)

To repeat, repeal of the entire law was sought by the Trump administration, and individual coverage rules have also been challenged. Even if a service is covered, however, benefits may be skimpy. Potentially costly care, for infertility, difficult pregnancies, genetic tests, cancer treatments, or major surgeries, among others, rarely is fully insured, and can generate daunting bills.

The ACA enabled states to create their own insurance marketplaces or, if they declined, the feds set one up for them.

There are four types of ACA health plans—bronze, silver, gold, and platinum. Medical care covered by the ACA is the same in all four plans. The amount you may pay for health care differs. Bronze plans have the lowest premiums and highest out-of-pocket payments for covered health care. On the other end, platinum plans have the highest premiums and the lowest additional out-of-pocket costs.

In insurance geek-speak, the actuarial value of these plans begins at minimums of 60 percent for bronze plans and increases by 10 percentage points for each metal stage until it hits 90 percent in platinum plans. Actuarial value is the average percentage of that metal plan's covered medical expenses that marketplace insurers will pay. The percentage you pay will differ based on how much care you use, and could be higher or lower than these "metal" averages.

The ACA offers potentially large tax subsidies to help people afford marketplace plans. They are keyed to costs of silver plans. People with employer health insurance generally aren't eligible for an ACA plan unless the cost of their employer coverage exceeds affordability thresholds that are tied to the employee's income and family size. Many ACA eligibility measures and amounts of tax subsidies are based on official Federal Poverty Level guidelines.

The Internal Revenue Service handles the law's tax details. Renowned for inscrutable forms, its ACA tools are surprisingly clear and helpful, including an online flowchart that walks you through the eligibility rules for premium tax credits. Never big on splashy titles, the agency's Publication 5187 is useful. Other riveting reads include the Instructions for Form 8962 and Form 8962 itself (this is the form you file for the ACA subsidies). Lastly, the IRS maintains an online premium tax credit summary page.

The premium for the second-cheapest silver plan available in your state is used to determine the amount of your tax subsidy. You are free to purchase any metal ACA plan and apply this subsidy toward that plan.

Here's an example from Kaiser that takes a hypothetical person through this process:

1. Pat is 30 years old and estimates her 2020 income will be 250 percent of poverty (about $31,225 per year).

2. Suppose the second-lowest-cost silver plan available to Pat in the marketplace is $500 per month.

3. Under the ACA, with an income of $31,225 per year, Pat would have a cap of 8.29 percent of income for the maximum payment she would owe for the second-lowest-cost silver plan.

4. This means that Pat would have to pay no more than $216 per month (8.29 percent of $31,225, divided by 12 months) to enroll in the second-lowest-cost silver plan.

5. The tax credit available to Pat would therefore be $284 per month ($500 premium minus $216 cap).

6. Pat can then apply this $284 per month discount toward the purchase of any bronze, silver, gold, or platinum plan.

This is mind-numbing stuff, even with the help of an ACA navigator. Kaiser has an ACA calculator that parses this complexity, using seven straightforward questions about where you live, your income, and family size.

ACA plans may provide cost-sharing help for plan deductibles, copays, and coinsurance payments. These supports, linked to incomes, are available only on silver plans. For people with the lowest qualifying incomes, these subsidies can boost the actuarial value of a silver plan to as high as 94 percent, meaning the person or family would have out-of-pocket expenses of only 6 percent for health expenses covered by the plan. Healthcare.gov has an online tool you can use to see if you qualify for this help.

ACA premiums have stabilized after years of sharp price swings and affordability problems. Kaiser provides an online map of state-by-state availability of private ACA insurance plans. It shows many areas with only one or two plan choices.

USE ONLY IN CASE OF EMERGENCY

The ACA offers what it calls catastrophic coverage to those younger than age thirty or older people who have qualified on hardship grounds. Here are the ACA's allowable reasons for such exemptions, and the federal government's links to expanded explanations:

1. You were homeless.
2. You were evicted or were facing eviction or foreclosure.
3. You received a utility shut-off notice.
4. You experienced domestic violence.
5. You experienced a death in the family.
6. You experienced a natural disaster—a fire, flood, or other natural or human-caused disaster that caused substantial damage to your property.
7. You filed for bankruptcy.
8. You had medical expenses you couldn't pay that resulted in substantial debt.
9. You experienced unexpected increases in necessary caregiver expenses due to caring for an ill, disabled, or aging family member.
10. You claim a child as a tax dependent who's been denied coverage for Medicaid and CHIP, and another person is required by court order to give child medical support.
11. As a result of an eligibility appeals decision, you're eligible for enrollment in a qualified health plan (QHP) through the marketplace, lower costs on your monthly premiums, or cost-sharing reductions.
12. You were determined ineligible for Medicaid because your state didn't expand eligibility for Medicaid under the Affordable Care Act.

The coverage in catastrophic plans is comparable to the "metal" plans. They carry high deductibles, so you must pay all your medical expenses until reaching your deductible's ceiling. The maximum annual deductibles for these plans in 2020 was $8,150 and twice that—$16,300—for a family plan. Current ACA deductible limits are online at HealthCare.gov.

ABOUT THOSE INSURANCE "LITE" PLANS

Furor over the ACA quieted a bit since a federal court struck down its mandate requiring people to get coverage or pay a penalty for not doing so. Freed of the threat of penalties, some people roll the dice and simply avoid health coverage. Others look for less comprehensive plans, and marketing for them has boomed. More than 3 million people had these plans in 2019 and job losses caused by the pandemic doubtless have since increased that number.

Technically known as short-term, limited duration insurance, variously abbreviated as STLD or STLDI plans, they initially were approved for no more than three months and available to help people caught in an ACA timing bind. These plans were later expanded to a year and, once ACA mandatory coverage requirements went away, can be renewed forever.

I can find something good and bad to say about any insurance plan. Compared to ACA plans, the coverage provided by short-term plans looks weak.

The key is to do your homework and not to take anything at face value. This can be tough given the upbeat tone of plan marketing campaigns. Even if such statements are untrue, there generally is scant oversight by state insurance departments to police them.

Short-term plans don't have to cover preexisting conditions or the ACA's ten essential benefits. Renewals are not guaranteed, so a person who becomes ill during a plan year might need to find other ACA coverage the next year.

These plans do have low and attractive premiums. You don't get much for your money and often face high deductibles. If you want to know more, Milliman, a large actuarial consulting firm, has produced a guide.

Your checklist should include:

- What's the plan's annual deductible?
- What are the co-pays and coinsurance rules? (Return to Chapter Two if you need to revisit these and other basic health insurance terms.)
- Does it have an annual out-of-pocket maximum and what is it?
- Which preexisting conditions are covered; which are not?
- If your preexisting condition is covered, is your premium going to be increased because of it?
- What are the coverage limits on the things it does cover, such as doctors' visits?
- Does it cover prescription drugs and, if so, what are the terms?

Having raised more caution flags than you'll see at a NASCAR pile-up, I still think there can be circumstances where a short-term plan makes sense. Just be aware that the burden is on you to learn exactly what a plan does and does not cover, and what you might wind up paying for the care it does cover.

Insurers also offer supplemental plans to help people pay steep deductibles on their ACA plans. Again, insurers don't provide benefits for free, so make sure you know exactly what such plans cover.

PRAYING OR PREYING?

Religious "sharing" ministries offer a version of a self-insured plan that isn't a licensed insurance product and may provide little or no assurance that your health claims will actually be paid. Some ministry programs are professionally run. It's essential to make sure up front that you know what you're getting.

More than a million people reportedly have such plans, which have risen in popularity as health insurance costs soared beyond what many families can afford.

Ministry programs have long been popular among, well, folks who actually are religious. They had some appeal to older people who mistakenly believed ministry plans would exempt them from the need to get Medicare or avoid late-enrollment penalties if they later decided they wanted Medicare. False on both counts.

More recently, the same regulatory rollbacks that encouraged the growth of short-term plans encouraged new ministry programs, including some that are neither religious or particularly ethical. As with short-term plans, buyer beware here! Make sure you know what you're getting, including more than a "best intention" statement that you will actually receive the benefits promised by a plan.

THE VA: A MODEL WORTH EMULATING?

The Veterans Health Administration (VHA), part of the Department of Veterans Affairs (VA), has about nine million veteran enrollees served through a separate national health system staffed with more than 300,000 employees who operate about 170 medical centers and nearly 1,100 outpatient clinics. Another five million mostly younger veterans have not yet applied for VA benefits but many are expected to do so as they get older.

Despite perceptions it provides substandard care compared with private health care systems, studies regularly find VA care comparable or even superior to private care. It provides care that often is much cheaper than commercial health plans and is authorized to bargain more effectively for lower prices than can Medicare and Medicaid.

The agency's negative optics also stem from an episode a few years ago when veterans faced lengthy waits for care that were covered up by the agency. This led Congress to enact new rules making it easier for VA enrollees to get care at non-VA facilities. That program has been slow to take hold. Critics on the left view it as part of an effort to privatize the agency; critics on the right are reluctant to support a program that is government-run, universal health care for veterans.

For these and other reasons, the agency is chronically under-funded, according to Suzanne Gordon, a VA benefits advocate who explains the program at length in her book, *Wounds of War*. More than one in eight budgeted staff jobs go unfilled amidst rising demand for services. Gordon expects the pandemic will cause soaring demand for VHA care as veterans with other health insurance lose their jobs and face growing financial stresses.

"The system is going to have a lot more people wanting to get in," she said in an interview. Veterans should enroll and get their foot in the door, she advises, even if they don't currently plan to use VA services.

A related piece of advice is to understand the eight eligibility priority groups used by the VA. They are complicated and, she notes, can be changed by the president and Congress. Even if veterans are denied VA coverage today, they may be eligible later if the rules change. Past changes have turned some categories into veritable kitchen sinks.

VA eligibility requires two years of military service and, in most cases, an honorable discharge. There is growing pressure to open eligibility to some veterans with less than honorable discharges, many of which were caused by Middle East battlefield stresses.

The eligibility categories depend on a person's specific service record, with the most generous benefits provided to those with service-related disabilities. The agency conducts an extensive survey each year of how veterans use its services and what they think of their care.

Here are the eight priority groups and how many veterans are in each:

1. Disabled veterans with service-connected disabilities of 50 percent or more. Veterans determined to be unemployable due to service-connected conditions (2.2 million).
2. Disabled veterans with service-connected disabilities of 30 to 50 percent (730,000).
3. Veterans who are former prisoners of war, Purple Heart recipients; discharged for a disability that was incurred or aggravated in the line of duty, with service-connected disabilities of 10 to 30 percent, awarded special eligibility classification under Title 38, U.S.C., § 1151 ("benefits for individuals disabled by treatment or vocational rehabilitation"), and, those awarded the Medal of Honor (1.25 million).
4. Veterans who are receiving aid and housebound benefits from the VHA, and those determined to be catastrophically disabled (185,000).
5. Nonservice-connected veterans and those not eligible for disability benefits whose incomes are below agency thresholds. Veterans receiving VA pension benefits. Veterans eligible for Medicaid (1.7 million).
6. Veterans with no service-connected disabilities who are eligible to receive compensation. Veterans exposed to ionizing radiation during atmospheric testing or during the occupation of Hiroshima and Nagasaki. Project 112/SHAD participants. Veterans who served in the Republic of Vietnam from January

9, 1962, to May 7, 1975. Persian Gulf War veterans who served from August 2, 1990, to November 11, 1998. Veterans who served on active duty at Camp Lejeune for at least thirty days between August 1, 1953, and December 31, 1987. Currently enrolled veterans and new enrollees who served in a theater of combat operations after November 11, 1998, and those who were discharged from active duty on or after January 28, 2003, are eligible for the enhanced benefits for five years post discharge (500,000).

7. Veterans with gross household income below the geographically adjusted income limits for their resident location and who agree to pay co-pays (375,000).

8. Veterans with gross household income above the VA and the geographically adjusted income limit for their resident location, and who agrees to pay copays (1.6 million).

Only a fifth of VA enrollees depend on the system for all of their care. The other 80 percent also have one or more types of Medicare (51 percent), the military's Tricare coverage (21 percent), and private health insurance (28 percent).

Making informed decisions about coordinating benefits is important for veterans with multiple types of health coverage. Those programs are covered elsewhere. I'd add only that they are especially relevant when it comes to drug coverage.

The VA generally charges less for drugs than other insurance and its drug benefits are heavily used by veterans with other health coverage. Priority Group 1 enrollees pay nothing for prescription drugs. Members of other groups pay no more than $11 a month in drug co-pays but there is an annual cap on their benefits. The agency maintains an online list of preferred generic drugs, which have a $5 co-pay.

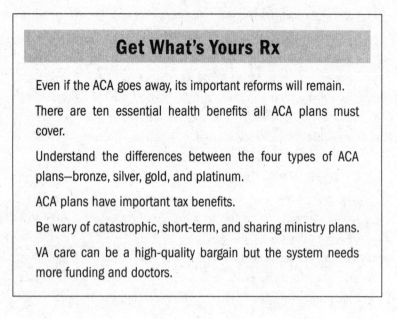

Get What's Yours Rx

Even if the ACA goes away, its important reforms will remain.

There are ten essential health benefits all ACA plans must cover.

Understand the differences between the four types of ACA plans—bronze, silver, gold, and platinum.

ACA plans have important tax benefits.

Be wary of catastrophic, short-term, and sharing ministry plans.

VA care can be a high-quality bargain but the system needs more funding and doctors.

HEROES II

The Insurance Claims Expert

Marsha Meytlis

Marsha Meytlis is in her early forties, the parent of two young sons, and an accomplished health data scientist with a doctorate in machine learning. As she tells her health care story, it quickly becomes clear that she is suited to relentlessly attack problems by acquiring whatever information is required.

None of which prepared her for the twin medical challenges of her young sons, received one after the other a few years ago. Meytlis agreed to share her story. She did not want to identify her sons and husband, in order to protect their privacy.

Her older son was diagnosed with autism and her younger son was evaluated as having growth "developmental delay." Immediate and intensive intervention for each was required, triggering therapies with different specialists, with no immediate end in sight.

"We were concerned when he was in his late twos," she said when discussing her older son. "We noticed that he wasn't speaking as well as his peers, and we became concerned. So we went for an evaluation to a developmental pediatrician. And she dropped this bomb on us of the autism diagnosis.

"It was only like three months after we got the autism diagnosis, that I found out that the younger one also had developmental delays," Meytlis said. "But with the younger one, it was easier because I had already done a lot of research for the older one. . . . I always felt like I was one step ahead of the game, because I could leverage the information that I had already learned was appropriate for the older one. . . . When the older one turned four, and the younger one was only six months, I already knew what the younger one would need when he turned four.

"We started learning about speech therapy, about occupational therapy, about physical therapy," she said. "We started learning about Applied Behavior Analysis. . . . I started researching on the Internet how to get all of those therapies."

Meytlis and her husband had well-paying jobs in New York City. They would need their incomes to deal with the therapist bills that rapidly appeared and mounted. "We did have enormous medical bills. Luckily, our income is pretty high so we were able to afford it. It's been crazy. When we did our tax returns last year, I think our total medical expenses were like around $100,000."

The traditional approach to therapy, Meytlis decided, would not work for them. With multiple weekly appointments with different therapists for each son, driving to appointments would be possible only if she left her job. She made the decision that for this to work, the therapists would have to come to her sons.

Through persistence, meticulous record keeping, and the willingness and skills to push back against unfavorable health insurance coverage rules, Meytlis is able to get the care her sons need and pay for it. Having been covered in recent years by three different health plans, she has mastered the nuances of how the system works and of how to work the system. Her "PhD" in health insurance began with the fact that behavioral therapists willing to make house calls are not in insurer provider networks.

"I have to pay everything up front to a lot of the therapists," she explained. "I would start submitting claims to the insurance and get either fully or partially reimbursed, and basically I had to become a medical billing expert. And I quickly learned that it was a lot of work, because even when you're supposed to get reimbursed, insurers make mistakes, and they don't reimburse you correctly, and then you call the insurance and you would be on hold for hours, and they would say that they would fix it, and then they won't fix it."

A tip for others, she added, is that health insurers will assign the same person to handle claims from high-volume users of health care. Having someone who knew her sons' medical histories and ongoing care needs has made a big difference.

Another key lesson was not so positive. New York State has some of the nation's strongest mandated health insurance benefits. It covers things not required by the Affordable Care Act and thus not standard under employer insurance plans. State insurance rules, Meytlis learned, do not have to be honored by self-insured employer plans.

These plans are governed under rules set up by ERISA—the Employee Retirement Income Security Act of 1974. It is commonly thought of as protecting pensions but also plays an important role in defining health benefits for employees with self-insured plans.

Meytlis's own employer plan was self-insured, she said, and its limitations included, for example, declining to cover more than fifty speech therapy sessions a year. "My kids get four sessions a week, so obviously fifty sessions per year is nothing." Fortunately, her husband's health plan covered unlimited therapy sessions, so they switched to his plan.

Her next challenge was getting insurance to cover non-network therapy bills. This required her to master insurer coverage exceptions and become knowledgeable about health care billing codes. Different insurers use different terms. Meytlis learned them all. In-network exceptions, gap exceptions, and benefit-level exceptions all mean the same thing, she said. "It means that you get an out-of-network provider covered at the in-network benefit rate."

The key to prevailing, she learned, was proving her sons' therapists were the only ones in the area who could provide the care they needed. At-home therapy is defined by different billing codes than in-office therapy. Finding those rarely used common procedural technology (CPT) billing codes allowed her to document the uniqueness of her in-home therapists. "It became easier as I became more of an expert," she recalled.

Still, claim rejections are common and insurance appeals thus became part of her skill set. Insurers have two levels of internal appeal, she found. Some have a third level where rejected claims are evaluated by independent experts. "I wrote letters with evidence for the appeals," she explained. "Sometimes, internal appeals get what you want, but in some cases the third external appeal is necessary where a third party reviews your case.

"The [therapy] providers that I have right now, they don't know anything about insurance because they're out of network," she said. "They expect me to pay them up front. When they started working for me, they didn't even know how to create an invoice for insurance. So I had to figure that out myself, and I had to give them a sample invoice and then teach them how to create an invoice for me that then, later, I would be submitting to insurance."

Along the way, Meytlis learned that insurance claims departments are not fans of fax technology. She is. "My best friend is FaxZero.com," a free online facsimile service, she said. Insurers that use online portals for claims processing can lose documents and there are limitations on what portals can accept, she learned. "Getting stuff through faxes works much better."

In Meytlis's world, finding and keeping talented therapists is the prime directive.

"I don't engage in price negotiations because when you start negotiating they don't really value you as a client," she found, "and then they will cancel sessions [and] you will be their last priority. . . . Once I find a good provider, I really value that provider because it's very difficult to find good providers. So, I'm willing to even pay them even more than what they charge, so that they will keep me, so that I will be a priority to them."

The price of eternal vigilance has been high. Meytlis scans all insurance company correspondence and puts it in an online Dropbox account. "You just have to be very organized about everything to make this work."

MEDICARE COVERAGE, COSTS, AND CONCERNS

One in five people in the United States with health insurance has some type of Medicare—nearly 54 million aged 65 or older and another roughly 10 million with disabilities. I'm going to lay out basic program rules, enrollment choices, and money tips. These fundamentals haven't changed since my Medicare book was published, so check that out for more detail; the Get What's Yours site posts annual program updates.

Medicare was enacted in 1965 and included Part A (hospitals, nursing homes, and, later, hospice care) and Part B (doctors, outpatient expenses, and medical equipment).

Part A is funded by part of a person's Social Security payroll taxes. Monthly Part B premiums pay about a quarter of Part B expenses. The other three quarters are subsidized and paid by the federal government (to the tune of more than $350 billion a year and rising).

In 2003, Congress approved creation of Medicare Part D drug plans, which are sold by private health insurers. It also approved rules that encouraged private insurers to expand Medicare managed care plans. They had foundered as HMOs but have since flourished as Medicare Advantage plans. (MA plans are technically referred to as Part C of Medicare.)

Part A pays complete costs for all but the longest hospital stays once a person has spent enough money to satisfy the program's deductible. This is not an annual deductible but is levied on each sixty-day "episode of care" a person needs during a calendar year. Part B's annual deductible and monthly premiums are adjusted annually for inflation. Here are the current enrollee costs.

Although Medicare provides broad coverage, it has holes. It does not cover routine dental, vision, and hearing care. It does not cover long-term, custodial care that many older persons require, such as help bathing and toileting, dressing, fixing meals, and shopping. And if you step outside the United States for care, forget about Medicare covering your non-emergency care (unless you live near the Canadian border and can't easily get to a U.S. health care facility).

Lastly, Part B pays only 80 percent of the expenses for things it does cover. To guard against catastrophic health expenses, about 10 million Medicare users buy private Medigap supplement insurance plans. After you've paid deductibles, these plans pay covered expenses not fully paid by Parts A and B.

The terms of Medigap plans must adhere to federal coverage standards. They otherwise are sold and regulated at the state level. Because each type of Medigap plan (identified by different letters of the alphabet) must cover the same things, you should look for the lowest cost letter plan that meets your needs. There is a federal guide to Medigap plans that is updated each year.

FIGURING OUT IF YOU NEED MEDICARE

For starters, no one is legally required to get Medicare. The issues about when to sign up revolve around making sure you have health insurance, which people want, and signing up in a timely manner to avoid late-enrollment penalties, which people don't want.

The traditional enrollment scenario is when a person is nearing age 65 and either does not have health insurance or will lose their health coverage. If you are in this group, you will have an initial enrollment period of seven months, which begins three months before the month in which you turn 65, includes your birthday month, and extends three additional months after your birthday month.

Complying with this seven-month window avoids late-enrollment penalties. The more important issue here is to sign up for Medicare soon enough to avoid a break in your health coverage. And while there's a seven-month window for getting Parts A and B of Medicare, the window for getting a Part D drug plan is only sixty-three days.

The lesson here is, don't dawdle!

Habits change, and many people no longer retire when they turn 65. People who continue working and have employer health insurance generally do not have to sign up for Medicare. They can keep their employer insurance plans to provide primary health coverage, regardless of how old they are.

When they do want Medicare, they will have an eight-month special enrollment period that starts when they lose their employer coverage. If they sign up anytime during this window, they can avoid late-enrollment penalties. Again, that's not nearly as important as making sure their health coverage does not lapse.

If you anticipate keeping your employer plan past age 65 and then signing up for Medicare later, call Medicare before then (1-800-MEDICARE) and find out when your coverage will take effect.

There are two important exceptions to these general rules.

People who work for employers with fewer than twenty employees generally are required to get Medicare as their new primary insurance when they turn 65. Such small employer plans will cease to provide primary health coverage but will provide secondary coverage. This can be useful to help pay for covered health expenses that are not fully paid by Medicare.

The second exception involves prescription drug coverage. Under Part D rules, employees with group health insurance who are eligible for Medicare (because they are age 65 or older or, if younger, disabled) must have employer drug coverage at least as good as a typical Medicare Part D plan. This is called the "credibility" test and it used to be a no-brainer because employer drug plans were pretty good.

The rise of high-deductible plans and other employer plans with skimpy benefits, however, means that more and more employer drug plans are not credible. Your employer must certify each year whether its drug coverage is credible. If it's not, you are supposed to get a Part D plan when you turn 65. I used the phrase "supposed to" because I suspect lots of older working people do not have credible workplace drug coverage and neither they nor their employers nor, I suspect, Medicare, lose any sleep over it.

Technically, if your employer coverage is not credible, and you fail to get a Part D plan, you will be charged late-enrollment penalties when you eventually get Medicare and a Part D plan. More on penalties in a bit.

MEDICARE FOR PEOPLE STILL WORKING

It's possible to have primary health insurance through an employer plan and also enroll in Medicare at age 65 or later. In the past, this rarely made sense. Today, those high-deductible health plans mean you could pay several thousand dollars in covered health expenses out of your own pocket before your employer coverage begins helping pay your medical bills.

In this situation, it can make sense to get Medicare to provide secondary, or supplemental, protection. The annual deductible for Part B in 2020 is less than $200. After that, it can pay 80 percent of covered expenses for doctors, outpatient services, and medical equipment. The typical monthly premium for people is slightly more than $144—here's that link to current rates again—and this needs to be figured into your evaluation of whether Medicare makes sense.

It also can make sense to get Medicare and simply drop your employer plan. This decision will require some homework and careful communication with your employee benefits office to make sure there are no unpleasant surprises in dropping employer coverage. Some employer plans require people to get health coverage as a condition of employment. Others specify that you can't reenroll in an employer plan after dropping it.

Dropping employer coverage will also affect covered spouses and children. I regularly get questions from readers asking about Medicare family plans. Sorry, folks. There are no such plans. Medicare covers only individuals. This means that you need to arrange for health coverage for other family members.

Spouses and children will continue to get primary coverage from small-employer health plans even if the employee has to get Medicare.

MEDICARE FOR AMERICANS OUTSIDE THE UNITED STATES

As noted earlier, Medicare does not provide health coverage outside the United States. Some Medicare Advantage and Medigap supplement plans do provide emergency foreign coverage, to a maximum of $50,000.

Millions of retirees live outside the United States. Many return regularly and wonder whether they should keep Medicare when they're outside the country so that their care is covered when they return. The answer is a clear "Maybe!"

For those who regularly return to the States, it is not realistic to drop Medicare and then reacquire it when you're back in the States. There can be a long lag between reenrolling and your effective coverage date.

The better calculus is to factor in the cost of basic Medicare, which will let you see any doctor in the United States who accepts Medicare. If you're eligible for premium-free Part A, the annual cost of Part B is about $1,735 a year, based on 2020 premiums.

Many expats get cheaper and often better coverage outside the United States. For them, coming back to the United States for care may not make sense. For people who regularly come back for lengthy U.S. visits, maintaining their Part B is worth serious thought. Given the outrageous costs of one medical mishap or ER visit, $1,735 a year looks like a bargain.

People who plan to live outside the United States for a lengthy period and then return should do the math. When a retired person without Medicare wants to sign up, there is a 10 percent late-enrollment penalty applied to Part B premiums for each year they did not have Part B. This penalty does not go away but remains in place so long as the person has Medicare.

The "math," in this case, involves comparing the annual cost of Part B with the most likely number of years an expat expects to go without Medicare. Multiply $1,735 (it will grow to reflect future inflation) times the number of years you plan to live abroad. Couples should multiply that by two.

To keep the math simple, say a person goes without Medicare for 10 years and then returns to the United States. They would incur 10 years of late-enrollment penalties, adding 100 percent (10 times the annual 10-percent penalty) to their lifetime Part B premium.

Of course, they would not have paid Medicare for 10 years while outside the United States. In this simple example, it would take them 10 years of paying penalties before their cumulative out-of-pocket expenses exceeded their savings from dropping Medicare while out of the country (Your Medicare IQ score will not be reduced should you want to reread this item.)

DO YOU WANT ORIGINAL MEDICARE?

There are two major Medicare pathways. The first is original Medicare, often called basic Medicare, with a stand-alone Part D drug plan and perhaps a Medigap supplement plan. The second is Medicare Advantage, including a bundled-in Part D plan. This one does not permit a Medigap plan because MA plans have annual out-of-pocket limits on medical expenses (these exclude its Part D plans, which as I'll explain below, do not have such limits).

Both packages provide broad coverage, insure people with preexisting conditions, and protect enrollees from surprise bills.

Original Medicare includes Parts A and B and permits people to use the services of any doctor, hospital, or health provider in the country that accepts Medicare and is willing to abide by Medicare's allowed payment schedules. On paper, more than 95 percent of the nation's health providers accept Medicare. In practice, it can be hard in some parts of the country to find providers willing to take on new patients. Of course, the same can be said about commercial health plans used by younger consumers.

Allowing people to access care from their preferred providers anywhere in the country continues to be a major appeal of original Medicare. It's the favored choice of people with retiree health benefits, because their retiree plans provide secondary coverage that complements original Medicare.

About 10 million people get a Medigap plan to protect them from things not fully covered by original Medicare—principally its payment of only 80 percent of covered Part B expenses. Medigap premiums can be pricey, and this "full" package of original Medicare can cost substantially more than a comparable MA plan.

Employers pay a large share of the cost of employee health plans. Medicare enrollees pay all of their Medicare premiums. Many new

Medicare enrollees thus get pocketbook shock when their out-of-pocket premium expenses rise, often sharply.

OR MEDICARE ADVANTAGE?

Medicare Advantage plans have become increasingly popular and now account for more than 35 percent of Medicare coverage. Unlike basic Medicare, MA plans can include insurance coverage for routine dental, vision, and hearing needs. They often pay for gym memberships, are expanding telehealth services, and cover a growing array of nonmedical needs.

The umbrella term for these needs is "social determinants of health" and you'll be seeing them in all types of health insurance plans. They include things like transportation to medical appointments, home-delivered meals for folks coming home from hospital stays, and home-safety items such as bathroom grab bars.

MA plans provide out-of-pocket limits on medical care, thus providing protection similar to Medigap plans. Many people find MA plans easier to use than original Medicare because all covered health care use is tracked by a single insurer, whereas people often deal with separate entities for original Medicare, Part D plans, and Medigap.

MA plans are cheaper than original Medicare. For people with few health problems or prescription drug bills, some MA plans with modest coverage parameters can cost little more than their monthly Part B premium, which people with MA must pay in addition to any premiums for their MA plan.

Low-income people may not have to pay Part B for either original Medicare or an MA plan. Medicare has four savings programs that are linked to Medicaid, which is regulated by different state plans. You can contact your state's Medicaid office to learn whether you're eligible. The next chapter provides more Medicaid details.

Medicare's oversight agency, the Centers for Medicare & Medicaid Services (CMS), has consistently changed its rules under President Trump to favor private MA plans over original Medicare.

Beyond a tilt toward private sector solutions, this policy is driven by a widespread notion among health experts of all political hues that original Medicare is not financially sustainable. Original Medicare is known as fee-for-service medicine. Consumers do not need prior approval before getting care. Whether they need it or not, any care covered by Medicare and deemed medically necessary for a particular patient will be provided and Medicare will pay for it.

Surveys consistently find that people with original Medicare demand more health care than they need. With few exceptions, doctors, hospitals, and other care providers are only too happy to provide it, and Medicare will pay such bills.

There are lots of reasons the government lays out more and more money each year for health care. Fee-for-service Medicare is at the top of this list.

The Congressional Budget Office projects that federal Medicare spending (after accounting for the Medicare premiums and program costs paid to Uncle Sam) will more than double over the next ten years, rising from nearly $700 billion in 2020 to more than $1.4 trillion in 2030. Even with economic growth, it will take up a bigger share of spending, amounting to 4.4 percent of the entire economy in 2030 compared with 3 percent in 2020. You can add hefty pandemic costs to this projection.

Medicare Advantage plans, by sharp contrast, are what's known as managed care plans where private insurers are gatekeepers between consumers and their health care. There is solid evidence that MA plans can direct and manage patient behaviors in ways that lead to healthier outcomes *and* lower prices. Even if you hate insurers, this is an outcome worth supporting.

The Medicare Payment Advisory Commission, known as MedPAC,

oversees the program for Congress. It has long recommended that Medicare move to such value-based care. If it does, expect other insurance programs to eventually follow suit. MedPAC's reports help demystify CMS's often impenetrable Medicare regulations. Its sibling program, MACPAC, does likewise for Medicaid.

While the insurers' gatekeeper role is what make MA plans affordable, it represents the biggest concerns the plans pose for many consumers and health advocates.

The plans often require people to get prior approval for care and, in evaluating such requests, they can and do say "no." Some of these are egregious and refusals get written up as horror stories, as they should.

To the extent that MA managers focus a person's care on evidence-based procedures and personal behaviors linked with healthier outcomes, patients can benefit and so can the rest of us. The problem is that MA plans have disturbing public optics. They pocket too much of their savings as profit while appearing to frequently deny care. This certainly hurts their case.

Another issue with MA plans is that they restrict your care choices to doctors, hospitals, and other caregivers that have contracted to be in a plan's provider network. If you go outside this network, the plan may hit you with steep fees or not cover you at all. Also, provider networks occasionally change during the year, forcing consumers to scramble for new doctors.

Narrow-network, HMO-type MA plans are the least expensive. They tend to have the smallest network of approved providers and the steepest penalties for getting care outside this network. (All Medicare plans protect people from the kind of surprise bills for non-network care that has plagued many people with employer insurance plans.)

MA plans thus can be problematic for people with serious health care needs. If you're in this boat, you need to carefully review the terms of an MA plan before getting one. This should include making sure your preferred doctors, including specialists, are in a plan's network. MA plans are regularly cited for using poorly rated nursing homes and other health providers. You need to do your homework to provide the best outcomes for you and your family.

THE D IN PART D STANDS
FOR DUMBFOUNDING

Part D drug plans have annual maximum deductibles set by Medicare—$435 in 2020. Payment obligations for specific drugs depend on which of several pricing tiers they are placed in by insurers. Plans generally have five tiers—preferred generics, other generics, preferred branded drugs, other branded drugs, and specialty medications (translation: the expensive ones). General program rules are set and overseen by Medicare; it maintains an online set of current rules.

Once a plan's annual deductible has been met, insurance benefits kick in. Your payments will depend on the drugs you take, of course, plus charges for co-payments (a flat dollar amount) and coinsurance (a percentage of the drug's price) that apply to whatever pricing tier your plan has selected for each of your drugs.

In the inexplicable wackiness that has attended Part D plans since their creation, your insurance simply stops once the total costs you and your plan have paid out exceed a defined spending threshold—$4,020 in 2020 (the limit rises each year with inflation).

This total is only for drugs covered by the plan and only if you have filed a claim for plan coverage. If you decide to buy a four-dollar subscription drug from a non-insured provider, your spending will not be included in your Part D calculations.

Once you and your plan have hit the $4,020 threshold, you will enter what's called the "coverage gap" and, once there, you must pay the entire costs of your drugs by yourself. To soften the blow, Medicare has limited what drug companies may charge you to 25 percent of their normal charges for your drugs. Of course, that's 25 percent of what often is a hefty price tag, and one that may have no relationship to underlying drug maker costs.

Relentless price increases for drugs—feel free to insert your epithet of choice here—have greatly increased potential out-of-pocket costs in Part D plans. You will not exit the coverage gap in 2020 until you alone (not you and your plan) have paid $6,350 for covered drugs—up nearly 25 percent from $5,100 in 2019.

Once you reach that $6,350 figure, you enter what's called the "catastrophic" phase of your Part D plan. Here, you may pay only a few dollars for each prescription and never more than 5 percent of the cost of your covered drugs. Five percent for an expensive drug can still be a big number. And there is no out-of-pocket limit on drug spending in a Part D plan.

For example, I take an expensive brand-name medication, still under patent protection, whose manufacturer charges me more than $5,000 a month. I hit the catastrophic phase of my Part D plan in February each year! Even so, I still must pay more than $275 a month for this drug. By the way, my insurer pays 15 percent of that $5,000-plus amount, and Uncle Sam pays the other 80 percent! This means that taxpayers ultimately pay for my medications. This includes you, so thank you, readers!

Like I said. Dumbfounding.

THE A, B, AND D OF
PRESCRIPTION DRUGS

Drugs are covered by all parts of Medicare, depending on where they are administered:

Part A—hospitals, skilled nursing facilities, and nursing homes
Part B—doctors' offices and other outpatient settings, including surgery centers and outpatient care at hospitals
Part D—self-administered prescription drugs

A canny friend of mine receives an expensive drug injection. He could inject it at home himself. He prefers to have the injections done at his doctor's office. The reason is not the free lollipops. It's the fact that Part B covers his office injections, whereas Part D would cover him for at-home injections.

Part B pays only 80 percent of covered care. My friend has a Medigap supplement plan that pays the other 20 percent. His out-of-pocket cost for this expensive drug thus is $0, compared with several thousand dollars if he gave himself the shots at home.

I don't know whether to report him to the authorities or nominate him for a savvy-shopper award.

GETTING HELP PAYING FOR DRUGS

Drug companies work with health foundations and other groups to fund patient assistance programs that help people afford their medications. Such programs are fine for consumers covered by employer insurance. However, they are viewed by Medicare as illegal inducements for patients to use a particular drug. The FBI has busted a Who's Who list of pharmaceutical companies for violating kickback laws.

Patients who accept financial help from one of these sources are not breaking the law, and who can blame them? We all want cheaper meds, and Chapter Fourteen explains how to get them.

Medicare's Extra Help program provides payment subsidies to more than 10 million Medicare enrollees whose incomes are low enough to qualify. Even if you're not sure, you should complete this Extra Help application. Millions of people eligible for Extra Help fail to apply.

TAKE ADVANTAGE OF MEDICARE'S
ANNUAL OPEN ENROLLMENT PERIOD

Existing Medicare beneficiaries are required by law to be sent detailed summaries during September explaining any major changes to their Medicare plans that will take effect in the next year. These are called "annual notice of change" or ANOC documents, and are often accompanied by a much larger document called an "explanation of benefits," or EOB, which, as its name says, lays out complete details of their plan's coverage. Increasingly, these documents are delivered electronically, although you have the right to request printed copies through the mail.

Unfortunately, you also have the right to ignore these documents and toss them in the trash. Sadly, surveys show that many Medicare beneficiaries do just that. They thus are unprepared to take advantage of their chances to choose more appropriate Medicare plans during the annual enrollment period that begins each year on October 15 and runs through December 7. People with MA plans have an additional open enrollment period during the first quarter of the year, during which they can change MA plans or move from an MA plan to original Medicare.

Passively keeping the same Medicare plans from year to year can be costly. Premiums, deductibles, co-pays, and coinsurance often change. The best plan for you right now may not be the best next year.

The details of private MA and stand-alone Part D plans are tracked by Medicare on its online Plan Finder site. The site allows you to enter your prescription drugs into Plan Finder and then see those plans that cover your drugs, with projections of their annual costs. Failure to take advantage of open enrollment looks a lot to me like throwing money away. Millions of people make this mistake, year after year.

WHEN GETTING MEDIGAP
CAN BE A PROBLEM

A person's initial enrollment in Medicare occurs either because they have no other health insurance when they turn 65 or they are leaving a private employer plan at a later age. During these initial enrollment periods, people have a six-month window that provides them preferred access to private Medigap plans. These are called "guaranteed issue rights" and in nearly all cases require Medigap insurers to sell you a Medigap plan. Even if you have preexisting health conditions, they must sell you a policy. And they can't charge you more for your coverage if you have health problems.

After you've had any form of Medicare for six months, you lose these guaranteed rights. Depending on where you live, insurers may then be able to charge much higher rates for Medigap plans and may not even have to sell you a plan at all. Medigap rules here are set by individual states. The Kaiser Family Foundation has a useful rundown of different state rules that's worth a look.

If you have a Medigap plan and are thinking of dropping it, perhaps in favor of Medicare Advantage, or have an MA plan and are considering dropping it for original Medicare and a Medigap plan, you should first call Medigap insurers in your state and find out what they would charge or even if they'd sell you a plan.

You can use Medicare's Medigap Finder to help narrow your list. Some insurance brokers have told me it's easy to change plans, that my concerns are unfounded, and I am causing unneeded stress for Medicare enrollees. Call me an ounce of prevention, pound of cure kind of guy.

Another problem with state rules confronts disabled Medicare enrollees who are younger than 65. Most *never* have guaranteed issue rights to Medigap plans. People with disabilities deserve rules that look out for them, not penalize them for being disabled.

AVOID LATE ENROLLMENT PENALTIES

Medicare's late-enrollment penalties snare many people who fail to sign up for the program within the correct enrollment windows. These penalties last a lifetime and may be harsh. They are applied to monthly premiums for Parts B and D of Medicare, adding 10 percent to monthly Part B premiums for each full year a person is late in enrolling, and boosting Part D premiums by 1 percent of the current national average monthly Part D premiums for each month a person is late in enrolling.

It doesn't take much space to describe these penalties and I'd gladly repeat this information twenty or thirty times if it convinced people to pay better attention and avoid them.

MEDICARE'S HIGH-INCOME
PREMIUM SURCHARGES

Medicare has become a means-tested benefit. Part B premiums are the same for 93 percent of us; about 7 percent of Medicare beneficiaries who are wealthier must pay higher premiums.

These premiums are set by rules requiring Medicare enrollees in the highest income brackets to pay 85 percent of the full price for the health care they get from Part B. If you ever find yourself playing a health version of Trivial Pursuit, you can score big by knowing that these surcharges are called IRMAA for short, and that this stands for Income-Related Monthly Adjustment Amount. There also is an IRMAA hit for Part D.

The income brackets used to calculate IRMAA charges are adjusted for inflation, although the top bracket will be fixed until 2028, when it also will become inflation adjusted.

IRMAA surcharges for the current year are based on federal tax returns for money earned two years earlier. It takes Social Security, which administers IRMAA, that long to get complete tax files from the IRS. The surcharges for 2021 normally would be based on returns for the 2019 tax year. People who get extensions on their filing times may experience a three-year lag. The coronavirus tax-deadline extension thus will result in lots of people paying 2021 IRMAA surcharges based on their returns for the 2018 tax year.

If you wondered how income is defined, you get yet another Trivial Pursuit score if you know that Social Security (which administers IRMAA) uses something called modified adjusted gross income. It's known as MAGI for short, and we're not talking about any wise kings here. MAGI consists of the figure on your tax return for adjusted gross income (AGI) plus any tax-exempt income you received that year.

I tried without success to find a clear definition of MAGI at IRS.gov, so here's one provided by TurboTax:

To calculate your modified adjusted gross income, take your AGI [adjusted gross income] and add back certain deductions. Many of these deductions are rare, so it's possible your AGI and MAGI can be identical. According to the IRS, your MAGI is your AGI with the addition of the following deductions, if applicable:

Student loan interest.
One-half of self-employment tax.
Qualified tuition expenses.
Tuition and fees deduction.
Passive loss or passive income.
IRA contributions.
Taxable social security payments.
The exclusion for income from U.S. savings bonds.
Foreign earned income exclusion.

Foreign housing exclusion or deduction.

The exclusion under 137 for adoption expenses.

Rental losses.

Any overall loss from a publicly traded partnership.

The IRMAA premium increases are not graduated but occur at specific dollar thresholds. It's thus possible that shaving just one buck from your MAGI could save a bundle.

Payroll taxes for Medicare also levy high-income surcharges on wage earners that were authorized by the ACA.

THE CONFUSION OVER COBRA

One last caution about Medicare rules involves employees who have lost or left their jobs and gotten COBRA continuation health insurance to help protect themselves and their families while they either look for another job with health benefits or seek health insurance elsewhere. These protections were created more than thirty-five years ago with passage of the Consolidated Omnibus Budget Reconciliation Act—hence the clever acronym.

These safeguards are welcome. My warning here is that when such a person turns 65 and becomes eligible for Medicare—*whether or not* they actually enroll in Medicare—COBRA insurers may stop providing them primary health coverage. Medicare becomes primary coverage in this situation, and COBRA policies are relegated to providing secondary coverage only for the covered health expenses that Medicare does not fully pay for. Few people know about this aspect of COBRA, and failure to get Medicare on a timely basis can have disastrous consequences. I've got the reader emails to prove it.

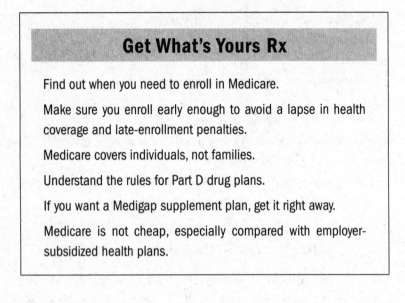

Get What's Yours Rx

Find out when you need to enroll in Medicare.

Make sure you enroll early enough to avoid a lapse in health coverage and late-enrollment penalties.

Medicare covers individuals, not families.

Understand the rules for Part D drug plans.

If you want a Medigap supplement plan, get it right away.

Medicare is not cheap, especially compared with employer-subsidized health plans.

MEDICAID: A PROGRAM
EVERYONE MAY NEED

Medicaid has surpassed Medicare as the government's largest health insurance and managed care provider, thanks to the Affordable Care Act's expansion option that most states have adopted. A projected 76 million people had some form of Medicaid in 2020. It provides multiple safety nets that include coverage for 29 million children, 11 million people with disabilities, 16 million low-income adults under age 65, 7 million who are 65 or older, and 12 million covered under the ACA.

Medicaid spending is split about 60–40, with the federal share ranging from 50 percent to more than 77 percent depending on a state's per capita income.

Access to Medicaid care can be a problem in some locales. Even where the feds pay most Medicaid expenses (including 90 percent of ACA coverage costs), it is still the largest budget expense for state governments. They regularly narrow eligibility in response to budget and political pressures.

Most people receive Medicaid through managed care plans that are increasingly offered by the same private insurers who dominate private and Medicare markets. Nearly 70 percent of the nation's physicians will see new Medicaid patients, although the figure is much lower in some places.

If you have a primary care doctor in a managed care plan, finding specialty care providers can be a challenge, even for the insurers who run the plans. Medicaid reimbursement rates generally are lower than those used by Medicare, which itself pays doctors less than what they receive from employer insurance plans.

The Trump administration has given states increased latitude, via Medicaid waivers, to depart from national coverage requirements. This has reduced access to the program through workplace waivers that require applicants to prove that they have been seeking employment. Support for waiver programs largely disappeared during the pandemic, as widespread job losses caused Medicaid enrollments to soar.

Still, research finds that access to Medicaid care is similar for those with Medicare and private health insurance. Access to care does not necessarily mean that it produces healthier outcomes, but Medicaid use is associated with better outcomes, particularly declines in infant and child mortality, plus later-life improvement in health and the abilities of these healthier children to hold better-paying jobs as adults.

Eligibility and coverage rules vary by state. The Kaiser Family Foundation collects and publishes much of this information; look at its 2020 report for details about your state. Use a search engine to find your state's Medicaid site.

LONG-TERM CARE

As you read in the last chapter, Medicare does not cover nonmedical care that disabled and older people often need, either in their homes or in nursing homes and other care facilities. Medicaid does, making these details important to a growing pool of possible beneficiaries.

This custodial care, as it's known, involves what are called the six activities of daily living (ADLs). These are a person's ability to be continent, to perform their own toileting, bathing, and personal hygiene needs, dress and feed themselves, and have enough functional mobility to get out of bed and move around their homes.

Private long-term care insurance covers only about one in ten older Americans, if that many. It's expensive and many insurance providers have run into serious financial problems.

As more older Americans require such care, rising Medicaid expenses for what are called LTSS—long-term services and supports—are increasing pressure on state and federal budgets. The two types of Medicaid programs covering LTSS are long-term care provided in a nursing home and home- and community-based services (HCBS).

Medicaid must cover anyone eligible for long-term care in a nursing home. States set their own eligibility rules in terms of a person's health condition and financial resources.

HCBS services, by contrast, are not mandated Medicaid entitlements. They are enabled through programs in which states seek waivers from the Centers for Medicare & Medicaid Services (CMS) to offer the benefits. HCBS services have been concentrated on people with disabilities. There is growing demand to offer them more broadly. Home care is cheaper than nursing home care, and people prefer it.

State generosity varies. Even those with the "best" HCBS programs may be way behind in processing HCBS applications, often due to shifting state budget issues. Waiting lists for eligible HCBS applicants are long and growing—wait times averaged thirty months back in 2017.

The shortage of such care would be even worse except that "many people don't know about" these benefits, said MaryBeth Musumeci, a Medicaid researcher with the Kaiser Family Foundation.

"Applying as early as possible" for such programs is helpful, she explained, because the initial application date establishes a person's place in line on their state's waiting list. She advises people to find their state's specific eligibility rules by getting in touch with their state's nonprofit aging resources agency. The National Association of

Area Agencies on Aging provides an online national locator to aging resources near you.

ALL IN THE FAMILY

At-home Medicaid care programs generally use the same functional eligibility criteria as does the nursing home long-term care benefit. As always, check with your state Medicaid program for details.

In some states, it's possible for family members to be paid by Medicaid for providing home-based care. This can be a significant monetary benefit for low-income households.

Advancing States, which works to improve state programs for aging and disabled residents, maintains a list of such states. Damon Terzaghi, a senior director at the organization, stressed that eligibility details vary among states and that waiver-based services are complicated.

"Not all of the programs in a single state will be administered the same," Terzaghi said in an email. "For example, you might have a waiver that is for individuals with intellectual or developmental disabilities that allows family members to be service providers, whereas a waiver for older adults in the same state may not. Similarly, some state-plan programs may not allow this to occur even if other waivers in the state do allow for it."

Lastly, eligibility definitions differ as to whether qualifying for service-based compensation requires the caregiver to be a "legally responsible person," a "relative," or a "legal guardian." "Legally responsible individuals" (such as parents and spouses) are allowed to provide services in cases of "extraordinary care," Terzaghi said. Other family members who are not "legally responsible"—grown children caring for their aging parents, adult siblings, or parents caring for an adult child—may qualify, too.

With that, here is the ADvancing States list:

Alabama, Colorado, District of Columbia, Florida, Georgia, Iowa, Kansas, Kentucky, Massachusetts, Minnesota, Montana, North Carolina, North Dakota, New Hampshire, New Jersey, New Mexico, New York, Oklahoma, Pennsylvania, South Dakota, Wisconsin, West Virginia, and Wyoming.

California is not on the list, but several of the state's waivers do allow some family members to be compensated for at-home Medicaid care. Its policy does not cover the broader category of legally responsible adults, which is the basis for inclusion on the list.

The California policy says that relatives may provide any waiver service, Terzaghi said, as long as the relative possesses the skill, training, and/or education to provide the service and that the individual meets the provider qualifications specified for that service. Relatives must meet the same requirements as other home-care providers and their performance may be monitored by state and local care agencies.

THE MEDICAID MONEY GAME

Medicaid does have coverage and financial details that apply to individuals and families regardless of where you live, so let's follow the money. Historically, only low-income people qualified for Medicaid's long-term care benefits, and they did so by passing income and asset tests. Often, they had to spend down nearly all of their wealth to do so. With the cost of long-term care often exceeding $100,000 a year, even many relatively affluent households may be facing a date with Medicaid in their futures.

Medicaid regulators use a standard "look-back period" of five years to judge whether a person's past asset divestitures were an inappropriate effort to avoid financial eligibility rules. Asset transfers that have occurred less than five years before applying for Medicaid may thus be included when evaluating that person's financial eligibility. As we'll see, there are important exceptions.

Whitney Gagnon, an attorney in New Hampshire with McLane Middleton, specializes in estate planning and elder law. Not all of a person's assets are "countable" toward Medicaid's asset test, she said. Besides a person's primary residence, certain life insurance policies may be excluded, as would certain types of irrevocable trusts and annuities.

Gagnon outlined long-term and immediate strategies for dealing with asset issues that can affect a person's later eligibility for Medicaid. The importance of state rules in determining Medicaid eligibility requires finding a competent attorney in your home state before acting on any general advice offered here.

The long-term strategy involves setting up and placing assets in what's called an irrevocable trust, Gagnon said. To avoid look-back sanctions, this needs to be done more than five years before the expected time when long-term care is needed. The key word here is "irrevocable," meaning that the person placing assets in the trust can never receive any principal back from the trust, she explained.

The assets in such a trust are thus excluded in determining a person's eligibility for Medicaid. The income generated by investments held by such a trust, however, can be provided to the person setting up the trust (the "grantor"). The trustee of such a trust can apportion the income among multiple recipients, which can come in handy if the person setting up the trust needs long-term nursing care and wants to qualify for Medicaid benefits. I'll explain more about this flexibility in a bit.

While creating such a trust can help someone qualify for Medicaid, Gagnon emphasized, it should be funded with assets that the person doesn't anticipate needing for living expenses and which are primarily intended to be conveyed to their heirs when they die. "We advise that people only transfer assets that they will never need or want," she said.

It's important not to put so much money into such a trust that the person finds themselves with insufficient funds to pay for other types of long-term care should they later need it.

There is a more immediate strategy that avoids the look-back rule and thus can be used once a person's need for long-term care has been established. This strategy, Gagnon explained, hinges on the fact that Medicaid has income and asset tests to determine the eligibility of the individual needing long-term care. There is, however, only an asset test for that person's spouse.

That spouse, commonly referred to as the community spouse, thus faces no income test. An immediate annuity can be created, with funding that escapes Medicaid's look-back rules of asset transfers. Income from the annuity can be directed to the community spouse without violating Medicaid rules.

"There's no specific limit in the guidelines," Gagnon said, "but in practice, usually, annuities that are over" $1 million "are denied."

Such annuities should be set up with limited payout terms geared to the ages and health of both spouses. "If the community spouse does not survive the term of the annuity," Gagnon said, "the remainder beneficiary has to be the state, and the state will receive a portion of the funds left in the annuity, up to the amount of the benefits that were provided to the spouse in the nursing home. We [thus] often try to get a very short-term annuity that we know the community spouse is going to outlive."

Because the community spouse faces no income test for Medicaid eligibility, a household that has set up an irrevocable trust can have its income shifted totally to that spouse.

As for home equity, the states have rules for equity levels that permit a person to still qualify for Medicaid long-term care benefits. States generally use the federal minimum of $572,000; a few have higher limits—up to $858,000.

"Nursing home residents do not automatically have to sell their homes in order to qualify for Medicaid, but that doesn't mean the house is completely protected," according to Medicaid experts in New York at Levene Gouldin & Thompson.

"The state will likely put a lien on the house while the resident is living and attempt to recover the property after the resident has passed away (but) the state cannot impose a lien if a spouse, a disabled or blind child, a child under age 21, or a sibling with an equity interest in the house is living in the house."

The equity limits cited here apply only when the entire home is owned by the individual seeking Medicaid. If a couple has joint ownership of the home, then only half its equity is applied to the test.

Lastly, and with due apologies for droning on here, equity value means the home's fair market value less any outstanding mortgages. So, if you have a mortgage on your primary residence, Gagnon points out, it can make sense to pay if off early or at least to pay off enough of the mortgage so that the home's resulting equity value is still in compliance with Medicaid eligibility rules. Paying back a mortgage with personal assets can be done at the last minute without violating Medicaid's look-back rules, she said.

SUPPORT PAYMENTS TO MEDICARE FOR LOW-INCOME MEDICAID ENROLLEES

Nearly 10 million Medicare recipients also qualify for Medicaid. As noted in the last chapter, there are four Medicare Savings Programs to help these dual eligibles pay for their Medicare benefits. There also is an Extra Help program to help people pay for their medications under Medicare's Part D drug program. More than a million dual eligibles either pay higher medical costs, go without care, or both, because they are unaware of these benefits. The federally funded State Health Insurance Assistance Program (SHIP) provides free Medicare counseling and has state offices able to help you understand if you qualify for any of these programs and then help you apply if you do.

THE ABLE PROGRAM

The Achieving a Better Life Experience (ABLE) Act allows people who became disabled before age 26 to benefit from 401(k)-like accounts that provide tax-free proceeds to help pay their personal disability-related expenses without compromising their eligibility for Medicaid. The accounts can be funded with up to $15,000 a year in post-tax money that may be contributed by anyone. The accounts have state-specified lifetime maximums in account balances that range from about $235,000 to more than $510,000. The Academy of Special Needs Planners maintains a directory of state programs.

(A state-by-state list, as of 2020, of lifetime maximums for ABLE accounts and Medicaid home equity limits may be found in Appendix 3.)

Get What's Yours Rx

Medicaid rules are set by individual states; they pay a third to a half of program costs.

Pandemic job losses have raised demand for Medicaid and created pressure for state budget cuts.

It can take a long time to get an appointment for Medicaid services, so apply early and document your place in "line."

Unlike Medicare, Medicaid does cover long-term care for people with low incomes and little wealth.

PART TWO

YOUR HEALTH CARE TEAM

HEROES III

The Letter Writer

Julie Greenwood

Julie Greenwood has coped with painfully debilitating psoriatic arthritis for nearly thirty years. She was born in July 1968 and her symptoms first showed up in 1991 after she got a perm at her hair salon in North Carolina. Her scalp felt like it was burning, and she assumed her hairdresser had simply left something on her scalp too long.

Shortly thereafter, she started noticing flaking, and thought it was from the perm mishap. In a few weeks, she had pain in her fingers and they later became swollen. She was then working for a chiropractor, who said her symptoms were indicative of the effects of psoriatic arthritis. She then went to a specialist, the diagnosis was confirmed, and she has been dealing with the disease nearly nonstop since then.

Greenwood said she has had a knee replacement, foot surgery, thumb surgery, and surgery to remove the ulna bone on the outside of one wrist. She's had so many steroid injections in her spine that it has deteriorated to the point where spine surgery may become necessary. She takes a bunch of drugs with unpronounceable names that seem to be missing vowels. She has regular physical therapy and water aerobics classes. She sees a psychiatrist, who helps manage her antidepressant and other medications, and a behavioral therapist.

After three decades, Greenwood has become wise in the ways of pain and the challenges of living a worthwhile life. Her daughter, Nora, was born in January 2002. She said her first husband walked out when Nora was only two weeks old, and that she's been married since 2014 to a wonderfully supportive man.

Millions of Americans cope with serious chronic conditions that can only be managed, not cured. Greenwood long ago learned that railing against what's "not right" would not get her far if she didn't figure out how to get the care and medications she needs. For her, fighting back has meant reaching out to people for support and trying to connect with people in human terms, not as faceless care providers or insurance company telephone representatives.

This lesson was driven home to her in 2004, when a new health insurer denied coverage for her to take Enbrel, an expensive biologic that had been working wonders for her. The insurer said that Enbrel was not medically necessary and that she could be treated with less costly medications. In increasing pain and at her wit's end, Greenwood sat down and wrote a letter that she sent to anyone she could think of, including her insurer, the Enbrel sales rep, and the maker of Enbrel, Amgen Inc.

Here are excerpts from Greenwood's 2004 letter:

> The first time I ever had any problem with psoriasis was about 12 years ago. I had no idea what was going on. I only knew that people would stop me and tell me that I had bread crumbs in my hair. The flaking continued to get worse and, at the same time, I was having severe joint pain. . . .
>
> All these years later, I have taken many different types of anti-inflammatory drugs, including Naprosyn, ibuprofen, Celebrex and Bextra. I have severe damage not only in my right pinkie finger but also in my right wrist. I am completely

unable to hold out my hand for change or turn it even half of the way that it should go. I am also worried about what years of taking this type of medication will do to my health.

My wrist has hurt so bad some days that I can't use my right arm to pick up my two year old daughter. Many times, I have had difficulties dressing myself and my daughter. Simple things, like picking up a dinner plate or taking change from a cashier, are still a major task for me.

When [my doctor] first mentioned Enbrel to me, I was very skeptical. I was terribly afraid of giving myself a shot. I had never even been able to watch anyone give me a shot before . . . could never even allow myself to see the needle that would be used. It seemed that this was a terrible choice in medication for my psoriasis/psoriatic arthritis.

My arthritis seemed to be getting worse, so I felt that I had to try this option, no matter how difficult. The first injection was very difficult. It took me 30 minutes to get up the nerve to inject myself. When I finally did, I couldn't believe how easy it was. Within 2 weeks, I was seeing miraculous results. For the first time in years, I didn't have to take any other medicine for my arthritis. The only thing I was using on my skin was Cetaphil and was already seeing significant clearing.

After another week, I felt like a human being again. I had human skin, which improved my self-image as much as it did my pain and discomfort. Enbrel was nothing short of a miracle for me. However, I had insurance thru my employer at that time, and in December 2004, I was no longer covered. . . .

It took a couple of months for me to get into really bad shape with my skin and joints again, but it did happen, and when it did, it was really bad. I knew what Enbrel could do for me, and still had a prescription for it . . . (But my new insurer has decided I do not have a medical need for this drug.)

I need Enbrel. It gives me a chance at life. It allows me to function normally. When I take Enbrel, I can play with my daughter. I can dress myself and my child. I can write and cook and type without difficulties. Enbrel allows me to work. This letter is to anyone who can use this information to help me get this medication for myself. If my insurance company feels that Enbrel is not medically necessary, I beg to differ. I have seen how good life is when you feel good. For the first time in 12 years, I know what it's like to feel good.

Shortly after sending her letter, Greenwood was approved for Enbrel and the trajectory of her life changed. In her case, and perhaps yours, reaching out in a nonthreatening way can be an effective way to fight back.

YOUR PERSONAL HEALTH PLAN

The loneliest feeling on the planet is when you learn that you, a child, or another loved one is facing a medical crisis—an accident that requires immediate medical treatment, the diagnosis of a life-changing illness, or some other event you feel unprepared for. You are vulnerable. You're likely not at your best just then in solving problems and worrying about the many tasks triggered by this news. The pressure to make informed decisions quickly may be intense.

One of the questions I asked health experts for this book was what they thought people should do to increase their odds of a successful outcome when faced with such a challenge. To a person, they emphasized the need to prepare for future needs by doing things in advance of needing care.

Prevention grabs few headlines when it comes to health care issues. That's a big mistake. It is a topic that can engender eye rolls from patients and attitudes such as, "Yeah, yeah. I already know that."

The coronavirus pandemic might have changed all that. We'll see whether its lifesaving preventive care lessons survive the pandemic itself. I can't do much here about that. I can explain the powerful link between preventive health care and significant health benefits— needing less care, spending less money, and living healthier and longer lives. Here are some compelling findings from experts:

If you exercise 30 minutes a day, five days a week, you can achieve a 50 percent reduction in cardiac mortality. *Dr. Dipti Itchaporia, American College of Cardiology.*

Cancer claims 600,000 lives a year and there are about 1.7 million new cancers each year. Many of those deaths and cases can be prevented through early screening. *Dr. Laura Makaroff, American Cancer Society.*

Flu killed 80,000 in 2018 yet fewer than 50 percent of Americans get annual flu vaccines. *Dr. John Brownstein, Harvard Medical School.*

Roughly 30 million people in the United States have high blood pressure, 25 million have high cholesterol, 10 million have diabetes. These conditions are relatively easy to treat if people know about them and act. Many don't. If they did seek preventive care, we could prevent 650,000 annual cardiovascular deaths, up to 150,000 stroke deaths, and 80,000 deaths from type 2 diabetes. *Dr. Eduardo Sanchez, American Heart Association.*

Obesity, a leading cause of chronic illnesses, is so much worse in the U.S. that it might more accurately be known as the American condition.

Prevalence of obesity, BMI ≥ 30, age-standardized estimates, 2016 or nearest year

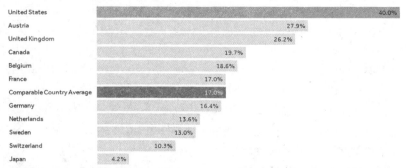

United States	40.0%
Austria	27.9%
United Kingdom	26.2%
Canada	19.7%
Belgium	18.6%
France	17.0%
Comparable Country Average	17.0%
Germany	16.4%
Netherlands	13.6%
Sweden	13.0%
Switzerland	10.3%
Japan	4.2%

Notes: BMI is Body Mass Index. Comparable countries here include Japan and the United Kingdom. Data for Canada and France are for 2015, data for Australia and Belgium are for 2014, and data for Germany are for 2012. Obesity data for Canada, Netherlands, and Sweden are self-reported.

Source: KFF analysis of OECD data

PLANNERS OF THE WORLD, UNITE!

"I travel internationally quite a bit for work," says UnitedHealthcare's Mike Baker, whom we met in the opening chapter. "I do a little bit of travel for pleasure and one of the places I go is [in Latin America]. And since I go there a fair amount, I know the telephone for the local hospital in the area that I go a lot, and have confirmed that there is somebody there who speaks English. I know the number for the State Department embassy there. And those things are in my phone. And I've needed them not once, but I suspect that because I go often enough, the moment when I need them, I'm going to want to have done that due diligence. And I get grief from my siblings and others for being *that* guy. I'm an operations person, and it's in my nature. But the time will come when I need it, and that's not the time when I will want to be Googling outside of my cell phone zone to find somebody who is not a great English speaker."

Planning extends to personal behaviors and lifestyle disciplines. The longevity benefits of taking good care of yourself can be enormous and flow disproportionately to those with money. Research done a few years ago found that people on top of the financial food chain lived more than fourteen years longer, on average, than those at the bottom, and that this longevity edge had widened by more than two years since the beginning of the twenty-first century. You might think, as I did, that rich people just bought better health care, and there is some truth to this. But the greatest contribution to life expectancy among the top 25 percent income group was preventive health care and exercise. And, for all you smart readers out there, education was a close second.

The message here is pretty clear: take care of yourself and you will live longer. Again, you already know this, right?

Baker is a bit extreme, even by his own account. He illustrates the potential value of health care planning. People often don't do this.

They lose out on a tremendous opportunity to prepare themselves for medical events that often are a surprise and that can pressure people into quick and perhaps poor decisions. Into this medical maelstrom would flow all of the issues created by our complicated and expensive health care system. Somehow, with the clock ticking loudly, you've got to find access to the best care at a price that you can afford, or at least a price that won't bankrupt you.

I wrote a book about Medicare a few years ago. Among its obvious and, to me at least, widely overlooked maxims was that people don't know what they don't know. When the topic is as complicated as Medicare or, in this case, all of health care, the implications are scary. Your health needs don't care what you do or do not know. They may not wait for you to educate yourself before you have to make consequential decisions, either for yourself or a child or other family member. No pressure, right?

KNOW THYSELF

Taking better care of yourself and your family begins with an informed understanding of your body and your family's medical history. There's a reason doctors collect this information. Couples who plan to have children should research their family histories for conditions their kids might inherit.

The U.S. Centers for Disease Control and Prevention (CDC) takes a deep dive into all of this. It explains links between aspects of your history and specific medical conditions and includes an online family history form that will help you compile a complete history and permit you to save this information and update it if needed. The site stresses that it does not store any personal information or share it with third parties. It does ask for your name. Color me skeptical! I'm guessing that large numbers of Jane and John Does have recorded their family histories here!

As mundane as you might judge them to be, family medical histories are "considered the most powerful tool that people can bring to their physicians," says Natalie Beck, a genetics counselor at Johns Hopkins in Baltimore. "If that information is brought to somebody who works in genetic medicine, we're trained to recognize the pattern of health issues that can run in families."

WHAT A HEALTH CARE HERO SAYS: "Get to really know your body, because doctors are great and everything but they see you once or twice a year. You know your body better than anyone else. If you have never done a breast or self-exam, you aren't going to know what is normal. Start today, and start to know your own normal. I just happened to find a lump on my testicle when I was doing my monthly self-exam."

—Justin Birckbichler, twenty-nine, public school technology coach, testicular cancer survivor

---

The CDC site has extensive genomics information. The issue of genetic tests for you and your children has moved from *someday* to *today*. More than 30 million Americans have swabbed their cheeks and waited to learn more about themselves and their heritage.

DNA tests from 23andMe, among others, are relatively cheap, and have contributed to rising consumer demand for more sophisticated genetic tests, which are not cheap and often not covered by insurance. Hospitals around the country are setting up high-end testing programs. The benefits of such testing may take years to be clinically proven, but people are making decisions now and not waiting.

23andMe had sold 10 million DNA testing kits as of mid-2019, when I spoke with Erin Trimble, the company's head of product partnerships. This included its Ancestry kit for $99 and the Health +

Ancestry service for $199. The company provides an expanding array of reports about genetic-related health issues that reflect the growing sophistication of the field.

As we learn more about the links between genes and specific health conditions, the logic of such low-cost services will increase. Use them as an inexpensive early warning system if you have reason to think you face elevated risks of serious health conditions linked to your family medical history. Don't expect test results to be actionable. They may indicate that additional (and more expensive) genetic testing is warranted. "We do encourage our customers to take their results to a health provider," Trimble says.

Beck, who left Hopkins after our interview to work for a telemedicine genetics company, cautions people not to expect definitive answers from direct-to-consumer DNA test kits. They are "likely not going to answer questions that people might have that are very appropriate, such as, 'Do I have an increased or decreased risk for '*xyz*.'

"And they also take the person's DNA and analyze it on a platform that is without the patient's medical and family histories, which are kind of the crux of genetic medicine," she added. Genetic counselors should take "all of that into account when we are evaluating a person, and helping them identify tests that would be informative and useful for their health care. So, there's not really like a one-size-fits-all type of [genetic] test."

Arguably the most significant tests that parents should track for their children are the newborn screenings automatically done for free at hospitals since the middle of the last century. The range of tested conditions has expanded, giving this single test the "largest impact on somebody's long-term life and health," Beck said. Some states include genetic screening as part of their newborn testing, she added, so make sure you check if your state is among them and exactly what conditions are included.

The National Society of Genetic Counselors maintains a directory to help you find a counselor. Prices—what's charged, what insurers cover, and what your out-of-pocket costs will be—are all over the place.

Concerns about the privacy of your genome are valid. Your genes can have life-changing effects on family members for generations, not to mention being a big deal for you. Blind DNA testing services are a response to privacy issues. Nebula Genetics began offering such a service in 2019, and others are sure to follow. If the testing service doesn't know the identities of its clients, that's a strong line of defense against others linking you to your genomic profile. Please do your homework before sharing your DNA results.

PREVENTIVE CARE

The cheapest health care is care you don't need and, if you take good care of yourself, may never need. Cue the "diet and exercise" music, fade into the sunset shot, and move on. I'll stipulate, as I did with assembling a family medical history, that you already know much of this stuff and either will or will not do the right thing. My job here is to nudge you.

Despite all we know about preventive care, even a lot of informed people fail to practice it. The consequences may be disastrous to them and certainly are disastrous for society. Each year, 1.3 million Americans die from largely preventable heart diseases and cancers.

In late 2019, Facebook launched a smartphone preventive health tool (that it promises is private) to focus on these two diseases. It partnered with the American Cancer Society (ACS), the American College of Cardiology (ACC), the American Heart Association (AHA), and the Centers for Disease Control and Prevention.

The guidelines for identifying screening and treatment needs for these illnesses are well known to medical experts if not to patients. Facebook has loaded these guidelines into a free app. The tool includes access to free preventive care for uninsured people at Federally Qualified Health Centers.

WHAT A HEALTH CARE HERO SAYS: "A lot of people they'll say, 'Oh, cancer runs in my family; oh, diabetes runs in my family; oh, fibromyalgia runs in my family.' And that's all they do. I strongly recommend that if you have an illness that's predominant in your family, you need to do your research on it, and become an expert, because you could be that person that becomes that family member with that illness. Have open dialogue with your family members to find out how is everybody's health? Lifestyle and fitness and nutrition play a key role to what can happen later in life. Life is life, and we're all dealt a set of cards. And it might not be the best hand, but you better play the heck out of that hand because you still have that opportunity to put on that poker face and bluff life; you still have the potential to win that hand."

—*Kristal Kent, forty-five, army
veteran, chronic fibromyalgia*

While you may tell yourself that you would seek preventive care if you needed it, the facts say otherwise. Screenings for the most treatable cancers, including breast, colorectal, lung, and cervical cancers, have stagnated, according to Dr. Makaroff of the ACS.

Despite her role as a disease prevention expert, she said that even she sometimes failed to talk about prevention to her own primary care patients. The culprit? "We just run out of time" because patient appointments are too short, she said.

Since the United States has priced itself out of being able to provide affordable health care to many of us, the world of preventive care deserves more attention solely as a means to save money.

The Affordable Care Act greatly expanded the list of largely free preventive health services that insurers are required by law to cover.

This list is overseen by several medical groups, most importantly a volunteer group of sixteen rotating health experts called the U.S. Preventive Services Task Force. Other groups include the Advisory Committee on Immunization Practices, the American Academy of Pediatrics, and the U.S. Health Resources and Services Administration.

WHAT A HEALTH CARE HERO SAYS: "Whether you have an acute or a chronic condition, at some point every one of us will be a patient and it is important to have access to and an understanding of your health care records. Sometimes different physicians and medical centers do not share patient information with one another; you should always have access to your own medical information. . . . Make an 'in case of emergency' list that quickly and easily has your medical resources listed in one place. List each of your doctor's names with their address, phone number and e-mail. List, update, and keep current medications and medical conditions. Once you have this list keep it at home and a copy in your wallet or purse. . . . Whether you use 'smart technology' or a pen and paper, many people have begun to monitor their fitness (counting steps, measuring blood pressure, and tracking sleep). In addition, patients now track their medication, symptoms, and side effects. Even a food diary can help people better understand their sensitivities to certain foods."

—*Amanda Greene, diagnosed in 1985*
with lupus, fibromyalgia, osteoarthritis,
and rheumatoid arthritis

The people who serve on the Preventive Services Task Force don't get paid for this work and disclose extensive information on professional affiliations to deal with conflict-of-interest issues. They review and evaluate available preventive treatments and provide letter grades to reflect their health benefits. By law, grades of A and B must be covered by health insurers under the ACA rules.

A list of top-graded preventive care measures is in Appendix 4 and has more than fifty entries. For all you Mike Bakers out there, review the list, discuss it with your primary care doctor, and agree on the procedures that make sense for you. Even if covered by insurance, your health profile may make some of them unnecessary, a topic covered in Chapter Eleven. If it makes you feel better, nearly no one takes full advantage of recommended preventive care procedures, according to a 2018 study. Here's a look at the percentages of people aged 35 and older who had high-priority recommended procedures for their age groups. See how you stack up:

Screening

Blood pressure	87
Cholesterol	82
Cervical cancer	75
Breast cancer	74
Colon cancer	64
Osteoporosis	63

Screening and counseling

Obesity	64
Tobacco use	62
Alcohol use	41
Depression	41

Vaccinations

Pneumonia   66
Flu   49
Shingles   38

Preventive medication

Aspirin use   46

Get What's Yours Rx

Preventive care is the cheapest and most effective health care.

COVID-19 has proven the value of preventive health care but it's not clear how long this perception will last.

A family medical history is essential to building a preventive care plan for you and your family.

Genetic tests are important early warning guides.

Learn which preventive health tests you should take; most are free.

YOUR PERSONAL CARE TEAM

Trudy Lieberman's urinary tract infection was not getting better when, in the fall of 2017, she and her family called for an ambulance to take her to a nearby New York City hospital. Two months later, she awoke from a coma after an array of life-threatening conditions plus some questionable care decisions. For those months and another month after she awoke, she was unable to speak or eat on her own because a breathing tube had been inserted down her trachea.

"My medical odyssey spanned four months, four hospitals, and two states," she later wrote. "During that time, my body atrophied: I would have to relearn to walk, get out of bed, sit in a chair, eat with a knife and fork, swallow scrambled eggs without fatally aspirating them." Her survival "was probably a mixture of luck, genetics, race, socioeconomic status, excellent insurance that erased the worry of high and surprise medical bills, and a family that fought so hard for me."

If anyone ever needed strong caregiving support from family and friends, it was Lieberman. And she had a formidable posse. "My family was armed to fight the health care system in a way that few families are. A rich network of my friends, professional colleagues, and journalistic sources supported them and were always ready with suggestions to hurdle the system's roadblocks. We created a ruckus when things went wrong. We asked questions. We knew how to be advocates for my health and fight against the obstacles."

Lieberman, in her seventies, has been writing about consumer rights for fifty years, most notably for *Consumer Reports* and the

Columbia Journalism Review. Health care is the focus of one of her five books. I know Trudy and confess to likely bias in retelling her ordeal; you can read it online in her own words.

Few patients were as well informed on health issues as Lieberman, although she had little ability to advocate for herself during much of her care. Her daughter took over, going around Lieberman's emergency room at one hospital and wiping down all the surfaces with Purell. When she did regain consciousness and a modicum of strength, Lieberman watched her caregivers closely. At one point, she forced herself to stay awake at night to make sure she was being administered the correct medications in the proper dosages.

People who are seriously ill in a hospital may be reluctant or simply unable to question their treatment. Lieberman was so concerned at one point during her long recovery that she switched doctors. She believes the decision contributed to her survival.

Lieberman was forced to confront some of the limitations of the consumer empowerment beliefs that have underpinned her journalism. "I realized that the notion that patients can use metrics and ratings to navigate their care becomes absurd once they are in a hospital. At that point, procedures and tests are condition-driven—that is, determined by illness—and patients are often in no position to bargain or choose."

One significant bright spot, as she noted, is that Lieberman and her family were spared financial distress, and possibly much more, because she had excellent health insurance—basic Medicare, a Part D drug plan, and a Medigap supplement plan that paid nearly all covered expenses not fully paid by basic Medicare. Once, a doctor billed her $400 for that part of his bill not covered by Medicare. Medicare later flagged the bill as improper because it prohibits such "balance billing" charges. The doctor sent her a check for the $400.

All told, Lieberman's total out-of-pocket expenses were about $5,000—out of medical bills totaling roughly $3 million! Not surprisingly, she is a big, big fan of Medicare, although her journalistic DNA recognizes $3 million is an unsustainable price for the health system to charge, even for care as extensive as hers. (Medicare undoubtedly settled her bills for much less.)

"All this nonsense about shopping around is just not very valuable once you have a serious illness and you are in a hospital," she told me two years later. "There is no way you can monitor everyone coming into your room. Whether they're going to balance bill, or whether they're in network or out of network. Most of the time, we didn't even know who these people were."

HOW TO BUILD YOUR PERSONAL
HEALTH CARE POSSE

Navigating our challenging health care system is a team sport. The patient can't do it alone. We seldom do much about it until an adverse health event is on the doorstep. We then go to Defcon 3 and become a Tasmanian devil of medical activity. This chapter is going to lay out all the things you need to do to build your health care plan *before* a medical problem occurs, including assembling what I am calling your health care posse and knowing how you would put it to work if it were needed.

Begin with a primary go-to person. Once you've decided who that should be, you need to sit down, face-to-face, and talk about what you'd like them to do and why. This conversation might be uncomfortable in spots. Do it anyway. A glass of wine may help this medicine go down.

Sometimes, your spouse—a logical primary helper—winds up *not* being the right choice. Here's a short list of what to look for in that person:

Availability. What good is a main helper if they're mainly unavailable? When you need to reach out to someone on the phone, which person is going to always pick up on the other end of the line?

Empathy. Your emotional needs may be as large as your medical requirements; you need to have a support person who can help you on both fronts.

Practicality. When my wife has a health problem, my first thought is to go find a roster of medical experts to provide her advice. Often, what she needs first is a hug. Next comes listening to what she has to say.

Once your primary posse member is on board, the two of you should talk about the need for other posse members and the roles you'd like them to fill. Like our master planner Mike Baker, you may never need to put this plan into action. Nevertheless, have a plan! The stakes are too high to wing it. If you've got children at home, of course, you already should be the head of their posse, and have a plan for them.

Whether you wind up with a posse of one or eleven, here's what posse members should be able and willing to do on your behalf:

- Make legally binding health decisions for you if for any reason you are not able to make these decisions yourself.
- Become an expert on your medical condition, including recommended treatments, finding the highest-quality care, and connecting with other patients who have gone through the same condition.
- Deal with the medical folks and institutions who wind up providing your care. This can include the care being provided, who is providing it, what they charge for the services, and advocating for your rights.

- Understand how your health insurance works, including what it covers, how to appeal claims denials, and how to wrangle over bills.
- Worry on your behalf about how you'll pay for treatment, including what it costs, what it should cost, and how to negotiate effectively to pay as little as possible.
- Coordinate with other people in your life to help handle your obligations, including grocery shopping and meal preparation, handling home maintenance appointments and repair visits, helping your kids and other family members.
- Keep posse members up to date on how you're doing.
- Listen to you, rants and all, and provide the emotional support you need.
- Do whatever else it takes so that you can focus on your treatment and recovery needs.

UNDERSTAND WHAT MIGHT BE WRONG WITH YOU

Major medical institutions and consumer medical sites are great tools to help you understand and evaluate your doctors' diagnoses and possible treatment plans. This is stuff you and your posse members need to know, and you should be on the same page here and not challenging one another with amateur diagnoses.

Rather than spending the next ten pages evaluating the relative merits of one site versus another, my advice is to visit a bunch of sites—see what they say, where they agree, and where they don't. It shouldn't take you too long to have a pretty good working understanding of your health situation, including follow-up questions to ask your doctors. Chapter Nine includes advice on how to talk with your doctors. Chapter Eleven discusses recommended care that you may not need and how to spot a bad medical diagnosis.

Increasingly, Google is becoming a good place to start. The

company's expanding commitment to becoming a major player in health care includes featuring clinically accurate sources among the first sites listed when people use its search engine to ask about health conditions and related medical terms. This is no accident. Google is exploring how to make big inroads (and big bucks) in health care, and realizes that its eponymous search engine must deliver accurate information if it is to be taken seriously.

Health care consumers aren't the only ones using such sites. Doctors and other health professionals use them, too. The leading subscription site for them is called UpToDate and is provided to 1.7 million people around the world by the professional services firms of Wolters Kluwer. It provides free patient access that lets you search for information keyed to specific health conditions.

Medical information can be complicated, and UpToDate reports can make for dense reading. Be prepared to spend some time here. The free entry for "headache" is more than two thousand words long. UpToDate's "Beyond the Basics" educational entries are useful in introducing and explaining the medical terms that your doctors and other expert caregivers may use when discussing your health diagnosis and recommended treatment. If you want full access from your computer or via a smartphone app, you can get weekly and monthly UpToDate subscriptions.

YOUR ADVOCACY POSSE

Beyond your core posse, you should build what I'll call your advocacy posse. These are people and organizations—most of whom you will never meet or know—who are dedicated to dealing with your specific medical condition and needs. If there is a virtue to social media that counters the many problems it has created, it may be found in online health support groups. Facebook says it has more than ten thousand private health advocacy groups.

"PatientsLikeMe, with more than 250,000 members, is the largest of the online health communities," Dr. Eric Topol wrote in his book *The Patient Will See You Now*. "There are hundreds of them that have cropped up in recent years, with cumulatively well over a million participating patients. Some are quite specialized, such as Crohnology, for patients with Crohn's disease and ulcerative colitis, which was started by Sean Ahrens, age twenty-five."

Further, the kindness, support, and help of others is essential to well-being, especially when it comes to health challenges. We knew this even before the coronavirus pandemic. I hope that appreciating the importance of social relationships will be one of its lasting lessons.

YOUR SOCIAL MEDIA POSSE

WEGO Health, based in Boston, helped me understand the intersection of health and social media. The company has evaluated what it calls "patient leaders" on social media platforms and has identified more than 100,000 of them. WEGO has not done this solely out of the goodness of its corporate heart. It packages this collective expertise and sells it to clients to inform their online health care marketing and sales efforts.

Jack Barrette, founder and CEO, acknowledged that client revenues are essential but said that the social mission of the company is the top priority. "There's just no one in this for the money," he said.

I walked through the typical Facebook engagement process with a Facebook health manager who would speak with me only if I agreed not to name him. Patient advocates often set up private Facebook groups. This makes sense on privacy grounds. People facing health challenges need somewhere to get guidance and support from people like them who understand what they're going through. They want to feel safe, not commercially exploited.

Using the Facebook search box, you can type in your health issue and append it to the phrase "support group." Facebook already divides its groups into categories. Health is one of them, so looking through groups in that category can be a good way to go.

Figuring out which group, if any, is right for you, is as much art as science, the manager said. First off, are you more interested in information or emotional support? Do you like the tone of the group? What information have group administrators decided to share with you before joining?

Many groups have created membership questionnaires to help people determine if they are a good fit for the group, and vice versa. Private group administrators—not Facebook employees—oversee member admissions and monitor the appropriateness of discussions. If a group's administrator believes someone is using the group inappropriately, they can drop that person from the group. Check out Facebook's community standards for additional details.

At my request, WEGO asked some of its patient leaders to provide advice on using social media. Careful engagement was their common theme:

Be careful about the kind of sensitive information that you share.

I don't really think there is a way to ensure that a social media site will protect your health information if you publicly share it.

If an online community does not have some sort of community and privacy guidelines outlined, I would proceed with caution, or find a different online community.

Be open in order to get what you need but be aware of what you post.

Read the Terms and Conditions carefully. I don't use my full name and certainly don't share a lot until I have been a member and seen how the group works together.

Maybe you want to only join private groups that are well monitored and mediated. Maybe you want to make your posts public and be a beacon of hope for others. Choose what is right for you.

I think when it comes to social media use, you need to work on the assumption that everything and anything you share could one day be "completely out there," and if you don't want that to happen, then don't post it.

Rather than worrying about the credibility of the platforms themselves, Barrette says the better advice is to look at the trustworthiness of individuals and groups using them. Harking back to the earlier days of broadcast television, he said, think of them as the big online networks that everyone must use. It's the programming—what's on those networks—that matters.

VISIT TWO WEBSITES AND
CALL ME IN THE MORNING

The National Financial Resource Directory is a patient support tool. Provided by the Patient Advocate Foundation, it goes well beyond financial help and includes an extensive list of other types of support groups.

There are separate entry paths depending on whether you have health insurance. The directory does a good job of breaking down what can be a stultifying number of possible health resources. It uses four pull-down menus that progressively narrow your search parameters: your age range, the state where you live, your medical diagnosis, and the type of assistance you're seeking. Once you've selected all four choices, you then launch your search. (Further details on using this directory are in Appendix 5.)

"One place we really fall down and that's going to be superimportant [is that] our system really fails when we expect consumers to do a good job of managing complex diseases and health problems," said Dr. Karen Joynt Maddow, an assistant professor of medicine at Washington University in Saint Louis. "We need to fix the system such that it doesn't put the onus on people. . . . I don't think the patient is the appropriate consumer for those details."

Appropriate or not, this is the system you need to deal with right now.

As emphasized elsewhere, health care is not a spectator sport. You need to be engaged and so do members of your health care posse. Whether you're a patient or a posse member, you need to be an advocate for yourself and for family members, said Maria de Jesus Diaz-Perez, director of public reporting at the Center for Improving Value in Health Care in Denver. You need to do your homework. "If you don't have a basic understanding about how things work, you cannot be an advocate," she said.

ASSEMBLE YOUR MEDICAL RECORDS

Having current and comprehensive medical records is essential to successfully navigating any serious encounter with health care. As we've seen, medicine has become so complex that even doctors and other medical experts need help keeping up with it all.

Ideally, your primary care physician's office is the best place to house and maintain your complete medical records. It may need some help and prodding to do so, so don't be shy about making sure they have all your information. You may need to call other health care providers and nudge them to provide your treatment history.

Your smartphone should have a file that links to your medical records. Key posse members should have this on their phones, too. Yes, this may be a hassle. Do it anyway.

As with other health situations, the "trust but verify" approach is best here. Assuming someone has your records is a mistake. Assuming that organizations with access to your records will give them to you quickly is a bad idea. You do have the legal right to your hospital records. Getting health providers to honor those rights may be hard. They also may charge a fee.

In a 2018 study, researchers contacted 83 top-ranked hospital systems with facilities in nearly thirty states. On the telephone, all 83 told researchers they would provide personal medical records. When researchers posed as health care consumers in the actual process of requesting records, the results were much different:

- All the hospitals stated in the telephone calls that they could do so, but only about half of them disclosed on their authorization forms that they were capable of releasing entire medical records.
- More than 40 percent did not reveal fee schedules on their authorization form or on the web page from which the authorization form was obtained, so patients were often not aware of the potential costs associated with requesting medical records.
- Nearly 50 hospitals charged fees for providing the records that were higher than the $6.50 flat fee recommended by HIPAA's regulator for electronically maintained records. One hospital wanted to charge more than $540.

"Studies have shown that patients want access to their records," the study's authors said. "When patients have access, they have a better understanding of their health information, improved care coordination and communication with their physicians, and better adherence to treatment. . . . Complicated, lengthy, and costly medical records request processes continue to inhibit patients from accessing their records."

THE FINE PRINT

People can't step up to help you in encounters with the health care system unless they are legally allowed to act on your behalf. These permissions often are geared toward people with serious illnesses who may be near the end of their lives. You should have them before you reach that point.

Prepare for Your Care provides helpful guides and checklists for the kinds of decisions you and your posse members may face. Advance directives, comprising a health care proxy and a living will, can be downloaded for your state. The guidance includes instructions to complete legally binding versions of these documents.

A health care proxy, a health care power of attorney, and a durable power of attorney are different terms for similar legal instruments. They let designated posse members (a spouse, parent, or child) make medical decisions on your behalf should you be unable to speak for yourself.

A living will sets out the types of medical care you want in an emergency situation. Do you want doctors to do whatever they can to keep you alive? Do you want ambulance medics and other health care professionals to try to resuscitate you should you stop breathing? Do you want to be hooked up to a machine and intubated so that you can stay alive while doctors try to restore your health?

You might be able to handle all of this with some online searches that will lead you to any number of legal sites with the forms you need. I recommend getting an attorney and, if you have the time and money, doing them all at the same time: a will, a durable power of attorney, a medical power of attorney, and a living will. The terms may differ based on the laws where you live. The objective of these documents is to set forth your end-of-life wishes that you want your legally empowered advocates to insist be honored by doctors, hospitals, and other caregivers. State rules vary here, so make sure whatever you have done will be honored in your home state.

Once you have these forms properly executed, notarized, and printed, put them in a safe place that is known to family members and make sure your primary posse member has a set. In addition to printed copies, get digital versions and then email them to the appropriate people in your posse. Send yourself a set, too, so they can be accessible from your smartphone. Medical emergencies may not leave calling cards. You may need access to these documents at any time or place.

Social Security and Medicare have separate rules and forms about who can represent the interests of a beneficiary. Your health insurer may require its own set of proxy representation documents.

The Health Insurance Portability and Accountability Act of 1996 (HIPAA) was designed to protect the privacy of your medical information. Doctors, hospitals, and other licensed caregivers cannot discuss your medical condition unless you've signed a HIPAA waiver form or have designated someone as your medical power of attorney. There are general HIPAA release forms approved by legal and health care organizations. Hospitals often prefer that you sign their version of this form.

Even when you think you've taken care of all your possible health situations and have armed your posse with the proper approvals to make decisions on your behalf, your health care preferences can still be thwarted by care situations beyond your control—most notably a trip to the ER provided by an ambulance.

Health care workers in these situations are there to save your life, not read living wills or health care proxies. For these situations, you may need what are known as provider orders for life-sustaining treatment. Commonly known as POLST documents, they may be called something else where you live.

A POLST order must be signed by your doctor or other licensed caregiver. It sets forth your care preferences and directs emergency care workers to follow them. POLST terms and forms differ around the country, making this state directory essential.

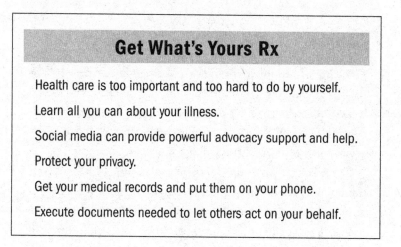

Get What's Yours Rx

Health care is too important and too hard to do by yourself.

Learn all you can about your illness.

Social media can provide powerful advocacy support and help.

Protect your privacy.

Get your medical records and put them on your phone.

Execute documents needed to let others act on your behalf.

HEROES IV

The Social Media Maven

Julie Croner

Julie Croner had the first surgery on her left knee when she was in fifth grade. Her doctor at the time, she recalled, said, "'You were probably born with a deformed meniscus and then through dancing and softball, you injured it.' And I thought, okay, whatever, I was a little kid. I really didn't think twice about it.

"Ever since then, every year I had knee problems," she continued. "I was either in physical therapy or I had a brace or I was on crutches." In middle school, her orthopedist suggested that something else might be causing her knee issues and suggested that she see a rheumatologist. She saw two. One didn't find anything amiss; the other diagnosed her with psoriatic arthritis.

Because of her young age, that doctor did not want to put her on "heavy-duty drugs" and recommended she just treat her symptoms as they occurred. Born in September 1985, Croner recalled that there was no Internet at the time she was in middle school and that finding out about psoriatic arthritis was difficult. She recalls many arguments with her mom where she questioned a diagnosis that she felt applied only to old people.

Managing her symptoms included two more knee surgeries in high school, "because there was a chronic inflammation problem" that needed to be treated. By and large, she functioned more or less normally through college and was into a career as an information-technology consultant at a large firm when her immune system began aggressively attacking her. That was in 2012.

"That's kind of where everything really started to go downhill because, lo and behold, I really did have psoriatic arthritis and going in and having this surgery whenever I had a flareup really exacerbated it," she explained. "And I ended up, from the summer of 2012 until December of 2012, just being in excruciating pain. My knee was so swollen I couldn't really walk on it."

This was the beginning of Croner's growing skepticism over the advice she was receiving from her doctors. Her orthopedist said it was "in my head . . . he just wasn't giving me answers." She responded by requesting "all the tests you can give me." She vividly recalls the date and details when he shared those test results with her.

"December 17, 2012, I will always remember the look on his face. He came in the examination room and said, 'Well, there is something wrong with you. It's called avascular necrosis. I know what it is. I've seen it before. But I don't really know how to treat it, and I don't really know where to send you. You'll probably need a knee replacement at some point in your life. Like, good luck!'"

Her pain became so bad that Croner went into the hospital over Christmas and had yet more tests. "'You definitely have psoriatic arthritis,'" she recalls being told. "'You have a lot of things going on right now. You've got avascular necrosis, and you've got complex regional pain syndrome,' which means the knee and the nerves in my left leg, they were stuck almost in a loop of pain."

The advice was to not put any weight on her left knee and immediately find a doctor who would do a knee replacement. "No one wanted to touch me" and do such a procedure because of her other health issues. She kept looking and looking for a solution.

"I lost track at twenty-nine different providers I went to trying to look for answers," she said. "And every time I went to one, they just gave me another pill. . . . I ended up being on nine different pills and two different injections."

Croner's pain became all-consuming, forcing her to leave her job. She spent the first half of 2013 "in bed in my parents' basement not wanting to move, in so much pain, and so depressed. I had never really been an anxious person before, but I started having really bad anxiety attacks anytime I would need to leave the house."

Croner had actively used Facebook. She stopped communicating with her friends as her pain worsened because she was "depressed at seeing them living the kind of life I had been living." With nothing to do, nowhere to go, and still in need of answers, she turned to Twitter and looked for help.

It was a good call.

"I stumbled upon all of these patients in different Twitter chats, just coming together talking, kind of commiserating in their misery together, and I found such a beacon of hope within all these patients, because it was the first time that I was like, 'Oh my god, I'm not the only person sitting in bed in so much pain! There are other people (like me) out there!' And I started connecting with them and I started talking to them on a regular basis, and I started asking them, 'What do you do to manage your pain?'

"It was those patients online who made me really realize that doctors absolutely have their place," she concluded, "but I am the driver of my own health and I can't just rely on the doctor to give me answers. I need to go out and seek the answers and empower myself with knowledge, too."

Croner became a voracious health care reader, tapped her consultancy skills, and made a spreadsheet about her life over the next six months—her diet, her activities, her meds, and her moods.

She correlated these with her shifting pain conditions and even built her own fatigue and pain scale. "I realized that there were so many things in my life that were contributing to my pain."

Driven by this knowledge, plus her continuing pain, Croner took control of her life and changed her diet, began yoga and other exercises, and practiced meditation.

"And [with] all these things together, I really started to rein in my psoriatic arthritis," she said. "As I did that, and I did it really because of guidance that I found online from patients . . . I got my body to the place where it wasn't fighting itself and now it was calmed down enough that I knew I could take care of the avascular necrosis. . . . I could handle dealing with my knee."

What she couldn't accept was her twenty-nine-doctor odyssey. "I still went to doctors and they still weren't telling me answers. So, again, I went online to these patients that I knew were there and a huge support system for me, and I found patients talking about this stem cell procedure that they got that was called Regenexx and how it regrew parts of their bone and they were back to living their life. And of course, it seemed too good to be true at first."

It wasn't. Off Croner went in March 2015 to the Centeno-Schultz Clinic in Colorado, for a weeklong therapy that extracted cells from her hip, along with "a lot of blood," which was reinjected into her knee ("like fertilizer," she said) along with her stem cells.

Quickly, her knee started producing its own healthy bone cells, leading to a 40 percent strength reading after six months and 60 percent after a year. "My knee was solid," she says, with healthy bone surrounding "the dead part."

On crutches for three and a half years, and "taking opioids every single day," Croner looks back at the procedure now and says, "It was just life changing to me." After three months, she was off all her painkillers and has had no pain or other serious issues since. She met her future husband in late 2015 and they now have two children and a third on the way.

The trajectory of her professional life changed as dramatically as her health. Going back to consulting was no longer appealing.

"It was the people online talking about their experience that really helped me get my life together," she realized. "I had been taking so much from patients that I needed to give back," she said. After "everything I've been through, I had to use it for good. . . . Patients first started inspiring hope in me, and then I thought, I need to inspire hope in patients."

She began blogging, connecting "with the most amazing people, who have become lifelong friends." Croner has since worked with health foundations, nonprofits, pharmaceutical companies, and others, becoming a social media patient advocate and connector. "I look at what I can bring as not just my own story but the collective story of the thousands of people that I connect with online."

In 2016, when Croner had begun feeling well enough to go back to work, she got a call from Jack Barrette, the head of WEGO Health, whom we met in the last chapter. Her patient leadership work had caught his eye and he offered her a job to lead and further build the company's patient leader network. For Croner, it has been the ideal job, allowing her to work remotely from her home in Pittsburgh and providing her the exposure and support to expand her impact.

"Now, I feel I've almost grown to another level," she said, "where I want to help inspire all of the other patients who are online sharing their story to get out there and tell more people to do so to inspire others."

9

YOUR PROFESSIONAL CARE TEAM

Finding a great fit with a primary care physician is the Holy Grail of better and less expensive health. I want to explain why, provide actionable advice, and put this decision in the context of the evolving sophistication and complexity of health care.

People who develop and maintain relationships with a primary care physician (PCP) live longer and healthier lives than those who don't. They wind up using less care—fewer ER visits, less use of unneeded care, fewer prescription meds—and thus may spend less money than do people who "save money" by forgoing a continuing PCP relationship. Other variables are at work, including education, wealth, and the values a person places on exercise, diet, and health care planning. These attributes are expressed through, and enhanced by, having an ongoing relationship with a trusted primary care doctor.

"I think that people who have had that in their life, or experienced it for a family member or themselves, get it, but a lot of other people don't get it," says Dr. Jennifer DeVoe, who chairs the department of family medicine at Oregon Health & Science University in Portland. "Many people haven't needed it so they're like, 'Why do I need this? I can just go to an urgent care center or I can just look up Web MD or Doc in the Box, show up at Walgreens, and get my antibiotic.'

"It's not like having a primary care physician is going to make your whole life great and your experience perfect," she added, "but it is, I think, a key ingredient for navigating the system." DeVoe felt so strongly about the importance of having a family doctor, she said, "that part of my decision to go to medical school was knowing that I have no physicians in my family and feeling like every family needs a physician to help navigate [the health system]."

Finding a good primary care practice may not be easy. Healthier and younger people—more likely men than women—often have little interest in establishing an ongoing relationship with a primary care doctor. This even included some of the health experts interviewed for this book. With equal parts braggadocio and denial, they often pridefully eschewed formal health care relationships.

PEOPLE WITH PRIMARY CARE DOCTORS, BY GENERATION

Generation	Birth years	Population	% w/PCPs
Gen Z	1996–	73.6 million	55
Millennials	1981–1996	79.4 million	67
Gen X	1966–1980	65.7 million	76
Boomers	1946–1964	75.5 million	84
Silent Gen	1928–1945	28.3 million	85

Sources: Knoema, Accenture

This is a mistake. Younger people may think they're invulnerable, but a sobering report by Moody's Analytics found that millennials "are seeing their health decline faster than the previous generation as they age."

"This extends to both physical health conditions, such as hypertension and high cholesterol," Moody's said, "and behavioral health conditions, such as major depression and hyperactivity. Without intervention, millennials could feasibly see mortality rates climb up by more than 40 percent compared to Gen-Xers at the same age."

If its projections are borne out, millennials will face enormous

medical bills, which, because they are the largest population group, will add to already unsustainable national health care spending. By-products would include lower growth for the entire economy and dismal retirement prospects for millennials.

Seeing a physician on a regular basis is arguably the best way to spot and treat emerging physical and behavioral health needs in otherwise "healthy" people. Treatment costs at younger ages are less than dealing with problems in later years.

DR. WELBY, I PRESUME?

DeVoe's championing of a close patient-doctor relationship was tested during the last week of her father's life. In an emotional re-telling, she described her encounters with caregivers in the hospital where he died. An only child, she wrote:

> Most patients do not have a daughter who is a medical profes-
> sional to help them navigate the complicated health care system;
> however, this special combination of professional and personal
> knowledge does not have to be embodied in 1 person. A team of
> friends, family, and health care professionals can serve as naviga-
> tors and advocates. . . . Everyone should have a primary care clini-
> cian on his or her team from birth to death, in the hospital and
> out of the hospital, in sickness and in health. As daughters, sons,
> and medical professionals, we should expect nothing less from our
> health care system.

That system fails to deliver on DeVoe's expectations. According to the Organisation for Economic Co-operation and Development (OECD), the United States ranked 27th out of 36 developed coun-tries in the number of physicians per capita. At 2.61 docs per 1,000 people, the United States has roughly half as many doctors to serve

Practicing physicians, density per 1,000 population, 2016

Austria	5.1
Switzerland	4.3
Sweden	4.3
Germany	4.2
Australia	3.6
Comparable Country Average	3.5
Belgium	3.1
France	3.1
United Kingdom	2.8
Canada	2.6
United States	2.6
Japan	2.4

Note: Data for Sweden is for 2015.

Source: KFF analysis of OECD data

Peterson-KFF
Health System Tracker

its residents as do many other countries. Going across our borders won't help, either. Canada ranks 26th and Mexico 29th.

In the United States, the relatively low pay of primary care physicians, compared with surgeons and other specialties, makes them a particularly endangered species. "The Association of American Medical Colleges predicts a national shortage of between 21,100 and 55,200 family medicine doctors by 2032," *Modern Healthcare* reported. As explained elsewhere, particularly in Chapter Sixteen, the movement of health care out of hospitals and doctors' offices into clinics and virtual care will help reduce the impact of doctor shortages.

As anyone seeking an in-the-flesh PCP knows, finding one can take time. Here's how experts advise proceeding. The first step is to understand the range of physician choices permitted under your health insurance plan. HMOs and other "narrow network" plans can reduce your options. The advice here, as in many other facets of *Get What's Yours*, is to call your insurer and understand your options in selecting a physician.

Armed with a list of possible physicians, canvass family and friends for their recommendations. You will be able to build on their thoughts in the next chapter, which is a guide to how to identify high-quality health care providers.

Dr. Amit Pahwa, who educates future doctors at the Johns Hopkins University School of Medicine, says medical education bears little resemblance to the system that trained current physicians. Although he is only forty, that includes him. Rote memorization used to be a major focus of medical education. No more.

"Access to information today is phenomenal, both on the patient side and on the physician side," he said. "The big thing with medical training is that you don't need to know a lot of facts," so "what we really are trying to teach students and residents these days is the application of the facts."

Like you, doctors go online all the time to seek information helpful in treating their patients. UpToDate is the go-to place for doctors to get their own clinical questions addressed. Nearly 7,000 health care professionals write and review site contents.

On-demand access to current medical information and treatment protocols is changing the role of the physician from knowing everything to knowing how to find out everything. This is broadening the role of the physician and their practice, DeVoe said. "It's a traffic cop, it's a safety officer, it's a general contractor in a lot of ways, you know people have used that analogy as well, the quarterback for the team. There's lots of great analogies."

"Continuity of care matters," Pahwa said. "The more fragmented your care, the more likely you are to go to the ER or the hospital. People who have regularly identified PCPs tend to have a better overall prognosis for their mortality," he added. "Our primary care doctors are kind of the doctors that help keep patients out of the hospital, which is expensive, and out of the emergency department, which is also expensive. And they're there to think about things outside medicine, such as nutrition and physical therapy."

"One of the things we've gotten away from in primary care is the continuity piece," says Beth Bortz, head of the Virginia Center for Health Innovation. "We have moved to a system where we don't reward continuity at all. . . . We're all about immediate access, and there is some real value to that, but when you are seeing a different person every time, are you more likely to have" unnecessary care or miss needed care?

In scouting out a PCP, keep an eye out for how much support their practice provides them in the way of nurses and other non-physician assistants. This should include behavioral health, a fundamental part of health care that is often stigmatized and considered a separate discipline. A social worker can be invaluable in helping people with nonmedical needs that can have a big impact on their health. Depending on your health needs, and those of your family, finding such augmented skill sets in a physician practice can be crucial.

NEW MODELS OF PRIMARY CARE

As you review a list of new physicians, or even consider changing your current physician, look at new types of physician practices that are becoming more popular.

In direct primary care (DPC), your PCP does not accept insurance and provides all of your routine care for a flat fee that usually ranges from $60 to $90 a month. For this, you get much better access to doctors and longer appointment times. You must pay the practice's fees out of your own pocket, but many employers will reimburse these payments. Some types of DPC plans include health insurance. Make sure you know what level of care your plan would include if you pursue this option.

If you need care outside the practice, your insurance would help pay those expenses. The burden of dealing with health insurers could fall on you, so it's important to know these details up front.

DPC fees generally include all aspects of your care, including clinical and lab services. The lack of insurance company involvement permits doctors to focus on practicing medicine, harking back to the kind of access to doctors that was common forty and fifty years ago. DPC practices may be similar to concierge medicine, which generally costs more and usually provides help with insurance claims.

Accountable care organizations involve practices that take on some financial risk with their patients' health insurers. In this model, an ACO would receive a fixed amount of money (capitation is the formal description of such payments) each year to care for a patient. If they didn't need to spend all that money, the practice would keep some of the savings. If the patient's medical costs were higher than the fixed payment, the ACO would have to pay some of that higher spending. Some ACOs have struggled to find the right balance of risks and rewards.

When looking for a primary care practice, keep these new models in mind. They are popular with doctors who feel they allow them to focus on the quality of care instead of the volume of treatments and tests a patient receives.

QUESTIONS TO ASK YOUR PROSPECTIVE DOC

What should you look for? Trust, competence, and empathy.

"One of the things would be is it someone you click with?" DeVoe said. "Is it someone who seems happy, and are they going to stick in their practice for a while? Is it someone who can take care of your family? Is it somebody who has a great team—nurses, social workers, pharmacists, connected to a network of specialists."

Do they have a philosophy about health care similar to yours? she added. "Are they going to do every single test and run up my bill or are they going to say, 'Hey, this is something that we can just watch for a while and wait and be a little bit more conservative.'" A good doctor is going to be likely to ask you many of the questions you would ask yourself.

"If you find someone that is bright and competent and empathetic to your issues and a good listener, and is inquisitive . . . they're going to want you to ask those questions and then partner with you to investigate some of those resources."

It can be immensely helpful, DeVoe said, if patients treat a prospective doctor like they would like to be treated. "You would be surprised at how rare it is these days" for patients to treat doctors as human beings, she said.

Experts provide these additional questions patients should ask:

- How easy is it to get a same-day appointment?
- Does the practice reserve open slots for patients needing care right away?
- How long is the typical annual physical? Does the practice schedule other wellness visits during the year?
- Does it provide vaccinations and other shots in the office or outsource such work, and what are the cost implications to you?
- Does the practice consider costs in its treatment recommendations?
- Where does it send people for ambulatory surgery, MRIs, and other tests, especially blood work, and are these locations in your insurance plan's provider network? The federal Centers for Medicare & Medicaid Services (CMS) supports an Ambulatory Surgical Center Quality Reporting Program that can help you evaluate outpatient facilities available for your

use. Healthcare Bluebook can provide cost ranges for specific ambulatory procedures and common tests.

A printable list of questions is in Appendix 6.

UNDERSTAND YOUR DOCTOR'S GATEKEEPER ROLE

Odds are, your primary care physician is going to be the gatekeeper for access to other medical specialists and hospitals. It is entirely appropriate to drill down into these topics with a physician before becoming a regular patient. You need a PCP who is a great health coach and can assemble the best team of specialists to meet your needs.

Increasingly, new doctors are being taught how to respond to a wider range of patient concerns, said Dr. Pamela T. Johnson, a professor in the Johns Hopkins Medicine Department of Radiology. "Many medical schools, including ours, have integrated the principles of quality, safety, affordability, and appropriateness into the medical school curriculum, . . . and also how to have conversations with patients about" these matters, she said.

Whatever practice you select, then, should have someone who knows insurance well and can help you understand what your care will cost and how your care will be affected by your insurance coverage. Your doctor should help with medical affordability issues. This is a fundamental expectation, not a "stretch" request.

HAVING THE MONEY CONVERSATION

Having money discussions with your physician's office is not only acceptable. It's mandatory. Affordability concerns cause people to forgo health care. Doctors increasingly know this. In late 2019, the

American Medical Association formally asked medical schools to train new physicians about health care finance.

Pahwa says cost issues now are commonly taught to medical students, including understanding the online tools that doctors can use to provide pricing and cost information for patients when discussing treatment options with patients. "We can do something called test scripts," Pahwa said, "where we can fake run it [a procedure] against their insurance." This capability is only slowly moving its way into physician practices. Ask about it.

Dr. Caroline Sloan, who practices at Duke University Hospital, has developed a list of money issues that doctors should be prepared to address. "Given these financial burdens, and the impact they have on people's medical care, health care providers need to talk to their patients about out-of-pocket costs," she wrote in a research paper coauthored with Dr. Peter Ubel at the Fuqua School of Business at Duke.

"Most doctors know nothing about costs," she told me during a phone interview. "My theory, which I'm studying now, is that most doctors don't understand how health insurance works. Patients need to be aware" of this.

For their part, she observed, "patients don't feel comfortable bringing up costs with doctors because they fear it will lead their doctors to ration care. . . . And doctors don't feel comfortable bringing up costs with patients because they feel it will lead patients to think they will ration care."

With a nod to the late author Stephen Covey, here is Sloan's list, including her summary thoughts, of "The 7 Habits of Highly Effective Cost-of-Care Conversations." They are aimed at physicians but illuminating to consumers, too.

1. You Won't Know If You Don't Ask. It is clearly time for physicians to screen for health care–related financial hardship in a systematic way.

2. Discuss the Cost Prognosis. Physicians regularly communicate prognostic information so that patients can make informed decisions and plan for the future. By the same token, we must keep patients apprised of their financial prognoses, so they can anticipate future expenses.

3. You Can Anticipate Many, If Not All, Costs. In frank discussions with patients, it should often be possible to anticipate many of these costs and develop plans for addressing them.

4. Be Systematic: Make Explorations of Out-of-Pocket Costs Routine. A cost-conversation screening system could quickly determine whether any problems exist, get around the shame that many patients feel about their financial difficulties, and clarify whom patients feel comfortable speaking to—clinicians or ancillary staff.

5. Integrate Cost Conversations into Your Workflow in a Way That Works for You. When patients needed financial assistance, various staff members resorted to researching insurance contracts, calling people in other departments, and using other creative workarounds.

6. Enlist Your Ancillary Staff. In addition to having more flexibility to incorporate cost-of-care conversations into their daily workflow, the familiarity of office staffers with cost-of-care considerations often aligns much more closely than those of physicians with patients' needs.

7. It Gets Easier, and Better. As physicians have more cost-of-care conversations, they get better at them. . . . Cost-conversation practice certainly will not make us perfect, given the logistical and informational barriers that exist. It will move us closer to the kind of patient-centered care that characterizes the ideals of our profession.

OTHER MEMBERS OF YOUR
HEALTH CARE TEAM

While a primary care physician is likely your key caregiver, the role of specialized physicians is crucial for people with known health issues, and especially for those with chronic conditions who require ongoing treatment.

Use the tools in the next chapter to evaluate the best caregivers for your health needs. If your insurance plan is not friendly to a preferred provider, talk to that provider about other insurance plans. Think ahead about whether you'd go out of network and pay more money to see a preferred specialist. If the answer is yes, how much more would you pay?

Beyond primary physicians, specialists, surgery centers, and hospitals, I would add clinics and pharmacists to my health care support list. Health care is moving away from hospitals and doctors' offices to freestanding clinics and retail stores.

PCP visits are on a steady downward arc, notes physician Eric Topol, author of *The Patient Will See You Now*. Beyond a shortage of PCPs and high costs, he said, "surely a contributing factor is that there are many emerging alternatives, from retail clinics with nurses to do-it-yourself (DIY) care."

This is borne out by surging growth in the numbers of nurse practitioners and other non-physician caregivers, many of whom work at freestanding consumer health facilities.

Drive through your neighborhood and look for new storefront health providers. They are becoming the gas stations and bank branches of our times. CVS Health, Walgreens Boots Alliance, Walmart, and others are opening in-store clinics at a record pace. See Chapter Sixteen on retail health care for more details.

For those without insurance, clinics can be a cost-effective alternative to the ER for most of a person's health needs. The National Association of Free & Charitable Clinics has 1,400 member clinics that provide free care or charge for it on a sliding scale linked to a patient's financial situation. Their patients tend to be people who make too much to qualify for Medicaid or can't afford to pay the deductible for the insurance they do have.

NeedyMeds has a searchable directory of more than 13,000 free or low-cost clinics. Many also offer a sliding scale of prices pegged to your income.

Hospitals have become major developers of walk-in clinics. Access and affordability may be more attractive than going to the hospital's own ER, and neighborhood clinics can be an attractive way for hospitals to generate new business for their expensive inpatient facilities and surgeons.

If you do have health insurance, call your health insurer for coverage details and possible restrictions. I know I am a broken record here, but you are paying thousands of dollars a year for your health coverage. You have the right to get whatever information you need to get the best value for your money.

Finding a local clinic that can meet your and your family's unexpected health needs is important. Seek guidance from friends and neighbors.

Lastly, find a good pharmacy and a pharmacist willing to make the time to talk with you. Your health insurance might constrain this choice. Even so, the selection of a pharmacy can have a big impact on your health and what you pay for it.

Pharmacists have been freed from archaic rules that prevented them from speaking with you about drug costs and your physician's prescriptions. They can be gold mines of information and informed help about your care needs.

Once you've assembled all the members of your care team, put their contact information lots of places—your phone, your refrigerator, your bedroom, and your car. Make sure the key people in your health care posse have this information.

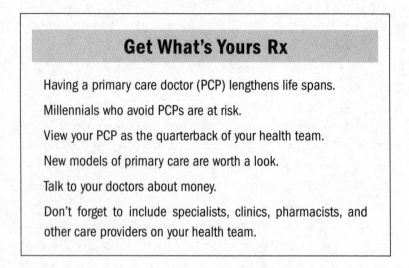

Get What's Yours Rx

Having a primary care doctor (PCP) lengthens life spans.

Millennials who avoid PCPs are at risk.

View your PCP as the quarterback of your health team.

New models of primary care are worth a look.

Talk to your doctors about money.

Don't forget to include specialists, clinics, pharmacists, and other care providers on your health team.

10

WHAT QUALITY LOOKS LIKE

There are enough health care ratings services, social media groups, and search engine forums to fill a chapter fifty times as long as this one. Downsizing this task requires careful thought about what's important to you and, if you're a caregiver, to the person whose welfare is in your hands.

Patient experiences, for example, are the stuff of countless posts and tweets. Basing a care decision on what other people say is rarely as good an idea as finding doctors and hospitals whose work produces the highest clinical outcomes.

Even here, it can be hard to compare doctors or hospitals because the health profiles of the people they treat may be different. Some models try to apply risk adjustments to such comparisons. It's not easy, and often not something that is explained to consumers trying to select a doctor or care facility.

Further, general grades may not help. What you're looking for is the best care for you, not for an average or typical patient:

- What are your health needs?
- Which doctors and hospitals are in your local market?
- How much choice of medical providers is permitted under whatever insurance plan you have?
- Does your health condition require you to get treatment first and ask questions about quality later?

This chapter will look at doctors, hospitals, nursing homes, outpatient surgery centers, and specialty care providers. Urgent care centers are covered in Chapter Twelve.

When you have time to consider your care choices, your job is to search for the best clinicians and the best place for them to provide your care. Nothing is more important here than finding the right doctors for you. Unfortunately, doctors currently are the weakest link in terms of publicly available medical-quality ratings services and tools.

PHYSICIAN QUALITY
RATINGS AND REVIEWS

Here are the things that influenced people the most when selecting a physician, according to a 2019 survey conducted by Binary Fountain, which provides digital and online reputation services to health care firms and professionals. (The last item, CAHPS, is a government program—the Consumer Assessment of Healthcare Providers and Systems.)

Personal recommendations:	52%
Online ratings/reviews	48
Location	36
Hospital affiliation	36
Gender	32
Insurance coverage	27
CAHPS survey scores	22

Here are the online platforms that people use most frequently to vet doctors and where patients posted reviews:

	To vet	Reviews
Google	54 %	49
Hospital/facility website	48	40
Facebook	45	57
Healthgrades	42	40
Instagram	29	30
RateMDs	23	22
U.S. News & World Report	21	21
Twitter	21	24
ShareCare	21	23
WebMD	20	18
Zocdoc	16	15
Yelp	14	12
Snapchat	14	16
Vitals	13	14

I'd use patient reviews only after I had narrowed my search to a few doctors. Even here, looking at unfiltered and especially anonymous reviews may be a confusing and even stressful waste of time. Rely instead on ratings services based on evidence-based comparisons.

ProPublica, a nonprofit investigative news site, provides useful Vital Signs about physician performance, including flagging conflicts of interests with drug and medical equipment companies. It tells you how to find out if a doctor has been disciplined at the state level, with state-by-state details on how to find this information.

When looking at the linked ratings tools above, look at their methodologies, understand what they are rating, and determine the relevance of the rating to your situation. My review found that *U.S. News & World Report* and Healthgrades provided the most evidence-based information for their physician ratings.

Guroo.com, a specialized ratings site, recommends not taking any ratings or reviews at face value without getting answers to these questions:

- Who owns the site? Is it a nonprofit or for-profit site?
- Do doctors pay for their own reviews?
- Are reviews or ratings anonymous? Is there any way to tell if a reviewer is a patient?
- Is the information complete? Do you notice any missing doctors in your area?
- Does the website disclose how often information is updated?
- How many ratings does a doctor have? More is better here.

Doctors, of course, are well aware that their reputations and even livelihoods may be determined by online patient reviews. Some are not above trying to game a review site with phony reviews of their own. For this reason, I'd put sites based on anonymous reviews at the bottom of my search for quality doctors.

The United Hospital Fund did a thorough review of ratings sites in 2017 and came up with a checklist of quality information that consumers valued. (You can see how well it aligns with your own thinking; details are in Appendix 7.)

The federal Agency for Healthcare Research and Quality (AHRQ) has identified four indicators of "standardized, evidence-based measures of health care quality"—prevention quality, inpatient quality, patient safety, and pediatric quality. Its extensive listing of measures likely is more detail than you think you will ever need. However, if you're like me, there is never too much detail when it comes to performance data on *your* medical needs or those of a loved one.

WHAT TO ASK A TELEHEALTH PROVIDER

Telehealth, as noted in Chapter One, was battle-tested during the coronavirus pandemic. The evaluations of how well various providers performed are still coming in.

Virtual care can evoke images of high-tech treatments supported by smartphone apps, wrist devices, and home-based WiFi gadgets providing real-time monitoring of health conditions. In reality, most telehealth involves calling a doctor or other licensed clinician on the phone and discussing your health issues

The range of recommended telehealth care includes allergies, bladder or urinary tract infection, bronchitis, coughing, diarrhea, fever, migraine or headache, pinkeye, rash, seasonal flu, sinus problem, sore throat, and stomachache.

Isolation and loneliness related to stay-at-home orders and other pandemic lockdowns have made behavioral health calls—especially video chats—increasingly common. Sending photos or using a video tool expands the range of applicable telehealth services. Even before the pandemic, for example, dermatology was becoming an attractive market for virtual care companies.

Although telehealth use was jump-started by the pandemic, most experts think it will become a permanent part of mainstream health care treatment. Longer-term adoption rates will be affected by the permanent, post-pandemic coverage decisions of regulators and health insurers.

Business consultants at Mercer see the telehealth transition as nothing less than possibly "the new foundation to rebuild health care," particularly among the large percentages of people who currently do not have primary care doctors.

Twenty-six percent of Americans do not have a primary care physician and the number goes up to 45 percent for millennials, Mercer observed. "Convenience could be a game-changer to support engagement with a primary care provider, which in turn supports early identification of health issues and care continuity."

McKinsey, the business consultants whose report was cited in Chapter One, projects that permanent adoption of telehealth services could replace substantial percentages of in-person care, including 20 percent of emergency room visits, 24 percent of office visits, and 35 percent of home health-aide care.

Further, new models of virtual care could be combined with traditional care to provide services not currently available. "This model also enables clinicians to better manage patients with chronic conditions," the report said, "with the support of remote patient monitoring, digital therapeutics, and digital coaching, in addition to virtual visits."

Dr. Joseph Kvedar is a professor of dermatology at Harvard Medical School, a telehealth expert, and president of the American Telehealth Association. The best telehealth for you, he advised, is from your own doctor and requires nothing more than a telephone line and perhaps the ability to send your doctor a picture from your smartphone.

Next in line would be the increasingly ubiquitous telehealth programs offered by health insurers through telehealth companies. Insurers are "unlikely to have contracted with a provider of services that hasn't convinced them that there's a certain level of quality" in the provider's work, Kvedar said.

The third "tier" of telehealth providers that he would endorse would be retail services affiliated with CVS Health, Walmart, Walgreens, and other well-known companies that are expanding into consumer health care. Their services will be closely vetted, he said, "because they have other reasons to care about their reputation to you as a customer."

Kvedar recommended that consumers ask how a telehealth provider was trained and credentialed. Providers should be "board certified," which is shorthand for having been approved to practice medicine. The American Board of Medical Specialties provides a free Certification Matters tool where consumers can check a doctor's accreditation.

Your telehealth provider should share results of your treatment with your PCP to maintain the continuity of your care. "If they don't ask you who your primary care provider is, that's a red flag," Kvedar said.

Insurance coverage and payments for telehealth also warrant your attention. Check with your insurer and health provider before initiating any telehealth care. Here are things to find out:

- Are telehealth services from my current doctors covered by my plan?
- What other designated telehealth providers are in my plan's provider network?
- What types of virtual care are included and excluded?
- Is prior approval from my insurer required before I receive care?
- Do I face any out-of-pocket costs for using telehealth services, either from my plan's designated telehealth providers or my own primary care physician?

WHERE MOST HEALTH INFORMATION LIVES

The Centers for Medicare & Medicaid Services (CMS) has the nation's largest pool of health care performance information. Nearly 130 million people are now enrolled in some form of Medicare or Medicaid, many with private insurance plans. CMS has been collecting health data for decades, and can slice and dice what ails us, what it costs to fix it, and how well or ill we are.

It analyzes this information using tens of thousands of treatment codes that permit comparisons of our care and the quality of the doctors, hospitals, nursing homes, and other places we go to receive that care.

The private health companies cited in this book draw information from databases created and maintained by CMS and other federal health agencies, many of which are housed in CMS's parent agency, the U.S. Department of Health and Human Services (HHS.gov).

CMS provides information about health care providers in these eight "compare" tools:

Physician Compare
Hospital Compare
Nursing Home Compare
Hospice Compare
Inpatient Rehabilitation Facility Compare
Dialysis Facility Compare
Home Health Compare
Long-Term Care Hospital Compare

I found Physician Compare the weakest of the CMS tools, and a poor way to find a doctor. There are just too many to evaluate and the data on measures of physician performance are spotty.

At the time this book was written, Physician Compare could confirm only general information about a doctor. I then had to go to other ratings sources to drill down into their record. I found *U.S. News*, Healthgrades, and WebMD the most useful.

The story is different when you're looking for specialized care providers. Many of its tools make use of CMS's five-star ratings systems. There is some muddiness when it comes to differentiating among facilities with two, three, or four stars. Not so with the top and bottom. Carefully consider using providers with five stars. Avoid one-star providers.

CMS says it's committed to improving all its "Compare" ratings tools, including consolidating all eight so that they will provide a similar "look and feel" and display the same types of results.

For a serious search, the star ratings are only the place to start. Look at the specific safety, health, and care measures on which the ratings are based. When it comes to choosing a care facility, these CMS comparisons can help you narrow the choice. Then, it's time for some house calls.

Remember our master planner, Mike Baker? Here is how he went about searching for a care facility for his dad.

My father passed away a couple of years ago, and we were at a moment where he was coming out of a hospital and going into a SNF [skilled nursing facility] and that skilled nursing spot was in Tucson, Arizona. At the time, there were four or five choices, so we had a little bit of time to do a little research. We asked the physician that he was accustomed to seeing. But none of us had ever been in that position before, no one had asked folks at the hospital for a recommendation, and there were wild variations among us on our perspectives on what was a good facility and what was a bad facility.

And so I kind of performed my own assessment the same way that I do when I walk into a call center. I've been running call centers my entire professional life, and you can tell in 10 minutes how an operation runs. And I show up for a site visit and I walk into a bathroom. How clean are the bathrooms? Because that stuff matters in an operation. You walk by the bulletin boards. And is it May or June but there's awards up from March on the wall? Are there, you know, TVs in the break room, but the cable's not working? If there are little details that are missed, the big details are going be missed.

So I called the higher recommended nursing facilities. I called the front desk at 8 o'clock at night to see how long it took some-body to answer. I asked for a nurse on duty and saw how long it took to get someone's attention. I drove by and walked into a cou-ple of places. Could I get in and walk in? Was the desk attended at 9 o'clock and what was that environment like? And while that is certainly not a parallel for what the clinical experience is going to be, it gives you an indication, I think, to the kind of attention that's being put on the human beings that are a customer of that facility.

Finding a quality health facility is easy, right? Just be like Mike!

HOSPITAL QUALITY RATINGS
AND REVIEWS

There are more than a million physicians in the United States but fewer than six thousand hospitals, so finding the good ones involves a smaller haystack. There is extensive public information on health procedures and outcomes involving hospital care. Given the stakes of a hospital procedure—the possibility of life-altering care and perhaps life-altering expenses—digging deeply into hospital quality tools is a good investment.

Avoid making a decision based on a hospital's average or general ratings. Drill down to find the specific surgery or treatment you want to research. Look for hospitals that perform lots and lots of this pro-cedure. Practice does make perfect, or at least a lot closer to it than the nearby surgery center that does one such procedure a month. Be prepared for some complexity. These are not simple five-star ratings systems.

The Agency for Healthcare Research and Quality (AHRQ), a federal agency that reviews hospital-quality measures, recommends providers of five sets of measures that have been endorsed by the nonprofit National Quality Forum:

- AHRQ Quality Indicators
- National Hospital Quality Measures
- CAHPS Hospital Survey (Consumer Assessment of Healthcare Providers and Systems)
- ORYX
- The Leapfrog Group

Spending some time with these measures may be more education than you want. The Advisory Board, a health care business consultancy, has produced a series of briefs explaining the major hospital ratings providers:

- CMS Overall Star Ratings
- CMS Hospital CAHPS Patient Experience Star Rating
- Healthgrades Top Hospitals
- Healthgrades Patient Safety Ratings and Excellence Awards
- Healthgrades Outstanding Patient Experience Ratings and Excellence Awards
- Healthgrades Specialty Excellence Awards and 100 Best Hospitals for Specialty Care
- Leapfrog Group Top Hospitals
- Leapfrog Group Hospital Safety Grade
- *U.S. News & World Report* Best Hospital Rankings
- *U.S. News & World Report* Best Children's Hospital Rankings
- IBM/Watson Health 100 Top Hospitals

The *New England Journal of Medicine* evaluated the hospital ratings tools of CMS, Healthgrades, Leapfrog, and *U.S. News & World Report*.

"It is unclear whether current rating systems are meeting stakeholders' needs," the article said. "Such rating systems frequently publish conflicting ratings: Hospitals rated highly on one publicly reported hospital quality system are often rated poorly on another. This provides conflicting information for patients seeking care and for hospitals attempting to use the data to identify real targets for improvement."

The article's authors handed out these grades:

U.S. News:	B
CMS:	C
Leapfrog	C–
Healthgrades	D+

(My own list of recommended health ratings providers is in Appendix 8.)

The IBM/Watson Health list is useful for people whose treatment choices are not limited to their nearby community. The company said these hospitals delivered higher care *and* lower costs. Here are details of seven key evidence-based quality measures:

- Higher Survival Rates: Nearly 25 percent higher than those of peer hospitals.
- Fewer Complications and Infections: Roughly 19 percent fewer complications and health care–associated infections.
- Shorter Length of Stay: Half a day shorter stays after adjusting for differing mixes of treatment severities.
- Shorter Emergency Department Wait Times: More than 17 minutes shorter.
- Lower Inpatient Expenses: Average inpatient costs per discharge were 12 percent lower, or an average of $830 less for each patient discharged.
- Higher Profit Overall Margins: Nearly 12 percent more profitable.
- Higher Patient Satisfaction: Three percent higher.

NURSING HOMES

Whether you or a family member is the patient, odds are that a serious health issue is involved. This may require a long-term stay or recovery from major surgery. In either case, the patient may not be in a great position to look out for themselves and will be relying strongly on the home they select to provide quality care.

The coronavirus exposed the widespread weaknesses of nursing homes in caring for older and disabled people. Inadequate funding, staffing, and equipment, including widespread shortages of qualified staff, were more the rule than the exception. As detailed comparative studies of nursing home procedures and performance emerge, they will be an important source of future quality information.

Even before the pandemic, documented cases of poor and abusive care were so common that CMS began flagging homes on Nursing Home Compare that had broken its care rules. Still, this tool is not highly regarded. *Health Affairs*, a prominent medical journal, assessed Nursing Home Compare and found its work on patient safety "to be weak and somewhat inconsistent, leaving consumers who care about patient safety with little guidance."

The Long Term Care Community Coalition provides details on nursing home staffing levels and how much time is available for per-patient care. "Staffing is perhaps the most important factor in a nursing home resident's quality of care and the ability to live with dignity," according to Liz Seegert, a health researcher at George Washington University who has reviewed the coalition's work.

Seegert said the coalition's site was easier to use than Nursing Home Compare and presented comparative information on the numbers of nursing home residents, staffing levels for licensed nursing professionals, the amount of time that care is available each day, and the amount of daily staffing hours for non-nursing time, which may include nonmedical counseling and staff for residents' social activities.

Lori Smetanka, executive director of the National Long-Term Care Ombudsman Resource Center, advises people to begin their search for extended care by checking out resources near them. Local affiliates of her program and those of the National Association of Area Agencies on Aging provide free assistance.

This help should include details on available area resources, free or reduced-price benefits the person may qualify for, and help deciding whether a nursing home is even the right solution, or if day-care programs and in-home services might be better.

I have long been a fan of an outpatient care program called PACE, which stands for Program of All-Inclusive Care for the Elderly. Its centers provide health, counseling, and activities programs where participants can spend the day. They include transportation and support services to help participants in their homes. Unfortunately, there are fewer than 50,000 PACE slots in the entire country. If you can find one near you, please take a careful look.

If a nursing home is appropriate, it's essential to make one or more on-site visits, and consider separate visits during mealtime and later in the evening. In doing so, Smetanka said, "make sure you use all your senses" and she means this literally. What does the home smell like, what are the sounds you hear, what do you see in terms of staff-resident interactions, are residents socializing during their meals, and the like.

Review the contract you would be expected to sign in order to become a resident, particularly what rights a resident has. A key issue here, Smetanka noted, is that homes often prefer that residents waive their right to sue and instead sign a contract that includes binding arbitration to resolve any disputes, including allegations of poor care or staff abuse of residents. Under rules adopted in 2019, you have the right to cross out that provision in the contract, and the home is still obligated to accept you as a resident.

OUTPATIENT SURGICAL CENTERS

Ambulatory surgical centers (ASCs) and hospital outpatient departments (HOPDs) have become go-to places for elective surgeries and charge lower rates than hospital inpatient procedures. ASCs tend to be cheaper than HOPDs. If a doctor or surgeon recommends you use a particular facility, you should ask—politely, please!—whether they have a business or contractual relationship with that site. There is loads of research that says prices, but not necessarily quality, go up when doctors and care facilities have business relationships.

Unfortunately, ASCs and HOPDs lack the fact-based comparative rankings that exist for physicians and hospitals. Word of mouth is important here, so ask your friends and colleagues if they have used an outpatient facility and what they thought about the experience. In reality, if you respect and trust your primary care doctor and the surgeon or care specialist they recommend for your procedure, you are going to use the outpatient site those professionals use. I could not find data on how many surgeons use multiple outpatient facilities. I doubt it's a large number.

The Leapfrog Group has added outpatient facilities to its hospital ratings. Its initial set of ratings was scheduled for release after *Get What's Yours* went to press. It will include only institutions that have provided data to Leapfrog. As noted with Leapfrog's hospital grades, providing a single grade to an institution may not reflect patient safety outcomes for different surgeries.

The ASC Quality Collaboration collects performance information on more than 1,600 participating ASCs (performance data as of the third quarter of 2019). Average industry performance is of limited value. Ask the ASC you choose for its metrics regarding your intended procedure.

Get What's Yours Rx

Don't make care decisions based on average quality ratings.

Find ratings for your specific illness or needed procedure.

Reputational ratings are often suspect and can be "gamed" by providers.

Consult several ratings services where possible.

The pandemic has revealed major weaknesses in U.S. health care and will lead to better ratings tools.

HEROES V

The Patient Advocate

Karen Moore

Karen's husband, James, died of sepsis in 2009 when he was only forty-two, related to what she now feels was a highly contagious strain of meningitis that she suspects he contracted at Parris Island, the U.S. Marine base where he worked as a chef. Karen was a wedding planner and did a lot of weekend events in and around their home near Savannah, Georgia. James would pitch in at these events and help with food preparation.

On Friday, May 1, James began to feel sick after he got home from work. The couple thought his symptoms—watery eyes and congestion—were the results of a spring allergy. Over the weekend, the couple did two weddings on Saturday and two more on Sunday, she recalled. After getting home from Sunday's second event, James developed a fever and his temperature neared 103.

The Moores had recurring weight problems. James recently had changed his diet and lost sixty-five pounds, Karen said. He had a full physical in mid-April, she noted, and his blood work and health status were excellent.

"I told him he should go to the emergency room," Moore said. He said the next day was Monday and that he could see his primary care doctor then.

"We didn't make it," she said. By 6 a.m. on Monday, May 4, James became violently ill, with vomiting and diarrhea. Karen called for an ambulance and they got to the hospital around eight.

Nineteen hours later, James was dead.

Karen, who was born in July 1968, has relived those hours countless times since 2009, in no small measure because she, too, contracted sepsis in 2016, spent nine days in a different hospital, and required nearly a year to regain her health. She has compared her care with that of her husband and decided to learn all she could about sepsis. This has included a year of study to get a health coaching certificate and extensive advocacy work in Georgia and nationally on behalf of sepsis patients.

James was in the hospital for eight hours before being admitted to intensive care, she said. During this time, he was under observation and Karen was told he had a blood infection and might be highly contagious. He was not diagnosed with sepsis, a virulent immune-system response to infections that is often a quick killer. He received no intravenous fluids or antibiotics.

By the time James was admitted to intensive care at 4 p.m., "that was eight hours too late," Karen now says. "In sepsis, every second counts. Diagnosis is critical." By nine on Monday evening, the hospital told Karen that James's prognosis was grim and that she should go home to get some rest, which she did. At 2 a.m., the hospital called to say she should return.

"By the time I got there it was about 2:50 and he was already gone," she recalled. "When I got out to park the truck, it was funny. The one thing that I remember is I heard birds chirping, and I remember birds don't chirp at 3 a.m., you know, and I just instantly knew that he was gone."

Once she was inside the hospital and had been told her husband was dead, Karen was asked if she wanted to see the body. "It took me two hours of just sitting there before I had the strength to actually go in and see him," she said. "I was just in total disbelief. . . . I was just taking him to the hospital, and nineteen hours later he was gone.

"My husband was such an amazing person. He was one of those people [that] his light just shined so brightly. He was just loved by everyone."

When Karen later fell ill herself, her first thoughts were that she would die just as her husband had done. "I'm living his story all over again," she recalled. "I was on my way out the door, too."

The hospital ER that received Karen had a protocol in place for treating sepsis. Her sepsis was diagnosed within thirty minutes of her arrival. Karen now says she received excellent care, in sharp and sad contrast with James's care.

"Everything that should have been done" for him was not done, she now says. "I really believe that there is probably a ninety-eight percent chance that he would have survived, had there just been a different level of care for him."

Karen's advocacy work began with insights about her own life and how she needed to live it. Her diet changed and, over time, she eliminated meat. The weight came off. She began to share her "personal journey" on social media, and the positive response led her to reach out to people on a more organized basis. This led to her studies, the decision to leave wedding planning and become a health coach, and efforts to encourage the creation of better treatment protocols for sepsis.

Moore's personal work has included overcoming the assumption that doctors always know best and thus deferring to their judgments. "For a long time, that was my mind-set, which was totally wrong."

Looking ahead, she said, "the thing that's important to me is making sure that people understand what sepsis is, they understand the signs, [and] they know how to advocate for themselves when they go to the hospital."

PART THREE

NEW HEALTH CARE CHOICES

11

UNNEEDED AND
MISDIAGNOSED CARE

Americans get too much care they don't need and too little care they do need. These twin problems—unneeded and misdiagnosed care—plagued medicine long before Hippocrates asked an Athenian to say "Aah" more than 2,500 years ago. They are fueled by doctors with the best of intentions and those who are not well informed or paying more attention to their wallets than their patients' needs.

Whatever the causes, Americans consume too much health care, boosting the nation's annual medical bills by $750 billion to $1 trillion. This waste is driven by health providers who encourage it and consumers who demand too much care, often because they don't know the true cost of that care.

At the same time, millions and millions of Americans receive the wrong medical diagnosis. Their doctors either treat them for the wrong maladies or don't uncover their true health needs and thus fail to treat them at all. Patients can be complicit here, failing to communicate effectively with their physicians. Whatever the causes, misdiagnoses are a huge, largely invisible medical problem.

Like much else in *Get What's Yours*, you can benefit from the development of evidence-based online tools drawing upon decades of health treatment results. These tools identify how to spot unneeded and misdiagnosed care and the steps you can take to avoid it.

Google can be your friend here. Research studies are issued regularly that change long-held standards of care. Inserting stents to unblock arteries was the commonly accepted protocol before late 2019, when research found that drugs alone worked as well as a bypass.

THE CHEAPEST CARE IS THE CARE YOU DON'T NEED

The good news about unnecessary care, often called wasted care or low-value care, is that this problem has been solved—on paper. Beginning in 2012, the American Board of Internal Medicine (ABIM) began assembling recommendations from leading clinical groups and medical societies about low-value treatments.

Today, its Choosing Wisely initiative has grown to encompass roughly 600 sets of low-value treatment guidelines from nearly 90 medical societies and other clinical experts. There is a smartphone app (search for "Choosing Wisely") that lets people choose from 115 or so sets of common, low-value medical treatment situations that are explained in plain English.

Percent of sicker adults who have experienced medical, medication, or lab errors or delays in past two years, 2016

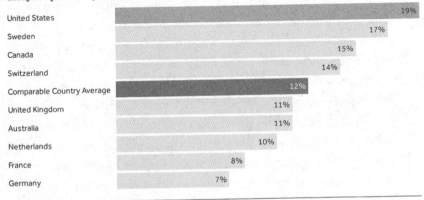

United States	19%
Sweden	17%
Canada	15%
Switzerland	14%
Comparable Country Average	12%
United Kingdom	11%
Australia	11%
Netherlands	10%
France	8%
Germany	7%

Source: KFF analysis of data from "Mirror, Mirror 2017: International Comparison Reflects Flaws and Opportunities for Better U.S. Health Care" (The Commonwealth Fund, July 2017)

Peterson-KFF
Health System Tracker

Unneeded tests and treatments for lower back pain are a good example. Here are the headlines of Choosing Wisely's entry for this condition:

- You probably don't need an X-ray, CT scan, or MRI.
- The tests will not help you feel better faster.
- Imaging tests have risks.
- Imaging tests are expensive.
- When are imaging tests a good idea?

Other partners, including state health groups, have been using real-world health insurance claims experience to help determine the incidence of unneeded care. Milliman, the actuarial consulting firm, developed the MedInsight Waste Calculator to help researchers identify promising areas to reduce wasteful medical spending.

In the real world, unfortunately, progress to reduce unneeded medical care has been slow. It can take years for new clinical guidelines and treatment protocols to become widely accepted by doctors, let alone understood by patients. Further, there are strong incentives for ordering tests and procedures. They are covered by health insurance, often demanded by patients, and are perceived by many clinicians as a defense against malpractice claims.

A study found that doctors use as much unneeded care for their own health treatments as they prescribe to us, so expecting them to lead the way here is a dubious strategy. The authors of the study, "Is Great Information Good Enough? Evidence from Physicians as Patients," concluded that "Doctors have far more information about health, and the benefits and risks of tests and treatments, than most of their patients. . . . Yet when doctors need health care they act much like their patients."

We have been given little reason to question how much un-needed care we get or how to avoid it. It usually takes a wave of high-visibility media attention to change public perception. The national plague of opioid addiction, fueled by massive overprescription, is a sobering example.

A 2017 study reviewed the substantial research done since 2012 on the impact of Choosing Wisely's efforts. It found three compelling reasons for low patient engagement with efforts to reduce unneeded care:

- "Most Americans remain poorly informed about the costs and benefits of particular treatments."
- "Many patients still seek tests or treatment even when informed that they are unlikely to yield much benefit, because they have been conditioned to fear rare, life threatening events."
- "Many patients proceed with low-value treatment either because they distrust the evidence of its low value presented to them or because they suspect that the resources saved will only bolster an insurer's or provider's profit margins rather than benefit the public."

"There's a whole culture [change] that's going to have to happen on the consumer side, of moving away from 'more is always better,'" said Beth Bortz, head of the Virginia Center on Health Innovation. The center has researched low-value care using the Milliman tool.

"A lot of Americans think that more imaging, more testing, is always worth it," Bortz said. "I think a lot of times consumers don't understand the risks of unnecessary imaging, long term. You don't want more CT scans than you have to have."

Beyond the cost of an unnecessary test, she said, there is possible physical harm and longer-term cost and emotional impacts keyed to the results of that first unneeded test. Such "cascade" effects can occur when test results delay treatment, lead to other tests, or reveal other possible health issues, setting off yet another round of tests.

A research study of internists found that nearly all of them had experienced cascade effects from incidental test findings and that twice as many patient encounters produced no clinical significance versus those with meaningful medical implications requiring further treatment. About a third of the tests might have been unneeded, the doctors told researchers.

"Most physicians reported that cascades had caused their patients harm (86.7 percent), including psychological harm (68.4 percent), treatment burden (65.4 percent), financial burden (57.5 percent), dissatisfaction with care (27.6 percent), physical harm (15.6 percent), disrupted social relationships (8.7 percent), and death (0.2 percent)," the study found.

SOURCES OF WASTED CARE

A comprehensive study of health care waste defined six sources of waste. The language is dry; the cost implications are not.

Failure of Care Delivery
"Waste that comes with poor execution or lack of widespread adoption of known best care processes, including, for example, patient safety systems and preventive care practices that have been shown to be effective. The results are patient injuries and worse clinical outcomes." Price tag: $102 billion to $166 billion.

Failure of Care Coordination
"Waste that comes when patients fall through the slats in fragmented care. The results are complications, hospital readmissions, declines in functional status, and increased dependency, especially for the chronically ill, for whom care coordination is essential for health and function." Price tag: $27 billion to $78 billion.

Overtreatment or Low-Value Care

"Waste that comes from subjecting patients to care that, according to sound science and the patients' own preferences, cannot possibly help them—care rooted in outmoded habits, supply-driven behaviors, and ignoring science. Examples include excessive use of antibiotics, use of surgery when watchful waiting is better, and unwanted intensive care at the end of life for patients who prefer hospice and home care." Price tag: $76 billion to $101 billion.

Pricing Failure

"Waste that comes as prices migrate far from those expected in well-functioning markets, that is, the actual costs of production plus a fair profit. For example, because of the absence of effective transparency and competitive markets, U.S. prices for diagnostic procedures such as MRI and CT scans are several times more than identical procedures in other countries." Price tag: $230 billion to $240 billion.

Fraud and Abuse

"Waste that comes as fraudsters issue fake bills and run scams, and also from blunt procedures of inspection and regulation that everyone faces because of the misbehaviors of a very few." Price tag: $58 billion to $84 billion.

Administrative Complexity

"Waste that comes when government, accreditation agencies, payers, and others create inefficient or misguided rules. For example, payers may fail to standardize forms, thereby consuming limited physician time in needlessly complex billing procedures." Price tag: $265 billion.

Several states have used Milliman's MedInsight tool to look at the percentages of specific medical procedures found to be unnecessary.

Virginia and Washington studies looked at nearly fifty procedures and analyzed use patterns by examining millions of private health insurance claims filed by state residents.

"The two best health care tests in America are PSA [prostate-specific antigen] and pap smears," MedInsight product manager Marcos Dachary told me. "Then, with a straight face, you can say the two worst tests in America are the PSA and pap smears." Interpretation matters here.

"Understanding the patient, the patient's age, the patient's prior condition—all of that nuance or context allows us to weigh in appropriateness" to help determine if a procedure was warranted or unnecessary. The procedures used in the Virginia and Washington studies, he explained, were those where the clinical nuances had the least amount of wiggle room for interpretation by providers.

The Virginia Center on Health Innovation study used six procedure categories and found that between 20 and 100 percent in each were unnecessary. The Washington Health Alliance has gotten similar results in its studies.

Unnecessary and expensive MRIs for routine health concerns top the list, accompanied by annual tests and screening procedures that produce little benefit, along with prescriptions of opioids and other powerful drugs for lower back pain, headaches, and other normal aches and pains.

The incidence of low-value care is also widespread in Medicare, according to a 2018 analysis for Congress. "In 2014, there were between 34 and 72 instances of low-value care per 100 beneficiaries," the report said. "Between 23 percent and 37 percent of beneficiaries received at least one low-value service."

(A detailed list of health care you should avoid is in Appendix 9.)

WHAT'S A PATIENT TO DO?

Odds are you trust your doctors and are predisposed to follow their advice. If not, you'd probably look for new doctors. So, when your trusted health care professional says you need a medical procedure or test, you are conditioned to agree.

This can be a stressful interaction to begin with, especially if you're feeling bad and already think something may be wrong. Why would you possibly turn down an offer of care, especially one that is covered by your health insurance?

Hopefully, this chapter already has told you why you should at least take a time-out at this point. Without seeming to question your doctor's expertise, there are ways to give yourself some breathing room.

"Thanks for your guidance and suggestions," you might say. "I'd like to go home, give it some thought, and talk it over with my family. If I did go ahead, when do you recommend I have this done?"

A Connecticut collaboration with Choosing Wisely looked at ways that patients can protect themselves from unnecessary care. It came up with five questions to ask your doctor; groups in other states now use the list.

1. Do I need this test or procedure?
2. What are the risks and side effects?
3. Are their simpler, safer options?
4. What happens if I don't do anything?
5. How much does it cost, and will my insurance pay for it?

CHECKLIST FOR GETTING
THE RIGHT CARE

Several medical and patient safety organizations have developed widely used patient guides, including a four-page checklist to help you get the right care. Excerpts from that list, done jointly by the National Patient Safety Foundation and the Society to Improve Diagnosis in Medicine, are in Appendix 10.

ACCURATE DIAGNOSIS AND
SECOND OPINIONS

Sue Sheridan became a first-time mother more than twenty-five years ago. Her son was born in 1995. Like many newborns, he had jaundice. Unlike only a few others, he had a more serious condition that went undiagnosed by caregivers at her community hospital in Boise, Idaho.

"My son suffered brain damage from kernicterus [a rare form of brain damage in jaundiced newborns] that was not diagnosed to treat his newborn jaundice. [Jaundice is] very, very, very common," she said when I spoke with her late in 2019. "It's the most common newborn phenomenon. There are national guidelines out there. And nobody followed them. And he ended up with brain damage.

"A lot of patients don't even think about looking up guidelines," she said. "I wish I would have. . . . That was in 1995. He now has severe cerebral palsy."

Sheridan's exposure to the effects of a missed medical diagnosis was not over. "After my son's effort, four years later my husband died because he had a tumor in his cervical spine that was removed. We were told it was benign.

"What we didn't learn," she continued matter-of-factly, "was that twenty-three days later a final pathology report came out. By now, he was discharged. And it was a malignant cancer, and that document never got presented to the neurosurgeon. It got put in my husband's file—his medical records. And the neurosurgeon never saw it, so his cancer went untreated for six months. And by the time the pain came back, it was too late. And so my husband died [three years later] when he was forty-five."

Enduring these devastating family tragedies triggered Sheridan to switch careers from international trade financing to health care and, in particular, patient safety.

"My son's name is Cal. After he was permanently harmed for the rest of his life," Sheridan looked deeply into what was being done to protect patients. "I thought somebody was in charge of keeping us safe," she said. "I learned that no one is in charge of keeping us safe."

She then rattled off a list of a half dozen health agencies, including the Food and Drug Administration (FDA), the Centers for Disease Control (CDC), and lesser-known groups.

"None of the agencies is tasked with keeping us safe," she said, lamenting the absence of a health care equivalent to the National Transportation Safety Board, which investigates accidents and identifies ways to prevent them. "We don't have that in health care."

Sheridan cofounded Consumers Advancing Patient Safety (CAPS), which eventually led to advocacy work with the World Health Organization. She later had advocacy positions with the Patient-Centered Outcomes Research Institute (PCORI) and the Centers for Medicare & Medicaid Services (CMS). Since early 2018, she has been head of patient engagement at the Society to Improve Diagnosis in Medicine (SIDM).

Sheridan also fought to get a better deal for her family. She and her late husband, a physician, brought a malpractice action in 1997 related to their son. After a twenty-eight-day trial, the court ruled against them. She kept fighting, all the way to the Idaho Supreme Court. There the Sheridans won, triggering a substantial award to fund Cal's lifelong care.

After her husband's death, and with the knowledge learned during the grueling case involving her son, Sheridan settled out of court. "I just did not trust the system," she said in explaining her decision.

In addition to financial awards, Sheridan is proud that the actions over her son and her late husband's treatments included formal changes in hospital treatment policies. "Malpractice doesn't change the system," she said. "They wanted me to sign gag clauses and seal everything up, and I refused to do that.

"Diagnosis is the beginning of the journey, and the beginning of what we hope is the right treatment," Sheridan noted. "If you don't get the right diagnosis, you're getting the wrong treatment."

BAD MEDICINE IS A LEADING KILLER

I wish that Sue Sheridan's experience was rare, unusual, unexpected, or some other comforting word. It is not.

Each year, an estimated 40,000 to 80,000 people die due to medical diagnoses that caused them to receive the wrong medical care or no care at all. Even the lower range of this estimate is comparable to annual gun deaths. I'm hard pressed to find either epidemic more frightening than the other. There is, however, no public outrage over lethal medical mistakes.

This is likely because people don't know the scale of medical misdiagnoses. The range of death figures cited here is based on autopsy results, not guesswork. And while avoidable deaths are down slightly from estimates made twenty years ago, the death toll from bad or at least off-base medical advice remains enormous.

The incidence of bad diagnoses that do not lead to fatalities is broader still. A 2014 study found that about 5 percent of all medical diagnoses for outpatients were in error. Based on the number of people interacting with health care then, this worked out to 12 million cases a year.

WHERE TO START

Vascular events (strokes, heart attacks, pulmonary embolisms, and related circulatory conditions), infections (principally sepsis), and cancer are the three leading sources of misdiagnoses. The potentially deadly consequences of these events should put you and your personal health posse on high alert.

Women and minorities need to be particularly alert to bias in their diagnoses. They have been routinely excluded from disease research studies and remain underrepresented. As a result, their symptoms may lead to erroneous diagnoses.

A woman who presents in an emergency room setting with chest or back pain might be diagnosed with acid reflux or GERD (Gastro-esophageal Reflux Disease), Sheridan said. That might be true for men but she could be having or had a heart attack. Gender bias is worse for African-American women, who are at higher risk for stroke.

Unless your doctor tells you your condition is life threatening and requires immediate treatment, your initial response to a diagnosis involving these and other serious conditions should include asking your provider the treatment they recommend, where they recommend it be performed, and if there is a recommended time when treatment should begin.

Rather than hurtling ahead with a plan of care, this is a good opportunity to take a time-out. "Thanks for providing your thoughts on this," you might say. "It's a lot to take in all at once. Would it be okay if I set up a follow-up appointment soon to discuss this further?"

A diagnosis related to any serious medical problem should trigger an extensive and broadening circle of research among friends, medical professionals in your community, disease-specific sites, leading medical sites, and social media advocacy groups. As detailed in Chapter Eight, the Patient Advocate Foundation has a Resource Directory that permits you to enter your age, state of residence, and diagnosis, and search for help using various topical filters, including "legal or advocate" services.

SIDM has a patient toolkit that can help prepare you for a deeper dive with your doctor. It's an interactive form you can complete and print out that asks you questions about your medical condition and provides places to enter symptoms and any related personal or family medical history, plus a list of your medications. It allows you to record pain issues.

You should bring a complete copy of your medical records and make sure your doctor knows anything about you that may be helpful. Lack of complete or accurate patient records is regularly cited as a contributing cause of medical misdiagnoses.

We've already covered issues of how to speak with your doctor. Here is a list of care questions from SIDM's toolkit:

1. What is my diagnosis? What else could it be? And what's the worst it could be?

2. Why do you think this is my diagnosis? From test results? From my physical exam?

3. Can you give me written information on my diagnosis? A pamphlet? A website? [Remember Sue Sheridan's rueful thoughts on medical guidelines?]

4. Can you explain the test/treatment you want me to have?

5. What are the risks to the test/treatment you want me to have? What happens if I do nothing?

6. When do I need to follow up with you?

7. What should I do if my symptoms worsen or change, or I don't respond to treatment?

I would add an eighth question: Can you suggest a specialist who treats the condition you've diagnosed? I would like to make an appointment with them.

A variant of this sequence applies when the misdiagnosis may consist of the absence of a diagnosis—a missed call of an illness or condition. Doctors face much tougher medical issues than they once did, simply because the things that medicine now can treat have expanded, as have the tools and medicines for treatment.

"The explosive growth in medical evidence and new technologies ends up being a double-edged sword," the SIDM site notes, "making diagnosis more accurate but also more complex at the same time."

If your doctor or your child's doctor feels a health condition is not serious—"She just has the flu"—you should follow up with the "what else might it be" or "what's the worst it could be" question. Your doctor needs to hear your concerns, and in thinking about how to reply, they just might change their opinion and do you and your child a lot of good.

WHEN MALPRACTICE IS
ALL THAT'S LEFT

About a third of medical malpractice claims over a ten-year period that resulted in permanent injury or death to a patient were caused by diagnostic errors, according to a 2019 study by researchers at Johns Hopkins University School of Medicine that was funded by SIDM.

The study found that of the 21,743 malpractice claims from 2006 to 2015 that caused severe harm, 7,379 were caused by diagnostic errors. Additionally, 21 percent of the total malpractice claims during the same period were the result of diagnostic errors. The malpractice claims data came from Controlled Risk Insurance Company and represented an estimated 30 percent of all malpractice claims.

Researchers analyzed the extent of harm caused by diagnostic errors for the three diseases mentioned earlier: cancer, vascular events, and infection. They accounted for about 62 percent of all diagnostic error malpractice claims and nearly 75 percent of those claims caused severe harm to the patient, including death and permanent disability.

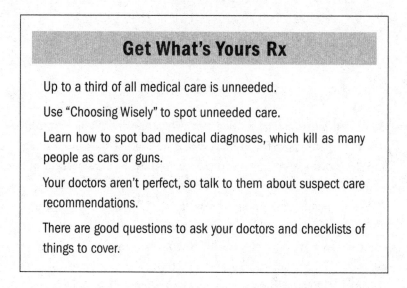

Get What's Yours Rx

Up to a third of all medical care is unneeded.

Use "Choosing Wisely" to spot unneeded care.

Learn how to spot bad medical diagnoses, which kill as many people as cars or guns.

Your doctors aren't perfect, so talk to them about suspect care recommendations.

There are good questions to ask your doctors and checklists of things to cover.

WHEN YOU'RE IN CONTROL AND WHEN YOU'RE NOT

All of health care can be divided into two parts—when you're in control and when you're not. The starkly differing health issues, timing, and decisions within these two spaces are health care's version of a Mars-Venus dichotomy.

When people crow about how well the U.S. health system works, it's because they're talking about situations where patients are in control. Here, we have choices for when, where, and from whom we get care. We have health insurance and the ability to plan for and pay our medical bills. We are not facing an imminent life-or-death crisis.

When critics lament how broken the health system is in this country, they're talking about the part where we are not in control. Where we need care right away or distressingly soon. Where our diagnosis does involve a life-threatening condition.

Or, while not necessarily life threatening, where we have been in a car accident, fallen down the steps, or broken a bone in a sporting or outdoors mishap. Off to the world of emergency medicine we go. We don't know who's going to treat us or how long it might take, how much it's going to cost, and whether our insurance will cover emergency expenses.

The most disturbing health care horror stories flow from this world of "no control" care, making it the more compelling place to start.

AVOID EMERGENCY ROOMS

By now, I hope you already know that a visit to the emergency room, or ER, can be damaging to your financial health.

Hospital ERs can and do slap their "facility fees" on top of whatever care you actually receive. These fees are justified as being the costs of providing and staffing emergency facilities before the first patient has even walked through the door. They make ER care expensive. And they've been incorrectly or even capriciously applied in so many situations that patients have good reason to wonder whose side their hospital is on.

Beyond facility fees, even if your insurance covers the ER you visit, you may have little control or protection against being treated by out-of-network doctors and other licensed clinicians who are not covered by your health plan. "In 2014, 20 percent of hospital inpatient admissions that originated in the emergency department (ED), 14 percent of outpatient visits to the ED, and 9 percent of elective inpatient admissions likely led to a surprise medical bill," according to 2017 research.

The American College of Emergency Physicians singled out four types of ER care where out-of-network doctors applied the most inflated charges, compared with in-network fees:

Breathing problems:	$841 vs. $326; 158 percent
Cuts, scrapes, and bruises:	$754 vs. $298; 153 percent
Abdominal pain:	$1,044 vs. $439; 138 percent
Chest pain:	$1,155 vs. $490; 136 percent

Here were the four most inflated charges it found from out-of-network physicians for common health problems that brought people into the ER:

Ear infections: $639 vs. $238; 168 percent
Open wounds: $633 vs. $236; 168 percent
Flu: $775 vs. $296; 162 percent
Bone fractures: $825 vs. $316; 161 percent

Medicare and Medicaid require doctors to accept lower payment rates than private insurers are willing to pay. Not surprisingly, patients with private health insurance are charged more for ER visits than people with Medicare or Medicaid. Insurers often urge consumers to seek care instead at walk-in clinics or their doctor's office.

Insurers may question whether you even need to go to the ER. UnitedHealth Group found in 2019 research that two-thirds of ER visits—18 million out of 27 million—were avoidable. It listed these ten common conditions as suitable for care at a clinic or your doctor's office:

Bronchitis
Cough
Dizziness
Flu
Headache
Low back pain
Nausea
Sore throat
Strep throat
Upper respiratory infection

The company found that hospital facility fees added about $1,070 to a typical ER visit and that hospitals charged ten times as much for lab, pathology, and radiology services as a typical doctor's office—$335 versus $31.

The average cost of treating common primary care treatable

conditions at a hospital ER was $2,032, it concluded. "That number is 12 times higher than visiting a physician office ($167) and 10 times higher than traveling to an urgent care center ($193) to treat those same conditions."

A study of Virginia ER visits found troubling percentages of what it called "potentially avoidable" ER visits. It listed five specific conditions, ranked them in order of the percentages of the time that ER care could have been avoided, and provided ER costs compared with what patients would pay at their doctor's office.

Respiratory infections:	$369 v. $77; 40 percent
Urinary tract infections:	$961 v. $78; 21 percent
Back problems:	$756 v. $80; 11 percent
Headache, including migraine:	$1,129 v. $83; 10 percent
Inner ear infections:	$262 v. $77; 8 percent

Some health insurers have limited coverage at some ERs, so if you have health insurance, make sure you're covered at nearby ERs. Please do this *before* falling off that ladder!

ProPublica, the investigative journalism nonprofit, makes it a bit easier through its "ER Inspector" tool. You can research nearby ERs based on important variables such as distance, wait times, patient satisfaction scores, and inspection-related violations.

Here are five variables ER Inspector will disclose:

Time Until Sent Home: The average time patients spent in the emergency room before being sent home if they weren't admitted.

Left Without Being Seen: The percentage of patients who left the emergency room without being seen by a doctor.

Time Before Admission: The average time patients spent in the emergency room before being admitted to the hospital.

Transfer Time: Among patients who later were admitted to the
hospital, the additional time they spent waiting before being
taken to their room.

CT Scan: Percentage of patients who arrived with stroke
symptoms and did not receive brain scan results within forty-five
minutes.

ProPublica suggests putting a note on your refrigerator listing
details for your preferred ER, your doctor, and your emergency con-
tacts. I would add some things.

I'm assuming you selected your preferred ER after making sure
your health insurance would cover care received there. Even so,
you should include your insurer's customer contact number. This
shouldn't be a problem, because I'm sure you're already keeping your
insurance cards with you at all times. Right?

What nearby health clinic might provide the care you think you
need at a much lower price than the ER? If needed, go back to Chapter Nine to refresh yourself about picking a health clinic.

Put a "TAKE ME WITH YOU!" reminder on the note.

IS YOUR AMBULANCE TAKING YOU
FOR AN EXPENSIVE RIDE?

All the price transparency and consumer empowerment in the world
can't counteract the reality that if you have a serious medical problem and call 911, you will have no choice about which ambulance
provider arrives at your doorstep.

If you do not have a life-threatening emergency or active trauma
requiring immediate attention, you have the right to instruct the ambulance to take you to the emergency room of your choice. You will
have no role in this decision, however, if the EMTs responding to

your call decide that your medical condition warrants the speediest treatment at the facility they judge to be appropriate.

The general rule is that the patient's choice is controlling unless their life is in jeopardy, said Rob Lawrence with the American Ambulance Association. Waving your health insurance card and muttering something about in-network prices may be to no avail here.

Medically necessary ambulance use is covered by health insurance. Your insurer's definition of medical necessity may differ from yours, but few people ever find this out before making that 911 call. I'm sympathetic but would repeat that failure to understand insurance rules is no defense in an appeal of a rejected ambulance claim.

Lawrence has an arsenal of facts and explanations designed to make ambulances appear to be among the good guys in health care. He knows this can be a tough sell, especially when it comes to the steady flow of horror stories about astronomical bills patients and their families are asked to pay for ground and, especially, air ambulances.

The key driver of ambulance prices, he said, is the concept of the "cost of readiness"—similar to ER facility fees. When you call 911, you expect an ambulance with trained EMS professionals to show up at your home within a reasonable time. In order to meet this service standard, the providers who work with local 911 response systems must have enough people and vehicles to meet expected peak service demands. They have to pay these people and maintain their vehicles whether or not anyone requests an ambulance.

Laws in some areas permit ambulance providers to charge you a fee if you call for an ambulance, EMTs examine you at your home, and decide you do not need to be transported to the hospital. Non-transport fees are not uncommon and these costs often are not covered by health insurance.

Increasingly, health insurers are using information from their insurance claims databases to evaluate ambulance services. They may have lists of who they like and who they don't, and can provide inducements to use preferred vendors or even deny coverage involving companies that charge a lot more than local market averages or have poorer service records.

Insurance companies often negotiate payments smaller than ambulance company initial bills, and ambulance firms often bill for the difference. This adds to an already unacceptable surprise billing burden that Congress is best positioned to rectify.

The message here, as elsewhere in *Get What's Yours*, is to get the facts by calling your health insurer—ahead of time if possible.

URGENT CARE CENTERS

There will be something approaching 10,000 urgent care centers in the United States by the time you read this, according to the Urgent Care Association (UCA). They are growing like crazy, courtesy of the soaring cost of health care at hospitals, long waits for doctor appointments, and large numbers of people without insurance or in high-deductible plans that drive them to seek lower-cost care.

In the process, these walk-in facilities are becoming the go-to place for non-life-threatening health problems that used to send people to the ER. They should be staffed with board-certified physicians and many have nurses. They can treat what ails you on the spot, including writing drug prescriptions.

Consumers have pretty much figured out when to go to a center and when they need more serious care. Only about one or two out of every fifty urgent-care visits winds up sending patients to an ER for more serious care.

More to the point, the UCA says the average cost of an urgent care visit is about $150 compared with more than $1,350 for a typical ER visit. A 2017 study in Texas found average costs in 2015 were similar at hospital ERs ($2,259) and freestanding ERs ($2,199)—but 13 times higher than the average urgent care center cost of $168.

That study found substantial overlap between ER and urgent care center treatments, with about a 60 percent overlap among the top 20 diagnoses for care in hospital ERs and a 75 percent overlap for freestanding ERs.

I would never recommend rolling the dice on your health just to save a buck. I am comfortable saying that you should consider whether an urgent care center makes sense before toddling off to a hospital ER.

Here are the things that typically send people into urgent care centers, the UCA says:

Allergies

Asthma

Burns, minor

Cough/cold/influenza

Conjunctivitis (pink-eye)

Dermatological conditions (rashes, infections, including incision and drainage as a procedure)

Dehydration

Ear infections

Fractures

Gastrointestinal disorders

Gynecology infections and disorders

Headaches/migraines

Influenza

Lacerations, including suturing

Pharyngitis (sore throats)

Pneumonia

Sexually transmitted infections

Sprains/strains

Upper respiratory infections

Urinary tract infections

Work-related illness, injury, screening, and wellness

Detection of complications of chronic illness

Detection and initial treatment of a more serious condition

Urgent care scenarios usually allow you time before you need care. Call the center you plan to visit. Ask about wait times and if it's staffed right then to handle the care you think you need. Centers accept health insurance, so bring your insurance cards.

Don't be surprised if your insurer has programs specifying recommended care centers. Insurers are drilling deeper into your health care choices, to save them (and perhaps you) money and drive care to centers they've identified as providing competent, cost-effective care. Insurers own lots of urgent care centers. So do doctors. Over time, these common ownership links will create coordinated care systems that position urgent care centers as part of your health care "team."

The state of independent measurements of urgent care center quality is behind the booming pace of center expansion and care. In my ideal "planning nerd" world, you would evaluate a few centers close to your home, do a bit of online research, and then visit what appeared to be your favorite choice to confirm your assessment and get comfortable with the people, office layout, and even parking availability. Then put the center's name and contact information on your refrigerator and in your phone.

HOW TO TAKE CONTROL
WHERE YOU CAN

The world of controlled need and access to health care is a more predictable place to be than rolling into some strange ER when you may be unconscious and barely aware of who's treating you, let alone whether they're in your insurance plan's provider network.

The earlier chapters of *Get What's Yours* were designed to prepare you to make informed decisions about this type of care. By now, you should:

- Know how your health insurance works.
- Have assembled solid personal and professional care teams.
- Know how to evaluate the quality of the care you need and how your insurance will affect your choice of caregivers.
- Understand how to decide if you need care and whether you've received an accurate diagnosis.

Knowing these things should prepare you for routine care needs. The story changes for two categories of serious health issues. The first includes cancer, heart attack, stroke, and other potentially fatal or life-shortening conditions. The second involves elective surgeries where the quality of your life is an issue. Except for cosmetic procedures, these tend to be covered by health insurance, though, we know, this often does not rule out crushing medical bills.

This is one situation where you can avoid surprises by finding out ahead of time how your insurer would cover you. Increasingly, insurers have special programs for patients with chronic health conditions.

Bundled care packages may be an option worth considering. These programs have been championed by the Centers for Medicare & Medicaid Services. They have been slow to catch on. In theory, they are great because caregivers must quote you a price for the entire episode of care you need—care and therapy to prepare you, the procedure itself, and post-treatment recovery and therapy. Payments to providers often are linked to successful outcomes, so those involved in your care have a financial stake in your well-being.

These packages are found mainly with joint replacements and other discrete events that have standard treatment protocols. As accountable care organizations become more prevalent, packaged care will become more common. Resistance to its adoption includes the slow pace of anything new in health care and provider concerns about being financially liable for outcomes beyond their control.

If you build a financial plan for a major health event—and you should—make sure it spans several years. Beyond the up-front costs of surgery, chemotherapy, radiation, rehab, and the like, you should ask your health providers about the extent and costs for ongoing, longer-term health care related to your condition. Your personal finances need to be prepared for a health event along with your body.

There's not much more I can tell you about finding the right people and places to treat serious illnesses and chronic conditions. When it comes to money and affordability issues, class is now in session.

WHEN ELECTIVE CARE MAKES SENSE

Whether you need a new knee or cataract surgery is largely up to you and your doctors. I would only urge you to do your homework. Be aware of typical surgical outcomes, including the rehabilitation realities of a new joint or bypass surgery. If you need surgery, look for providers who have implemented enhanced recovery after surgery (ERAS) programs that reduce hospital stays and support better patient outcomes. Work with people in your personal health care posse to plan for the full episode of whatever care you will undertake.

Most elective surgeries occur in outpatient settings. Costs vary depending on whether you are in a hospital outpatient department (HOPD) or an ambulatory surgery center (ASC) and, if the latter, whether that center does or does not have business ties to a hospital or physician group.

Medicare provides an online checklist of questions to help decide the type of facility to use; its questions include:

For your doctor:

- Which hospitals or ambulatory surgical centers do you work with when you perform this type of procedure?
- Which facility is the best place for me given my health status and medical history?
- Do you know if the facility you recommend accepts my health insurance?

For the facility:

- What if I have a medical emergency during a procedure at an ambulatory surgical center?
- Can you provide me data on outcomes for my procedure? Do you have any quality metrics to share with me about your staffing, care coordination, medication safety, and steps you take to prevent infection?

For your health insurer:

- Is this procedure covered by health insurance?
- Am I required to use a certain facility? Do I need prior authorization?
- Will my billed costs be different at a hospital outpatient department than an ambulatory surgical center? Will my out-of-pocket costs be different because of my insurance?

To drill down into the range of costs for your procedure, ask your doctor or outpatient care provider the billing codes for your procedure. Medical codes can rival the complexities of Talmudic scholarship. You can find help from current procedures terminology (CPT) codes that are widely used. It's likely your doctors won't know these codes but people on their staff or at the facility definitely will. After all, they need to know these codes to bill you and your insurer for the procedure.

To give you an idea of the range of costs you will face, here are lists of CPT codes and related health conditions for ten commonly performed outpatient surgical procedures. They are based on Medicare data. This skews the listings to older patients but will give you an idea of the range of payments that insurance companies may shell out.

TOP 10 ASC OUTPATIENT PROCEDURES

Rank	Code	Description	Annual Procedures
1.	66984	Cataract surg w/intraocular implant, 1 stage	1,252,835
2.	J0585	Injection, onabotulinumtoxinA (Botox)	759,997
3.	43239	Esophagogastroduodenoscopy (Egd) biopsy single/multiple	539,772
4.	45380	Colonoscopy and biopsy	464,136
5.	45385	Colonoscopy w/lesion removal	397,339
6.	64483	Epidural steroid injection in lumbar spine w/imaging guidance	319,592
7.	66821	After cataract laser surgery	283,574
8.	64493	Injection into lumbar/sacral spine w/image guidance	220,472
9.	62323	Lumbar interlaminar epidural steroid injection	195,648
10.	G0105	Colorectal screening; high risk individual	137,697

To get the spread for these procedures where you live, go to Healthcare Bluebook, enter your ZIP code in its free price-comparison tool, and then enter the CPT code for one or more of the ten procedures listed above. If the code doesn't work in the tool, try the name of the procedure.

In my ZIP code, for example, the range of costs for cataract surgeries was $1,307 to $16,638! The results included hospital-based surgeries.

WHEN THE BEST CARE IS
A PLANE RIDE AWAY

Increasingly, the best solution for elective health procedures may not be near your home. As we learned at the beginning of *Get What's Yours*, health insurers—particularly those administering employer-insured health plans—may recommend high-quality, low-cost care from a network of doctors and hospitals that are part of their "centers of excellence" (COE) programs.

Health insurers have done the homework to evaluate the quality and prices for the elective procedures they cover. As explained earlier, their quality and pricing tools are more sophisticated than those used by the popular ratings services.

Providers are included in their centers of excellence because they and their affiliates have demonstrated the highest-quality and most cost-effective results for their care. Better patient outcomes translate into fewer complications and thus lower costs to insurers and patients.

If you still want care near your home, you probably can get it covered. It may cost more than from providers in an insurer's COE network. To this extent, the insurers are asking you to shop for your care, with their COEs as recommended providers for certain procedures.

Outside the environment of insurance plan programs, the world of medical tourism is harder to navigate. More patients are seeking its benefits due to the rise in people without insurance, those with skimpy plans, and people who want cosmetic and other health procedures that aren't covered by insurance. In 2020, an estimated 2.2 million Americans will go outside the United States for some type of health treatment, according to Patients Beyond Borders, a medical tourism facilitator. (This was a pre-pandemic projection.)

This is a world of free enterprise health care where you may be paying 100 percent of all costs. In shopping for such care, the growth of data-driven quality and pricing tools has become invaluable.

In terms of quality, the Joint Commission is the major information source for international health care. It is the leading private service helping Americans evaluate the quality of hospitals in the United States and globally. It generates what amounts to a seal of health care approval, but only to organizations that have requested and paid to be evaluated and accredited. This gives me some pause, but the commission's work is widely accepted by health care experts.

For background, the group's glossary explains the care programs it evaluates and its different types of accreditations. This knowledge will, in turn, help you make sense of its accreditations for U.S. (QualityCheck.org) and overseas (WorldHospitalSearch.org) care providers.

In the United States, of course, there are lots of other ratings tools to help you find top-quality providers. The Joint Commission's global ratings are difficult to replicate.

Its global accreditations include certifications for these specific procedures:

Acute Myocardial Infarction (heart-related diseases)
Asthma
Cancer (all types)
Childhood Asthma
Chronic Heart Failure
Chronic Kidney Disease
Chronic Obstructive Pulmonary Disease (COPD)

Diabetes Mellitus (types 1 and 2)
End-stage Renal Disease
Heart Failure
HIV/AIDS Management
Joint Replacement (all types)
Osteoarthritis of the Knee
Outpatient Diabetes
Pain Management
Palliative Care (all types)
Primary Stroke
Transplantation (all types)
Traumatic Brain Injury

Americans undergo more than 18 million cosmetic and reconstructive surgeries annually in the United States and more are done overseas. Cosmetic care ratings are beyond the scope of *Get What's Yours*. Saving money on such care is not. As always, two credible sources of information are better than one; three are better than two, and so on.

The Medical Tourism Association has price comparisons for common procedures, comparing average U.S. costs with those in more than a dozen countries. These averages are a guide. Get specific prices from care providers before deciding where to get your procedure done.

Few hospitals have done more to lower costs while improving quality than India's Narayana Health. The story of how it did so is an impressive guide to the things that are generally *not* happening in U.S. hospitals.

Dr. Devi Shetty, the founder and head of the growing chain of Narayana hospitals, can perform an all-day coronary thromboendarterectomy for about $10,000. The U.S. price tag is about $200,000.

MediBid.com offers a reverse auction system for cash market

health care prices—in the United States and other countries. If you enter the procedure you're seeking, MediBid will canvass its network of providers and generate a list of responses and prices linked to your travel preferences. Its cost calculator provides a look at the range of savings for common procedures. The next chapter will explain how MediBid is used to help people shop for health care.

Get What's Yours Rx

Emergency rooms are the costliest place to get health care; consider urgent care centers and outpatient clinics instead.

You often can control ambulance decisions, saving money and improving your care.

Hospitals are costly care providers that even hospitals say you often should avoid.

Understand your elective surgery options and costs.

Your best and cheapest care may be in another state or country.

HEROES VI

The Warrior Mother

Cynthia Buness

In 2016, the medical journal *Pediatric Gastroenterology, Hepatology & Nutrition* (*PGHP*) published a piece titled "Oral Vancomycin Therapy in a Child with Primary Sclerosing Cholangitis (PSC) and Severe Ulcerative Colitis." PSC attacks the liver, has no clinically accepted cure, and its victims may require a liver transplant in less than ten years, assuming they are still alive.

Cynthia Buness was one of three authors of the paper.

The article presented the health and medical treatment history of a severely ill young woman who had been diagnosed with PSC. The language used will be well known to medical researchers. It was alien to me and, I suspect, you. I've included an excerpt in Appendix 11. Hats off if you can power through to the end. The point here is to emphasize that this is the language of medicine and the clinical vocabulary that Cynthia needed to master.

Cynthia was the first named author of the PGHP article, a slot normally reserved for the lead researcher. Her two coauthors were liver experts at the Mayo Clinic in Phoenix and Texas Children's Hospital in Houston.

Cynthia has no medical training. She is a Phoenix housewife and mom. And the person described in the article was hardly a random patient but her daughter, Areta. At the time the article was written in late 2015, Cynthia (born in November 1957) was fifty-eight; Areta (born January 1997) was eighteen.

Areta had struggled with digestive problems for several years and had kept them from her friends and others outside the family. A high achiever, she had managed to work through pain and incontinence issues and became a high-functioning athlete and endurance runner. Her difficulties progressed and forced a reckoning as she began her sophomore year—a time when many athletes begin competing for varsity team slots.

"Here she was," Cynthia recalls, "just entering her sophomore year in high school. And we were told [by her that] she had decided that instead of cross-country, that she was going to switch to badminton because there weren't bathrooms when you were out doing cross-country, and also she was just too thin.

"She was in the middle of the badminton tryouts, and we had this liver biopsy," Cynthia says. "And she went in the next day . . . and the results came back and it was absolutely, completely devastating. And I was frozen with these results because there is no treatment or cure and progression will lead to a liver transplant, or death, within eight to fifteen years, depending on how the disease progresses.

"It took me a little bit to get my act together" after absorbing the news that Areta had been diagnosed with PSC, an uncommon disease without patient numbers large enough to command much attention from researchers and pharmaceutical companies.

Once she did, "I started to teach myself." Armed with a thirty-five-year-old college zoology degree and the motivation of a committed parent, Cynthia taught herself about PSC, sought out leading doctors in the field, and fought (with diplomacy and respect, she advises) with Areta's local doctors.

After the initial PSC diagnosis, Cynthia's husband started Googling around and the search led to Dr. Kenneth Cox at Stanford, she said. He was recommending the treatment of PSC with what's called an "off label" (not clinically accepted) use of an existing generic antibiotic named vancomycin.

Cynthia then sought out a local liver expert at Mayo, Keith Lindor, and spoke with him about what she had learned. Lindor would later be a coauthor of the *PGHP* article and two others Cynthia coauthored. Dr. Cox also became a coauthor.

"He [Lindor] said, 'I think you need to try this drug,'" she recalls. But Areta's local doctors refused to put her on vancomycin and instead suggested a course of treatment that Cynthia feels may have prevented her later treatment from being effective.

"Nobody was really following this Stanford doctor's protocol," she said. And without the advice of Lindor and other experts, Areta and her parents might well have accepted the recommendations of her local doctors. They didn't.

"We had to take a leap of faith, and trust a doctor who, basically, nobody seemed to be listening to up at Stanford," she said.

Today, Areta is free of symptoms from a disease with no cure. The vancomycin therapy that did the trick is on its way to becoming a standard of care for some of those afflicted with PSC. Cynthia has become a relentless patient advocate. The course of this ten-year journey was often uncertain and can appear haphazard in hindsight.

At first, mistakes were made on the effective vancomycin dosage. This is when Cynthia learned there was no accepted protocol for using the drug to treat PSC. While their search for a treatment solution was proceeding, Cynthia was launched on her own effort to secure research funding to test the drug for PSC.

She went to physician conferences and paid her own way. "It's been a very big monetary commitment to me.

"In the beginning, I couldn't understand anything. I'd sit

there and it's just like I'm hearing Greek," she recalled. "And now, I can go and I understand everything that is talked about."

During the early period of her advocacy efforts, she said, "doctors did not believe that the colon was connected to the liver in this. And I just kept saying, 'You know, my daughter took a drug for acne and it changed the microbiome in her gut. . . .' And that's what caused this disease. And nobody believed me. And now, just last fall I published a paper with Stanford, Mayo, and UCLA that that's exactly what happened!"

Tapping Lindor and others, Cynthia has learned the arcane rules of medical grant writing, and has made several applications. She pulled together a group of PSC patients and their families as potential research subjects and sought funding to research pediatric (adolescent) and adult treatments. "We didn't really know the rules very well" at first, she said. "So we got rejected . . . but I kept trying." When we spoke in March 2020, Cynthia said that despite some success, much work remains.

Over time, she has become a fan of going to the top when she interacted with drug companies seeking research support. "I would always go to the CEO of the company."

During this time, Areta's symptoms had disappeared except on two occasions. The first was caused by her being prescribed a different brand of the generic. If you think all versions of a generic are the same, just ask Cynthia. This was easily resolved.

The second reappearance of PSC symptoms had no apparent causes. Areta was still taking the same version of vancomycin, which was made in China. Her husband learned the drug maker had changed manufacturing locations. Cynthia again went into research mode and began learning about the frequent quality problems in overseas generic drug production.

"Then I called the CEO of a pharma company that I know" to

discuss how the system works, she said. Generic drug companies "can tell you nothing's changed but there are so many things that can change and they can still tell you it hasn't changed."

"I started thinking maybe it was the capsules," she continued. "So, we started taking the drug out of the capsules . . . and within two days, she was better."

"The tragedy" with her detective work, she said, "is it's okay for her and for the six other patients who know me. But what about everybody else?"

Such knowledge motivated Cynthia's patient advocacy work. "You have to be diplomatic, because you can't tell doctors what to do with their patients. But you can arm patients with information, and I have a whole set of information that I send to patients."

And, of course, she remains motivated by her child. "Nobody understands what it's like unless you have a child or family member. Having a child with a disease like this—it changes you," she said. "I live on the verge of panic. Whenever she calls, I think, 'Oh, my god, is she calling because she wants to talk with me or because she's got a problem?'"

As for Cynthia, her broader goal is clear:

"I'm going to try to cure this thing. That's what I'm working on now."

13

SHOPPING FOR HEALTH CARE

Ralph Weber was living in Canada early this century when his now-former wife, Tess, developed a painful bunion that required surgery. What the couple discovered was that universal access to health care in Canada had created a long waiting list for this care. After more than two and a half years, and with her pain often unbearable, Ralph, a Canadian, and Tess moved back to her home state of California in 2005 so she could get the relatively simple operation she needed.

In 2005, insurers could and often did deny coverage if a person had a preexisting health condition, which Tess certainly did. "I knew it was a preexisting condition," Weber recalled, "so it wouldn't be covered [by health insurance]. So, I actually bid it out. I asked several people [surgeons] to bid on it." Borrowing a commonly used business practice, he issued what was basically an RFP, or a request for proposals. A bunch of health providers responded and after checking out their credentials, the couple chose the low bid.

"It was great," Weber said. "She got in the next day." The price for her bunionectomy was $2,200—about 10 percent of the price that people without insurance were charged at the time, and far below what the surgeon would receive by doing the procedure on someone with health insurance.

Weber did more than marvel at his good fortune. He started a business based on the experience and launched what he called MediBid in 2010. At first, he focused on other Canadians who were frustrated by long waits for care. The reputation in the United

States for sky-high health costs had deterred them from looking south for care.

What Weber found is that many doctors and surgical centers in the United States were and are more than willing to bypass the bureaucracy of American health care. Today, upwards of 120,000 health providers in the United States and fourteen other countries work with MediBid and will accept discounted prices for providing care.

Weber learned that building relationships with employers was a better way to grow his business than by marketing MediBid to individual consumers. Most of the company's nearly 300,000 enrolled consumers, who are called "seekers," are covered by employer health plans. MediBid also is used by health care sharing ministries— controversial health insurance substitutes where members agree to pay health costs for other members who need care.

MediBid's cost calculator displays expected charges for various procedures, providing a benchmark for the prices they receive when they use the service. Most bids are for elective surgeries (joint replacements, arthroscopies, colonoscopies) and expensive standardized tests (MRIs, CT scans, mammograms). For $100, a consumer can become a registered seeker and bid for a procedure. The fee is often waived by members whose employers work with MediBid.

A person can stipulate how far they travel for the procedure. Weber says the resulting bids will honor this request. He will toss in a low bid from farther away so the seeker can see the full range of their potential savings.

Medical tourism is known for providing cheap care at exotic destinations outside the United States. However, tourism today mostly happens inside the United States, within 250 miles of a person's home.

MediBid evaluates provider quality by looking at publicly available ratings tools, including many of the quality measures explained in Chapter Ten and the Joint Commission hospital certifications explained in Chapter Twelve.

Over the years, Weber has become an outspoken champion of health care price transparency. "The U.S. is the only country on the planet that has four prices for every procedure," he says, ticking them off one by one:

List prices are called chargemasters by hospitals. They are often not based on underlying costs at all, he claims, and are used more as the starting point for subsequent negotiations. These include **cash prices** that often are discounted by about 30 percent, and even lower **insurance company prices**. Then there's **the fourth price** that providers are often willing to accept from MediBid and others.

Ironically, Weber says, providing complete price transparency in health care might cause prices to increase, at least at first. Research studies strongly support the finding that there is little or no correlation between price and quality in U.S. health care. Weber believes, however, that consumers do assume higher prices mean higher quality, and thus would select more expensive care if shown a price list.

Such attitudes are changing. In research done for Patient Rights Advocate, founder Cynthia Fisher says, 75 percent of consumers said that high health prices did not necessarily reflect high-quality care.

It's possible MediBid's influence will be more as a trailblazer than a large-scale conduit to low-cost care. Founded in 2010, the company has only seven full-time employees, and Weber says potential investors are not exactly knocking down his door.

New Choice Health provides a similar pricing service. ClearHealthCosts is a crowdsourcing service—people report their real health costs and the site lets consumers search for pricing information for care near their homes.

For years, the Surgery Center of Oklahoma has drawn patients from across the country with low prices and price transparency tools. More such services are popping up.

The KISx Card program works with self-funded employer insurance plans to identify surgical providers that the program says will accept significant price reductions for expensive procedures in exchange for prompt, direct payments that avoid traditional insurance processing requirements and delays. "The savings to the employer is so substantial," the company says, "that they are able to waive employee deductibles while offering a cash incentive for engaging in the program."

Here is a list as of mid-2020 of possible savings from the top procedures offered by the KISx Card program:

Procedure	National Avg. Price	KISx Card Price
Lumbar Laminectomy	$77,000	$10,190 (87% Savings)
Thyroidectomy	$38,000	$6,100 (84% Savings)
Microdiscentomy Lumbar	$40,000	$9,600 (76% Savings)
Knee Arthroscopy w/Anterior Ligament	$35,000	$7,250 (79% Savings)
Ultrasound for Prostate Cancer	$50,000	$25,000 (50% Savings)
Breast Reconstruction	$30,000	$7,980 (73% Savings)
Total Knee Replacement	$40,000	$22,500 (55% Savings)
Anterior Cervical Discectomy	$40,000	$18,960 (53% Savings)
Total Hip Replacement	$45,000	$25,000 (44% Savings)
Total Mastectomy	$14,000	$5,500 (61% Savings)
Vaginal Hysterectomy	$13,500	$8,000 (41% Savings)
Cholecystectomy	$12,000	$5,865 (51% Savings)
Hemorrhoidectomy	$6,000	$2,560 (57% Savings)
Transurethral Resection of the Prostate	$9,000	$3,500 (61% Savings)
Carpal Tunnel Release	$4,000	$2,750 (31% Savings)

Hospitals have long been reluctant to share their chargemaster lists. The Trump administration has been sued by the industry over its issuance of price transparency regulations. Despite lawsuits and other delaying actions, the movement toward transparency seems more a matter of when than if.

The University of Utah Health System provides downloads of its chargemaster. The 25,000 items it contains supports the contention of many critics that such lists are too complicated for consumer use. Utah's major chain of private hospitals and clinics, Intermountain Health Care, provides a more reasonable 2,900-item chargemaster. The real value of these lists is unlocked when you can use them in discussions with health advocates and hospital financial counselors.

WELCOME TO HEALTH CARE SHOPPING

MediBid's Weber and Jeff Rice, the cofounder of Healthcare Blue-book, whom we met in Chapter One, are two of the many health care heroes in this book whose actions have been spurred by their own experiences with the health care system. If you want to shop for health care today, you can, thanks in no small part to what they and a small group of like-minded reformers have done.

The real costs of health care are coming in from the cold, so to speak, often over the objections of the parties whose prices are being disclosed—doctors, equipment, and drug companies and, as noted, hospitals.

This chapter will tell you how to find this information and how to use it to get a better deal in health care. When we come to Chapter Fifteen, which explains how you can fight back against out-of-this-world health care charges, you'll see how patient advocates use real cost information to drive down medical bills and convince providers to accept lower payments.

Cost information is one of three essential ingredients that have been missing from health care shopping. So is the knowledge among nearly all consumers that it's even possible to shop for better and cheaper care. Lastly, the need to even shop for care has been obscured by health plans. Insurers have misinformed consumers for decades, telling us we needn't shop for care because they have negotiated the best prices for us.

Behavioral research on consumer health care shopping largely has concluded that it's not happening, and that health care is different from autos or earbuds or other consumer products. Here are three reasons, as explained in a report from Altarum, a Medicare and Medicaid consulting firm:

1. The quality of care is not easy to ascertain, so simply giving consumers a list of "real" medical costs may not make their treatment decision much easier.
2. Physician recommendations have a big impact on patient decisions, whether or not physicians know the cost of their recommendation or the quality of care provided by their recommended treatment professional.
3. Health insurers are powerful middlemen between patients and their care needs, and their decisions on care may have nothing to do with the price or quality of that care.

Given these problems, the study said, "transparency tools have generally not been successful when it comes to incentivizing consumers to compare services and shop for the best price."

A later study by Altarum interviewed consumers about how they actually used some of the leading (as of 2019—some time ago by tech standards) consumer sites and web apps that deal with health pricing, quality, and scheduling medical appointments. "The findings reveal a deep divide between the information that consumers would typically seek and the information provided by the transparency tools," the study said.

Why? Dig a bit deeper and it turns out the absence of consumer shopping is not due to the lack of information and opportunity. It's because consumers are unaware it even exists.

"Consumers would not typically turn to a web-based comparator tool to select a provider," the study said. "Indeed, many were surprised to learn that tools like the ones tested in this exercise even existed.

"People generally thought that price depended upon what insurance they had but did not realize that prices can also vary among providers," it added. "Their primary goal was to obtain an estimate of the out-of-pocket cost, not to compare prices."

While consumers in general may still not know how to benefit from the widespread development of accurate and easily accessible information on health care prices and quality, you, dear reader, are not thus disadvantaged.

Shopping for health care takes effort. It will get easier as cost information and the tools to make use of it become widespread. Good tools exist right now, often controlled by insurers and other providers. They are used to promote preferred services and providers to insurance plan members.

Armed with pricing and quality information explained later in this chapter, you can shop for health care and, as other chapters in the book make clear, you're probably already doing so. As more people do it, they will be sharing their experiences on social media and stimulating more consumer activism.

This is becoming powerful stuff, especially when coupled with the slowly spreading recognition that there is little if any correlation between the cost and quality of care. Unlike the ill-fated and safety-plagued Yugo of auto lore, the cheapest health care can actually turn out to be as good or even better than expensive care.

With that in mind, here are a dozen tips about how to shop for health care:

1. When you get a diagnosis of recommended care from a doctor or other clinician, ask about the range of care options for the condition being diagnosed. There often are multiple options;

caregivers tend to have their preferred solutions, which may or may not be your best options.

2. Heed the lessons in Chapter Eleven and make sure the care is needed. Get a second opinion for any significant health treatment.

3. Do not accept averages—average costs, average treatment outcomes, and the like. You are not average and neither are your needs.

4. Do seek information that is as specific to your indicated treatment as possible. This may include understanding the medical billing codes that will be used in determining the charges for your treatment.

5. Find out who your doctor or treating professional recommends provide you the treatment. Use provider-quality tools (Chapter Ten) to evaluate that recommendation and decide whether to push back against it. This may be uncomfortable. Keep in mind that it's your health on the line, not theirs. If you have a good relationship with your doctor (Chapter Nine), they will respond positively.

6. Once you've agreed upon your treatment professional, contact their office and get the name or names of facilities where they perform your treatment. Make sure to ask them how many of these procedures they do in a month or quarter. I'm a big fan of the "10,000 hour rule," popularized by Malcolm Gladwell, which explained how people get good at what they do.

7. Call those facilities and ask them what their charge for your procedure or course of treatment will be at your insured, in-network rate. Try to find out the out-of-network charge and, third, what the cash-payment rate would be or even if they accept cash payments. Make sure to include the costs of an anesthesiologist in these discussions.

8. Use one of the health cost tools explained in this chapter to see the range of costs for your treatment in your local market—or as close to your local market as you can get. Some tools may have cost information at the specific-facility level; others may provide only area or regional averages.

9. Confirm with your health insurer that the treatment is covered as an in-network procedure. If not, use the information you gathered about non-network and cash charges.

10. If there are cheaper treatment facilities, call your recommended treatment professional and ask if he or she has privileges at any of these cheaper locations, and if they would consider providing your treatment there.

11. If not, use your knowledge of the range of treatment costs to ask the facility favored by your treatment provider if it would consider lowering your fee. The more expensive the charges at your expected treatment facility, the more leverage you are likely to have in such a discussion.

12. Once you've made your decision, call your health insurer again and review any prior authorization or related insurance approvals you will need.

AN EARLY TALE OF HEALTH CARE SHOPPING

Jeff Rice's shopping odyssey involved his twelve-year-old son's need for foot surgery. Trained as a doctor, Rice did his due diligence and found a highly regarded foot surgeon in St. Louis, about a three-hundred-mile drive from his home near Nashville.

The surgery would occur at an outpatient facility and would take about an hour. Rice knew the medical billing code for the procedure, provided it to the facility, and asked how much the surgery would cost.

"The quote [from them] was, 'We don't know, why are you asking?'"

And unfortunately, that was the attitude," he recalled. "They called me back and said it would be $37,000." For a one-hour, outpatient procedure.

Rice later learned that the charge the facility might accept for a claim processed through his health insurer was still $15,000 to $25,000. He called the surgeon, and asked him if there were other places in the area where he had operating privileges. The surgeon recommended another facility.

"'They're just as good [and] way more convenient,'" he recalled the surgeon telling him. "So I called them . . . and this alternative option was $1,500, instead of $15,000 to $25,000." Rice's son had the surgery, which was successful.

Rice saw the lack of available health care pricing as a business opportunity. The hard work of starting a company was compounded because Rice and cofounder Bill Kampine began Healthcare Bluebook in 2008, just as the great recession was stopping business funding in its tracks.

Rice and Kampine sought out employers who had decided to self-insure for their employees' care. This meant that the employers had assumed the risks and financial responsibility for their employees' health care needs. Some employers acted on the realization that their health insurers worked for them, and not, as it had often seemed, the other way around.

In these new third-party administrative agreements (insurers here are, in fact, known as TPAs) the insurers had to provide employers with details about their employees' use of health insurance.

This seemingly minor change was not minor at all. Employers now had access to what insured care their employees received, who provided it and where it was delivered, what doctors and hospitals billed for the care, and—this is a big deal inside a big deal—what they ultimately wound up accepting as payment for it from the employer's insurance plan.

We saw in Chapter Three what having this information has meant for Walmart. Even much smaller employers can develop the same intelligence if enough of them agree to share it, and this was the key to Healthcare Bluebook's business strategy.

The company got paid by employers for putting this information into an understandable framework that made sense to the employer and which could provide fair, apples-to-apples comparisons about the health care experiences of other self-insured employers.

Further, if an employer agreed to provide its self-insured employee health data to the company, it would receive access to the much larger pool of data being collected from other participating employers. It wouldn't know the identity of these employers or any personal details about any individual employee's care.

THE POWER IN BIG NUMBERS

As Healthcare Bluebook added employer health plans, the power of its data grew. Today, it has information from about five thousand employers insuring several million employees. Those employers can shop for health care and so can many of their employees. Your employer may be one of them or perhaps a spouse or friend works at one.

The company has collected enough information to list the actual prices paid to doctors and hospitals in every ZIP code in the United States.

It also knows about the quality of that care by analyzing billing codes associated with unsuccessful care—return visits to hospitals, repeated procedures, and other markers of complications following the initial delivery of care. Linking such codes to specific doctors and hospitals can create solid evidence about who's good and who's not so good at providing care.

For consumers, Healthcare Bluebook's "Find a Fair Price" tool provides the price range for care. It does not identify specific providers. That information is available only to people whose employers provide their claims information to Healthcare Bluebook and who have provided access to their employees. Its tools are available as smartphone apps.

If you do your homework and find the price for a procedure, the public tool will let you know how this compares with costs actually paid for the procedure by insurance plans covering people who got the care in your home market. If there is a nearby health provider willing to do the procedure for a cash-market price, the tool will identify that provider and the price.

THE HEALTH COST GENIE IS OUT OF THE BOTTLE

Despite its enormous cache of claims documents, Healthcare Bluebook hardly monitors all of health care. No tool does. Other information firms, nonprofits, and state governments provide similar data. As their numbers grow, so will the availability of broad, consumer-level pricing information.

The Health Care Cost Institute collects and analyzes claims information involving 90 million people—50 million with commercial insurance and 40 million with Medicare. Its data is used to produce reports on pricing trends that have had a big impact on consumers. Its Healthy Marketplace Index is lifting the veil on health costs.

By comparing the prices for the same health services in more than 110 metro areas around the nation, you can learn how your area ranks and how much health care people in these areas used. It turns out that people in high-price markets use less health care. To the extent that high prices discourage consumption, they already are health care shoppers.

HCCI uses its data to provide public pricing information via

Guroo.com. Guroo tracks nearly three hundred "bundles" of common health needs, explains the care provided for each, and provides average national, regional, and local costs.

In 2016, HCCI did a study about how much health care was "shoppable." "It should not be expected that someone [will] pull out his or her smartphone and research the lowest price emergency room before dialing 911," the HCCI report said.

For a health care service to be shoppable, it must be a common health care service that can be researched ("shopped") in advance; multiple providers of that service must be available in a market (i.e., competition); and sufficient data about the prices and quality of services must be available.

Here were the study's key findings:

- About 43 percent of the $524.2 billion spent on health care by individuals . . . was spent on shoppable services.
- About 15 percent of total spending in 2011 was spent by consumers out-of-pocket.
- $37.7 billion (7 percent of total spending) of the out-of-pocket spending in 2011 was on shoppable services.
- Overall, the potential gains from the consumer price shopping aspect of price transparency efforts were modest.

HCCI updated this study in early 2020 using the same methodology as in 2011. Based on comparable 2017 spending data, it found even less of health care was shoppable: 36 percent versus 43 percent earlier.

Procedures used in the study excluded from the definition of what's shoppable a lot of things that I'd argue are shoppable and becoming more so. Prescription drugs are defined as not shoppable. Really? You'll learn how to shop for them in the next chapter.

HOW TO USE PRICING INFORMATION
TO SHOP FOR CARE

FAIR Health has assembled details on more than 50 billion health and dental claims applying to commercial insurers and Medicare. It provides extensive consumer price information—including in-network and out-of-network/uninsured prices.

FAIR Health's information, unlike that of Healthcare Bluebook, tracks prices charged by health providers and not the amounts of money they ultimately agreed to accept in payment for their services. Make sure you know exactly what's being measured in any pricing tool you use.

Medicare prices are linked to its own system of codes—the Healthcare Common Procedure Coding System (HCPCS). Knowing what Medicare will pay for care can be a powerful lever to negotiate lower prices. It's even been given its own name—Medicare reference pricing. And it's being used by employers, health advocates, and consumers to get better deals on health care.

The state of Montana, for example, has tied health care payments for state-controlled insurance programs to levels that are about 2.9 times higher than Medicare rates. This may seem like a big difference. Commercial insurance payment rates versus Medicare, however, are often 4 to 5 times greater, or even more.

Medicare has a Procedure Price Lookup Tool that provides average national prices for outpatient procedures done at ambulatory care centers and in hospital outpatient centers. It was presented in a consumer-unfriendly format as I was writing this book and the agency says it will be improving its consumer pricing and transparency tools. Let's hope so.

Still, here's just one example of how invaluable Medicare pricing information can be. Let's take a colonoscopy, a common procedure.

The average price that Medicare reimbursed for a colonoscopy (flex-ible, with biopsy, single or multiple; code 45830) was slightly more than $500 at an ambulatory center and more than $780 at a hospital outpatient center.

Using Healthcare Bluebook, the commercial price of this proce-dure in my hometown ranged between $1,114 and an astronomical $10,764. Even the lowest price nearly doubles Medicare's payment rate for care at a nonhospital outpatient center.

We will return to this topic. Chapter Fifteen explains how you can use Medicare's payment rates to contest inflated health bills. Chapter Sixteen profiles emerging retail health providers that post public price lists, providing traditional health care providers with national competition.

STATES LEAD THE WAY TO CONSUMER HEALTH SHOPPING

As the Montana story illustrates, shopping for health care is being aggressively pursued at the state level. Absent national moves to tackle rising health prices, many states have not waited around for some political version of Godot. More than a third of the states have created databases of claims-based health care costs. They are known as all-payer claims databases. There is even an APCD Council that keeps track of what individual states are doing.

Eighteen states had mandatory insurance claims databases as of the end of 2019, meaning that insurers had to provide them claims information. Another seven states had databases where cooperation from insurers was voluntary.

The states with mandatory databases were Arkansas, Colorado, Connecticut, Delaware, Florida, Kansas, Maine, Maryland, Mas-sachusetts, Minnesota, New Hampshire, New York, Oregon, Rhode

Island, Utah, Vermont, Virginia (data submission voluntary), and Washington (also an existing voluntary program).

The states with voluntary programs were California (also a state program in implementation), Michigan, Oklahoma, South Carolina, Texas, Washington, and Wisconsin.

California, Hawaii, New Mexico, and West Virginia were implementing programs, and there was strong interest in establishing claims databases in ten states—Alaska, Idaho, Kentucky, Montana, Nevada, New Jersey, North Carolina, Pennsylvania, Tennessee, and Wyoming.

The Maryland Health Care Commission has a consumer-friendly "Wear the Cost" tool that provides cost and outcomes information for four common treatments—hip and knee replacements, hysterectomies, and vaginal childbirth deliveries. Prices vary greatly and there is no consistent correlation between price and quality. You can see details about knee replacements in Appendix 12.

I spent time in Denver with managers of the Center for Improving Value in Health Care (CIVHC), the program in Colorado that collects the state's health insurance claims information.

"A certain level of the population is going to do exactly what their doctor tells them," said CIVHC's CEO, Ana English. "Another level will reach out [for more information], but only to friends and doctors. . . . Another layer is going to seek any information wherever they can. That's a very small percentage of the population."

To move the needle, she added, awareness of real cost information needs to be increased, and more health care payers—employers and insurers—need to negotiate lower prices. "The change is not going to move at a rate that's acceptable until those questions" are dealt with, she said.

When this happens, change does occur, noted Cari Frank, CIVHC's vice president of communications and marketing. Medicare reference pricing is a popular approach.

"What we're seeing across the country is . . . employer coalitions are really ramping up and saying, 'This is not okay anymore. We're not okay paying five times the Medicare rate,'" she said. "And they're starting to negotiate with hospitals based on the Medicare rates."

Health providers often give price discounts to employers or even consumers. These discounts have little relationship to underlying costs. "The way that they have typically done it," Frank said, is by saying "'I'm going to give you a twenty percent discount off of my charges, or I'm going to give you a thirty percent discount off my charges.' And people think they're getting this great deal when, in reality, that charge is kind of based on nothing.

"Until we educate consumers about what drives the cost of health care, we're not going to make the right headway," she concluded. "Consumers have not cared about total cost but just what they paid, but if you're not looking at the total, you're not paying attention to the most important thing driving your premiums for the next year.

"But consumers don't make that connection, and why would they?" Frank noted. "They've never had to understand that before. And I don't hear anybody talking about that but us."

The odds are rising that actionable information will be available where you live. The 2019 Altarum study included a list of fourteen highly regarded health care price and quality tools.

In addition to Guroo, CIVHC, Maryland, and FAIR Health, they include the Illinois Hospital Report Card, Compare Maine, MNHealthScores (Minnesota), NH HealthCost (New Hampshire), Oregon Hospital Guide, Hospital Report Cards (Vermont), Health-care Pricing Transparency Report (Virginia), Washington State MO-NAHRQ, and My Health Wisconsin.

HOW TRANSPARENCY CAN SET YOU FREE

Like other early leaders in consumer health care, Cynthia Fisher started Patient Rights Advocate because of her own health system experiences. A successful entrepreneur and investor, Fisher has been making the transition from commerce to causes for several years. She founded and later sold the ViaCord umbilical cord blood and tissue business, which was based on a transparent pricing model.

"We set a standard on the direct-to-consumer medical service that was price transparent," she said. "And we gave all of the information to the parents on everything about that cell product that we collected, but also everybody anywhere around the globe paid the same price for that service. And they knew what they would pay and then [we said it would be] stored over the life of that individual for $100 a year, and that price would not go up. It would be a set price."

That transparent price, not coincidentally, was "at least half to sometimes one-sixth the price of the opaque, nonprofit hospital system that competed with us at the time."

As she got into advocacy work, Fisher recalled, her past experiences were contrasted with the medical horror stories that friends and family members brought to her. "It was really financial ruin that people were coming to me with," she said, including helping a friend with breast cancer file for bankruptcy.

"My nephew, my mother and dad's doctor. Everyone had a story, and I thought, you know, 'Houston, we have a problem.' The effects of today's runaway costs of health care are multigenerational," she said. "And it's devastated families. And it's not affected one or two generations. We're into a third generation."

Fisher wants the consumer to have a seat and a voice at the table and to empower that voice with transparent information about health costs. "Without knowing prices, we as a consumer, a patient, and our employers, have limited to no negotiating leverage," Fisher said. "And then we are expected to pay with a blank check whatever we're charged. . . . Our hospitals are showing people the protocol to become a beggar."

As an entrepreneur and advocate of business competition, Fisher thinks businesses can and should lead the way toward the kind of health system that nearly all consumers say they want.

"I believe firmly that we should be able to get to a price-transparent model in health care," she said. Consumers should "be able to have complete access to our health information, be able to get care anywhere, and then be able to shop for the best quality of care at the lowest possible price."

Get What's Yours Rx

You shop for cars; you can shop for health care, too.

Understand where to find and how to use health shopping tools.

Health care shopping tips you need to know.

Databases of insurance health claims are producing powerful consumer tools on health costs and quality.

States are leading the way—see if yours is among them.

GETTING AND PAYING
FOR DRUGS

Rich Sagall was a practicing family physician in Bangor, Maine, in the late 1990s when he became sensitized to the rising affordability problems his patients were having paying for their prescription drugs. "To be honest, I didn't pay too much attention to whether people could afford the meds I was prescribing, and I think that was typical of most physicians."

Sagall was alerted by a colleague to the growing number of patient assistance drug programs. The idea of gathering this information and making it available to patients occurred to him at the same time as he was teaching himself HTML, or hypertext markup language, the first set of tools that early Internet enthusiasts used to build websites.

Sagall and the colleague began building NeedyMeds. Its original focus was providing lower-income patients access to the patient assistance programs offered by pharmaceutical companies. After building the site on evenings and weekends, Sagall got some development funding, set up NeedyMeds as a nonprofit, and began spending more and more time on what was no longer a hobby. He said goodbye to his partner—a medical social worker who had decided to move on to other activities—and later stopped practicing medicine to devote all of his time to the venture.

"I feel that with NeedyMeds I'm impacting thousands more people than I ever could in private medicine," said Sagall, who later moved to Philadelphia and then Gloucester, Massachusetts, where he still lives.

The challenges of getting access to affordable drugs are largely different when it comes to whether your drugs are incredibly expensive brand drugs or generally inexpensive generics.

Pricing and access to brand drugs are largely controlled by the makers of those drugs. They have patent protection and patients taking them have little or no ability to find other drugs that can help them. Besides cost and access problems, these are the drugs that people often need to keep living or at least lead tolerable lives.

Some generics, of course, are also lifesavers. And not all of them are cheap. The indefensible insulin availability and pricing crisis was an unwelcome wake-up call to reexamine assumptions about generics.

Before tackling these two worlds of brand and generic drugs, your first visit should be with your health insurer.

UNDERSTAND YOUR DRUG COVERAGE

If you have private health insurance and take any prescription medications, you need to understand your insurer's coverage rules. They have several moving parts, each of which is relatively easy to follow:

- Find out your plan's annual deductible. If you participate in one or more drug assistance programs (explained later in this chapter), find out whether your plan will apply the assistance payments toward your deductible. Many employer plans do not, creating what amounts to a surprise charge that can influence your prescription decisions.
- Look for your prescribed drugs on the plan's list of covered drugs, which is called a formulary.
- Your plan has different levels or tiers into which covered drugs are placed—generics, branded drugs, and specialty

medications. Each tier may have different payment terms
for co-pays (a fixed dollar amount per prescription) and
coinsurance (a percentage amount based on the drug's price).
Find out how your drugs are covered and priced.

- Health insurers have favored relationships with pharmacy
chains, although none as close as CVS and Aetna, which was
acquired in 2018 by CVS. Your drug prices are likely to be the
lowest if you fill your prescriptions at your plan's preferred
pharmacy.

- The cheapest prices may be found for mail orders of ninety-
day prescriptions. Find out if this is the case with your plan.

- Plans require people to take a lower-cost generic if available.
You will get a gold star in this awards category if you talk
about your required meds with your prescribing doctors and
make sure generic equivalents are right for you. If not, your
doctor's office should contact your insurer to get approval for
the preferred medication.

- Medicare's rules on drug coverage are explained in Chapter
Five.

TAKE ADVANTAGE OF YOUR PHARMACIST

Pharmacists used to be prevented from talking with you about drug
prices. This gag rule has been ended, so one question you can and
should ask your pharmacist is, "Is there a lower price available for
this prescription?" It might be from another pharmacy or a discount
card. Or a different quantity limit or dosage.

A 200 milligram prescription med may cost no more than the 100
milligram version that you take. Pill splitting may be a great way to
save money. Check with your doctor or pharmacist. Odds are, getting
informed advice from the pharmacist will be easier.

Pharmacists are trained to spot adverse side effects from the

combinations of certain prescribed medicines. Flowing all your prescriptions through the same pharmacy can minimize such complications. This continuity of care means a lot more to me than the
occasional four-dollar discount drug.

Anyone who takes multiple medications will visit their local pharmacy more often than they do their doctor. Pharmacies are offering
a growing array of inoculations, tests, and even consultations with
on-site nurses and other health care professionals. As retail health
care is becoming more prevalent (see Chapter Sixteen), your local
pharmacy and pharmacist may become more important health providers.

WHERE TO FIND HELP
WITH BRAND DRUGS

Over the years, Rich Sagall has stuck to his original motivations.
NeedyMeds has expanded and now provides consumer assistance
programs that include:

- Pharmaceutical patient assistance programs, including online
  application forms (more than 340).
- Manufacturer coupons offering rebates, discounts or even free
  trials (more than 1,700 drugs).
- A national directory of $4 discount programs searchable by
  state, drug, and store.
- Drug formulation and dosage listings (more than 4,000).
- Diagnosis-specific assistance programs (more than 1,300).
- Free or low-cost clinics that charge on a sliding scale
  depending on patient incomes (more than 13,000).
- Organizations that help patients with application paperwork,
  either for free or a small fee (more than 800).

- Programs that bundle all available support and education programs for specific diseases (more than 50).
- Low-income government assistance programs at the state, county, and local levels (more than 700).

PATIENT ASSISTANCE PROGRAMS

Chandra Wahrgren is president of Ardon Health specialty pharmacy in Portland, Oregon. Ardon deals with costly medicines and, while it does want to make money, has relatively modest profit goals in comparison with the huge pharmacy benefit firms that dominate the drug business.

Ardon has adopted a "high touch" approach to helping consumers get access to their medications and understanding how to use them. A typical phone conversation with a new consumer will take half an hour.

In many cases, a goodly part of that conversation might be about the various patient assistance programs available to users of expensive drugs. Consumers could save money on expensive drugs through such programs if they better understood and used them.

"One percent of the population utilizes a specialty medication," Wahrgren said, "but specialty medications are reaching fifty percent of the overall drug spend."

Ardon locates financial support for about 85 to 88 percent of its overall customers and 94 percent of those who take brand-name drugs, she said. This is higher—perhaps much higher—than other specialty pharmacies. "It's been a core value" at Ardon, Wahrgren said. More to the point, its experience shows what's possible.

Even if your provider of specialty drugs does not provide the care and feeding that Ardon does, there's no reason you and other motivated consumers can't achieve its success rate.

"Eligibility rules require that patients not have access to any government programs such as Medicaid, Tricare [for active and retired military], and Medicare, mainly Medicare Part D," the company said. "A patient is not required to provide any income-based applications for most of the programs."

To illustrate a typical program, Ardon provided details for the assistance program for Stelara, a drug treating Crohn's disease that is made by Janssen Biotech, a unit of Johnson & Johnson. The list price for the drug is $11,756 a month, Ardon said. About 75 percent of patients pay less than $5.

(See Appendix 13 for Ardon's list of assistance programs for expensive drugs.)

Besides pharmaceutical company programs, many foundations provide support. Financial help is often targeted to specific diseases and health conditions, and may include income tests to qualify. FundFinder tracks foundation programs and includes contact details. These services are free.

Medicare's interactive guide to pharmaceutical assistance programs provides the closest thing to an official directory. NeedyMeds and RxAssist are other good places to find assistance, as is the National Financial Resource Directory, introduced in Chapter Eight.

Manufacturer support programs are not available to Medicare enrollees—perhaps the largest market for specialty drugs. Under the rules for Medicare Part D drug plans, the full price of specialty drugs is charged to patients and taxpayers may pay as much as 80 percent of the tab through Part D subsidies that shield patients from bearing the full brunt of high drug prices.

Medicare bans such support payments on the grounds they constitute kickbacks by inducing patients to use these expensive drugs instead of cheaper alternatives, thus saddling Medicare with the expense.

Federal investigations have found that many pharmaceutical

companies have tried to find a way around this rule by providing funds to foundations that, in turn, provide assistance payments to Medicare beneficiaries. Several federal prosecutions have found such charities guilty of violating these Medicare anti-kickback rules. There is growing pressure to ease or eliminate Medicare's kickback rules.

PHARMACY DISCOUNT CARDS

While Rich Sagall has been hunkered down in Gloucester, Doug Hirsch has been on the other side of the country in the Los Angeles area, building GoodRx into the nation's largest program helping consumers get access to cheaper drugs. It is noteworthy that many of the forces disrupting health care are driven by technology and do not require a lot of employees to change the way things are done. NeedyMeds has only about 30 people. GoodRx has around 350.

A veteran of Yahoo and Facebook, the fifty-year-old Hirsch started GoodRx after a personal encounter with health care that left him shaking his head—much the same motivation as other health care entrepreneurs you've met in *Get What's Yours*.

He founded the Daily Strength website in 2005, providing an online gathering place for people needing help with serious health needs. After selling that business in 2008, he recalls, he had an encounter at a local pharmacy that was similar to the epiphany that Healthcare Bluebook cofounder Jeff Rice told us about in the last chapter.

"I was handed a prescription by a doctor back in 2010, and I walked into my local Walgreens here and presented the paper prescription to the pharmacist and they said it would be about $500. And I hadn't ever really talked to my physician about that. There had never been any discussion of cost. It was just like, 'Here's a drug. You should consider taking this.' And $500 was more than I wanted to pay. And I had insurance, so why is anything $500?

"So I took the prescription back because I'm also thrifty and cheap. And I walked down the street to the other chain pharmacy and presented it to them, and they said it would be something like $300. And that was about $200 less for what I perceived to be the same product. My interest was piqued. So I brought it to a third pharmacy, where they said something higher—I think it was like $600. When I then walked out of the pharmacy, the pharmacist then came out of the booth, and ran into the parking lot chasing me and, very nicely, was saying, 'Well, I know I said $600, but maybe we can work something out and I can give you a better price.' And I thought, am I buying a used car, or am I buying health care here?

"For me, at this point I was like, okay, well, I have three price points for what I again perceived to be the same product, and no information that can guide me to making the most efficient purchase. So I did what any good entrepreneur should do, which is I went to Google and I typed in the drug name plus price. And nothing came up. There was literally nothing. There were about twelve states at the time that had some kind of legislation that said drug prices needed to be publicly posted. In six of those states the websites were broken. The other six were basically useless."

Hirsch got together with some friends from his high-tech days and concluded, "There seems to be no way whatsoever for people to figure out what health care products and services should cost. There's gotta be a way for us to decipher this.

"Everybody told us we were wasting our time. They all said, 'The drug companies set the price. You're wasting your time when you're worrying about generic drugs, because nobody cares about generics. It's all about brand drugs. And there's only one seller of a brand drug and they determine the price.'"

Undeterred, they went ahead and, as you likely know by this point in this story, Hirsch has been proven right. There is intense interest in generics and the discount card provided by GoodRx is now used in filling 3 percent of the nation's drug prescriptions.

More than half the nation's doctors tell their patients about GoodRx because they want their patients to take their meds, Hirsch said. The GoodRx app is used by roughly 15 million people a month. Enter the name of the drug and you will see prices in your area using the GoodRx card, group discount programs from retailers, and mail-order pharmacy offers.

If you have a drug plan, you should find out whether it makes sense to get the drug through your insurance plan or if the savings using the discount card are large enough to use it instead. Hirsch said 75 percent of GoodRx customers have health insurance.

Take your prescription to the pharmacy where you'd like to get the drug, show the price on your phone to the pharmacist, and get your meds. If you want the group price, you will need to join that group and should be aware of any related fees. If you decide on a mail-order pharmacy, you will have to provide billing and prescription details.

Despite the success of GoodRx and other discount drug programs, Hirsch said more growth will come as consumers become more comfortable with different ways of shopping for health care. "People often ask us 'Who's your biggest competitor?' " he said. "And our competitor is just people who don't know any better, who assume that the old way of doing things, which was to show their insurance card at the pharmacy, is all they need."

GoodRx and NeedyMeds have growing company in the discount drug advice and pricing business, including Blink Health, Family-Wize, and WeRx. You should look at multiple sites for the best prices for your medications at your preferred pharmacy.

Your shopping efforts should include multiple sources for comparative purposes. HealthWarehouse, an online pharmacy, recorded the lowest overall price in a *Consumer Reports* drug shopping test of pharmacies. Beyond price, finding a convenient location can be the deciding factor. Many discount programs are run by grocery chains and might be the preferred choice for regular shoppers even if they don't have the lowest prices.

Besides comparing prices for the drugs you take, here are Rich Sagall's discount-card tips:

- Never pay for a card—There are many good cards that are free. There is no reason to pay for a card since it's unlikely it would offer a discount any better than a free one.
- Never register for a card—The only reason to give your name and address is if the card is being mailed to you. If a card asks for your information, odds are it is selling this data to one or more third parties.
- Read the privacy policy—Make sure the marketer has a privacy policy that you agree with. It should explain what's done with your personal information. The gold standard is a program that says it will never share your personal information.
- Help line—All reputable marketers have a toll-free help line. Give the line a call and see how responsive they are. Do they have real people answering your questions or just a recording? If you leave a message, do they call you back?
- Shop around—Try different cards to see which offers you the best discount. Ask your pharmacist which has the best prices.

GOING OUTSIDE THE UNITED STATES

If you are planning to cross the border for your medications, or get them through an online pharmacy abroad, there are two things to know. First: it may be illegal. Second: it is unlikely you will be prosecuted.

People familiar with the practice say you generally can pass through customs without much hassle if you have no more than three months' worth of a medication, you declare it to customs agents, and you show them a doctor's prescription or a personal note attesting it is for personal use, along with contact information for your physician.

PharmacyChecker.com allows you to search for lower drug costs outside the United States. Here's a 10-drug sampler for 90-day prescriptions:

Drug	U.S.	Foreign
Premarin 0.625 mg	$ 624	$15
Januvia 100 mg	$1,594	$73
Crestor 10 mg	$ 969	$24
Advair Diskus 250/50 mcg	$1,437	$73
Spiriva Handihaler 18 mcg	$1,430	$72
Nexium 40 mg	$ 863	$19
Synthroid 50 mcg	$ 151	$14
Xarelto 20 mg	$1,561	$149
Zetia 10 mg	$1,261	$150
Ventolin HFA 90 mcg	$ 218	$69

A bigger risk if you're shopping abroad for medications is that you might not get what you paid for—and it might not be safe. "There's a lot of junk in the pharmaceutical world," Dr. Ken Croen, a primary care physician at the Scarsdale Medical Group in New York, told *Kaiser Health News* in a story about how to shop for drugs outside the United States. A company called Valisure will test your meds for safety if you decide to use it as your mail order pharmacy.

The Canadian International Pharmacy Association runs a site (cipa.com) that allows you to compare drug prices among dozens of pharmacies whose legitimacy it has certified. Its customers "tend to be people who live in the U.S., are on fixed income or low income and can't afford the medications where they live," Tim Smith, the association's general manager, told Kaiser.

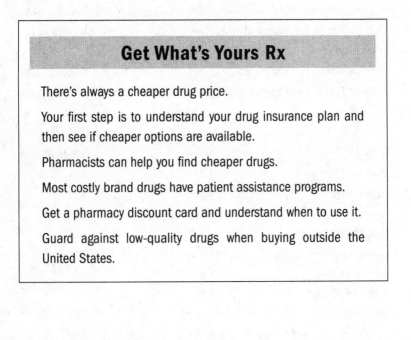

Get What's Yours Rx

There's always a cheaper drug price.

Your first step is to understand your drug insurance plan and then see if cheaper options are available.

Pharmacists can help you find cheaper drugs.

Most costly brand drugs have patient assistance programs.

Get a pharmacy discount card and understand when to use it.

Guard against low-quality drugs when buying outside the United States.

HEROES VII

The Warrior Daughter

Areta Buness

If there is a competitiveness gene, Areta Buness inherited it. Her mom, Cynthia (see Heroes VI), fought relentlessly for her daughter and continues to fight for other patients with primary sclerosing cholangitis (PSC), the rare liver disease that Areta must contend with for the rest of her life.

The story of the Buness family, of Phoenix, dots all the *i*'s and crosses all the *t*'s required to do battle with the American health care system. It begins with Areta, who was born in January 1997, and might not even have a story without a mountain of grit, a boundless determination to compete, and a consistent refusal to accept what other people said she could not do.

At three, she was taking taekwondo; at seven, she set an Arizona age-group record for the 5K; at nine, she was testing for her second-degree black belt. Later, she ran cross country and discovered lacrosse, which quickly became her passion. "I started playing it in seventh grade and I fell in love with it," Areta told me shortly after her twenty-third birthday. "I like sports. I've always liked running. It's a really fast-paced sport, super fun, and team oriented."

The seventh grade also marked a darker milestone. Areta went to a dermatologist to deal with teenage acne and was told to begin taking doxycycline, an antibiotic frequently prescribed for that condition. Shortly thereafter, she began experiencing diarrhea and began seeing a gastroenterologist. No one connected the dots between these symptoms and what, in hindsight, seems to have been a life-altering, adverse reaction to the doxycycline, which she continued to take.

"They didn't really give me any warnings or potential side effects of it," she says. "I started getting intestinal problems and diarrhea. . . . I continued taking it for months after I started getting symptoms because no one ever told me to stop."

The next year, the overachieving teen was in eighth grade playing lacrosse on a local high school team when she began experiencing pain and swelling in her ankle that became so severe she was forced to use crutches to get around. "We had no idea what it was, and eventually I went to the emergency room because it was really bad pain," she recalls.

ER doctors had no idea of what was causing Areta's distress. "They thought maybe it was a spider bite," she says. Initial tests triggered more tests and her visit turned into a hospital stay of about ten days.

"They connected the fact that I was having gastrointestinal symptoms with the fact that I had this random inflammation and swelling in my foot as a manifestation of the inflammation in my colon. It's called erythema nodosum," she said. After a colonoscopy, she was diagnosed with severe ulcerative colitis and began taking a "bunch of meds."

They didn't help. Her symptoms worsened and she began experiencing side effects, including throwing up in the middle of the night and passing bloody stools. "There was not like a drug that didn't have a bad side effect, and nothing actually improved my original symptoms," she said. Her gastrointestinal specialist concluded her colon would never get better and advised her to have it removed.

The Buness family decided to change doctors—not the first

time they looked for different caregivers in the face of opinions that involved life-altering and perhaps life-shortening advice.

Areta's symptoms did not go away. As a high school freshman, her weight plummeted to 85 pounds. She not only continued playing lacrosse but began running cross-country.

Now getting monthly blood tests from her new doctor, the test results one month for the first time showed elevated liver enzymes. This led to a liver biopsy and the PSC diagnosis. While receiving what appeared to be an accurate diagnosis was comforting on one level, she was told there was no treatment for PSC and that her liver would fail before she turned thirty.

Her mom, Cynthia, learned of a promising experimental treatment that "seemed too good to be true," Areta recalls. Her hepatologist "refused to even try it."

"I told him that I want to play lacrosse in college. I need to be able to take something that can help me. I can't just do nothing about this. And he told me that I might as well give up about trying to play competitive sports because I'm never going to be able to do that with my disease prognosis."

With that, her mom contacted the Stanford doctor who advocated an experimental treatment with the drug vancomycin, and the story about Areta's remarkable recovery then began to unfold.

This turnabout rests on a daunting health care regimen that Areta has followed since her sophomore year in high school. For a time, she began seeing a new doctor in San Diego who was willing to approve the experimental treatment. She flew there for a colonoscopy and multiple MRIs. These have since continued at other locations. She still has monthly blood tests. She takes 390 pills a month (thirteen a day).

Still passionate about lacrosse, Areta set her sights on the elite Stanford program. Her illness had affected her high school lacrosse performance enough to eliminate the chance for a scholarship. So, she buckled down on her studies and was accepted by the school based on academic merit.

"I wasn't recruited, because recruiting happens much earlier than I could actually gain muscle and absorb nutrients," she explained. "So, the coaches weren't really looking at me at all."

This would change.

As a walk-on to lacrosse, Areta made the varsity team. She felt she didn't measure up to the other talented players. She kept working, including getting and staying in the best shape possible. Her conditioning, measured by a wireless monitor that all players wore, gave her the opportunity she sought.

"I always crushed the team conditioning," she wrote in an autobiographical story published on the Stanford website. "I beat myself up if I didn't finish first in sprints. I got to the field 30 minutes early, at 6 a.m., to make sure I was warmed up. No matter how many times I got knocked down in practice or felt like I wasn't good enough, I reminded myself how hard I fought to be here. My spirit is strong even when my body struggles."

Early in her sophomore year, the lacrosse coaches posted team conditioning numbers. "Mine were the highest in everything, way beyond everyone," she wrote. "I had no idea. I was just playing hard in practice, because that's what I always do. One of the coaches said to the team, 'Areta's working her hardest every single day in practice and it's showing. We will always find a place for her because of this.'"

They moved her from midfield to attack. And started her in the next game.

Through it all, Areta kept her health condition private. "I

really didn't want anyone to know about my disease or what was going on with that, because I thought that people would think that was weird or feel bad for me in some way," she recalled. "And I didn't want that, because I didn't want people to feel that I couldn't do it, or couldn't take on hard classes or lacrosse or something like that. So I tried hard to really pretend that nothing was wrong, to the point that I [thought I] have to be better, I have to get the best grade in this class."

Areta now feels that keeping things to herself was not as helpful as having a support network. She participates in social media groups as a resource for others with PSC. Her disease contributed to her decision to get an advanced degree at Stanford in microbiology after getting her undergraduate degree there in 2019. She plans to use these skills to tackle the challenges of climate change rather than treatments for PSC and related illnesses.

"When you're told you can't do something, it makes doing it that much more special," she reflected in her Stanford story. "I wouldn't be where I am today without the inner strength that I began to learn when I was three years old in taekwondo. I'm grateful for the things that I can control, and I know that overcoming an obstacle just means that I'll meet another one."

15

HOW TO FIGHT BACK

Susan Null provides people in the New York City area with fee-based help to get a better deal on health care. She and her husband have thirty years of experience in getting blood from a stone—convincing health insurers, hospitals, doctors, and other providers to overrule denied claims, reduce their fees, or accept reduced payments where contested bills turn out to be correct (yes, health insurers are correct a lot of the time).

Null doesn't waffle in laying a lot of blame for poor health insurance outcomes at consumers' feet. "People make a lot of assumptions that when they have health insurance, they're covered," she said. "They have no idea what that really means. . . . I think that that ends up being the biggest problem.

"They proceed to seek services for their medical care without having a full understanding of what the impact could be for them financially; that's where it starts," she said. "They then go to a hospital or they go to see a doctor or they could go for a test someplace and, again, they're making the assumption that they have insurance, so they're covered. And then, all of a sudden, they get a bill for hundreds or thousands of dollars that they were totally not expecting. And they don't know how to unravel it."

Null's advice harks back to the mantra on preventive health care in Chapter Seven. Just as the cheapest health care is the care you don't need, the best claim rejection from an insurer is the one that doesn't happen because you've done your homework.

"People need to be assertive and aggressive," says Jill Hanken, a Virginia poverty rights attorney. "And they need help."

"There are state bureaus of insurance that need to be empowered" to help consumers at the local level. "We just need more people pushing back" against the insurance companies. "They're just getting away with murder. You've got to push back on these insurance plans, You've got to exercise your rights to appeal."

A 2019 study of health claims on state Affordable Care Act exchanges found a fifth of in-network claims were denied overall. Few of these denials are appealed. "Healthcare.gov consumers appealed less than one-half of one percent of denied claims, and issuers overturned 14 percent of appealed denials," the study said.

When you are going to have an interaction with the health care system, Null advised, whether it be with your primary care doctor or a specialist, call ahead and ask them what billing codes they expect to use in charging you for the visit. This is not done often, she said. It would save a bushel of regrets later on if it were.

Medical billing codes are the financial language of health care. Care providers must use them to get paid, so asking them for the codes related to your care is hardly unreasonable. Armed with these codes, call your insurance company to ask if your policy will cover treatment for the coded services. If so, what will it pay and what might you have to pay?

One other not-so-small thing. Do you remember phone calls to businesses where the automated voice says something like, "This call may be recorded for quality control purposes"? Well, Null advises, you should play this game, too.

When you call your health insurer and finally get through to a human being, ask them to make sure the call is being recorded. This will alert them that you mean business. Having a record of the conversation can help if there is a later disagreement about what you were told.

Get and write down the name of the insurance company representative on the call. Ask the representative for a reference number that can be used in later discussions (if they occur). And make a note about the date, time, and duration of the call.

"Ask them, 'Are you recording this conversation?' " Null said. "You can ask them to make sure that they do. Now, they will fight you all the way [not to give you] that phone conversation. But you can win."

Mike Baker, the claims expert with UnitedHealthcare, said consumers need to be aware that those much-maligned claims people whom we love to hate are often not even involved in early-stage denials.

"Particularly in health care," he said, "the majority of claims are adjudicated electronically using the information that's available to the robot at the time, and so I think rule number one is take nothing for granted, and don't accept no for an answer."

"Pick up the phone and call, or follow the steps, and appeal," Baker advised. Appeals often fall into gray areas and require human intervention by insurers. And when humans are involved, he noted, "there are two scenarios there that I think are relevant. . . . Humans are fallible . . . and humans can be influenced by the right information and circumstances."

Mistakes in coding—intentional and accidental—are so common that consumers should never accept a complex medical bill as accurate when they first receive it.

Journalist Elisabeth Rosenthal learned medicine as a Harvard-trained emergency room doctor. She covered what ails the U.S. health care system in her 2017 book, *An American Sickness*. She is now editor of *Kaiser Health News* and was earlier a reporter at the *New York Times*, where she wrote a groundbreaking series in 2013 and 2014 on medical costs, "Paying Till It Hurts."

Rosenthal briefly reviewed the evolution of medical coding complexities in a 2017 piece for the *Times*. "Seemingly subtle choices about which code to use can have large financial consequences," she wrote.

Often, coders for hospitals and doctors try to use coding that maximizes their revenue, while health insurance coders are looking to deny claims and save money. So-called upcoding—using codes that make patient health conditions appear worse, justifying higher payments—has become part of the medical billing lexicon.

Null's clients know little about medical coding and have a lot to learn about health insurance, she said. She has found the same true for many of the people who work for health insurers. "Often, the people who man the phones at the insurance companies at the first level, unfortunately, they don't really understand their product.

"Don't take the first answer," Null advised. "You have to work your way up, maybe one level, maybe two levels, maybe three or four levels of supervisors, until you get the appropriate answer, and even then, you may not like it, and then you're going to have to go through the appeals process."

Many of the people who hire Null don't do their homework and thus do not understand how to appeal or, if their appeal is rejected, why the insurer reached that conclusion.

"Then it [the appeal] gets denied because that wasn't the reason that the claim was actually denied [in the first place]," she said. "If you don't get the right answers at the start, you can't build your case." This brings Null back to her first message: "The first thing that you should do is make sure that you understand some of the basics about your plan."

Null belongs to a trade group of medical claims adjusters called the Alliance of Claims Assistance Professionals (ACAP). She says prices vary depending on the complexity of the client's situation. Hourly rates ($100 an hour is not unusual) often are used, as are rates expressed as a percentage of how much money the adjuster saves the client. Make sure you understand the financial arrangement ahead of time.

Null says her approach is to take on a client only when she is confident she can save them more money than her fee. Out of 20 callers, she said, she will give free advice to 18 of them and take on one or two as clients.

Timeliness is important, she advised. Don't wait months or years to tackle adverse health rulings. And don't wait to act until your medical bills have been referred to collection, at which point you'll have to deal with multiple adversaries and your credit rating may already have been damaged.

"So what we try to teach people to do is, don't do what most people do," Null said. "Don't immediately pay the bill because you think it's right, because there's a good chance there could be a mistake in it. And don't ignore it, either."

Null says sometimes her clients wind up needing to pay a hefty bill. "Sometime the facts will point to [the conclusion] that this is your bill," she said. "I think the biggest thing that people don't realize is that in most instances you can negotiate."

In bargaining, she may use publicly available lists of the lower rates that Medicare and Medicaid will pay for the same procedures. Doctors and hospitals accept these rates for Medicare and Medicaid patients, she noted, and some are persuaded by this argument to lower their fees for people with commercial insurance who normally are charged rates three to five times more.

After negotiations end, Null says she often can guide clients to payment assistance programs. Her goal is to bring the problem to an end and not have financial and emotional problems hanging over clients' heads.

NEGOTIATING FOR LOWER PRICES

By now, you're well aware that health care prices often have no relationship to either cost or quality. Hospitals and other providers may charge rates that don't reflect the real world. These so-called chargemaster lists are under attack, as we learned in Chapter Thirteen.

Our hospitals love us, to be sure; they just don't want us to know how they arrive at their inscrutable bills. They do have some logic on their side. If private health insurers, physician groups, and other powerful health care providers have access to hospital pricing details, that will make it harder for hospitals to negotiate favorable business deals with them.

Even without full transparency, you are not helpless in fighting outrageous bills. The cost tools covered earlier in *Get What's Yours* are available to use as leverage. They are largely the same tools that the big players use to negotiate better deals.

For starters, Medicare has enormous sway over payments to hospitals, doctors, medical equipment companies, and virtually anyone else whose cash registers ring with Medicare-related charges. It pays much less than employer health plans, and much, much less than the often ridiculous retail "sticker" prices that appear on provider medical bills.

Doctors and hospitals accept Medicare and Medicaid rates as payment in full for their work. Surveys show that providers can make money with those payments, although not nearly as much as they'd like. They make for an effective price floor in negotiating reduced medical charges.

One little-known tool reveals Medicare's prices for outpatient surgeries. These procedures are growing in importance, and outpatient care usually can be evaluated ahead of time. This tool can help reduce your medical bills; Medicare should expand it to more procedures.

To give you an idea of the possible negotiating power of Medicare prices, let's take another look at those ten commonly performed outpatient procedures at ambulatory surgery centers (ASCs):

TOP 10 ASC OUTPATIENT PROCEDURES

Rank	Code	Description	Number of Procedures
1.	66984	Cataract surg w/intraocular implant, 1 stage	1,252,835
2.	J0585	Injection, onabotulinumtoxinA (Botox)	759,997
3.	43239	Esophagogastroduodenoscopy (Egd) biopsy single/multiple	539,772
4.	45380	Colonoscopy and biopsy	464,136
5.	45385	Colonoscopy w/lesion removal	397,339
6.	64483	Epidural steroid injection in lumbar spine w/imaging guidance	319,592
7.	66821	After cataract laser surgery	283,574
8.	64493	Injection into lumbar/sacral spine w/image guidance	220,472
9.	62323	Lumbar interlaminar epidural steroid injection	195,648
10.	G0105	Colorectal screening; high risk individual	137,697

The Medicare pricing tool provides its payment rates for ASCs and hospital outpatient departments (HOPDs). I used it to look up payments for these ten procedures. I then went to Healthcare Bluebook and looked for the range of costs in my hometown that commercial health insurers had paid for these procedures. I omitted the Botox injection because Medicare does not cover it. The two colonoscopy codes were priced the same so only one entry is shown below. I've used shorthand descriptions in showing the results, which were startling.

OUTPATIENT CARE PRICE COMPARISONS

		MEDICARE PRICES		HEALTHCARE BLUEBOOK
Code	Procedure	ASC	HOPD	Cost Ranges
66984	Cataract	$977	$1,917	$1,307 to $16,638
43239	Esophago	$392	$761	$976 to $9,748
45380	Colonoscopy	$504	$979	$1,114 to $10,764

64483	Epidural	$394	$764	$522 to $1,630
66821	Laser	$255	$496	$559 to $7,568
64493	Lumbar I	$394	$764	$522 to $1,630
62323	Lumbar II	$308	$598	$522 to $1,630
G0105	Colorectal	$383	$744	$1,001 to $10,016

Knowing about true costs is a powerful tool in a consumer-driven health care market. Here are three related lessons:

1. **Lesson I:** If you have a choice where to go for care and there is no observable quality difference, skip the hospital in favor of a freestanding ASC.
2. **Lesson II:** Never, ever pay retail for health care!
3. **Lesson III:** Look up prices in your own area and use the differences to negotiate a lower payment to your care provider. If you have health insurance and feel your insurer was a sucker for approving such a large payment for your procedure, call them and say so. The more that consumers do their homework and complain about high prices, the sooner they will start getting better deals.

CLINICAL TRIALS

Clinical trials have long been a place where patients and families turn for access to experimental treatments and medications. Getting access to care that can save or extend a life is a long shot that people who have little or nothing to lose often are willing to try. Patients with a terminal diagnosis may seek to participate in clinical trials or donate their bodies to research to help find future cures and treatments.

The National Institutes of Health (NIH) operates ClinicalTrials. gov, the government's official record of clinical trials and a starting place for anyone seeking a trial that might help them, including related educational materials. The U.S. Food & Drug Administration created Project Patient Voice to report how patients have reacted to experimental cancer drugs.

Despite laws and regulations mandating that they furnish clinical trial information to the government, compliance by trial sponsors is spotty and some of the worst offenders are the biggest names in pharmaceutical and academic research.

"Of 184 sponsor organizations with at least five [clinical] trials due as of 25 September 2019, 30 companies, universities, or medical centers never met a single deadline," *Science* magazine reported in early 2020. "As of that date, those habitual violators had failed to report any results for 67 percent of their trials and averaged 268 days late for those and all trials that missed their deadlines. They included such eminent institutions as the Harvard University–affiliated Boston Children's Hospital, the University of Minnesota, and Baylor College of Medicine—all among the top 50 recipients of NIH grants in 2019."

Patient advocacy groups are solid sources for leads on clinical trials, and these recommendations may include trials that are not tracked by the NIH site. The Patient Advocate Foundation's National Financial Resource Directory includes clinical trials information.

In addition to checking ClinicalTrials.gov, look at AllTrials.net, a British effort to track clinical trials globally. Its efforts include a website dedicated to tracking U.S. clinical trials.

Nearly all clinical trials cost nothing to join. However, the boom in entrepreneurial medical research in recent years has brought with it the rise of fee-based clinical trials. Such "pay to play" research raises ethical red flags. The decision to participate is up to you. As always, do thorough homework before making a binding commitment. The NIH is working on advisory guidelines to help patients evaluate such programs.

Beyond mainstream drug and academic circles, Apple, Facebook, and other digital platforms are connecting consumers to virtual clinical trials that, over time, seem likely to help improve access to clinical programs. Wearable health monitors are booming and so are their real-time applications. Social media groups have become gathering places for patients, and can funnel them into clinical trials and related efforts to fight even orphan diseases that afflict small numbers of patients.

WHERE PAYMENTS ARE AS TOXIC AS DISEASE

Cancer is hardly the only disease where the financial impact of treatment rivals its physical damages. It is the biggest bad bear in the woods and the most studied. And it shares an unpleasant reality with victims of chronic illnesses—the financial fun never stops. Patients who may cope with Year One or even Year Two expenses often are unprepared for the bills that keep coming their way later.

"The problem of paying for cancer care is so vast that it has a name, financial toxicity, representing the 'other' toxic side effect of cancer treatment," two cancer experts wrote in 2016. "Patients who get into financial difficulty suffer high rates of emotional distress and lower quality of life."

"In a study we conducted with several colleagues," Dr. Scott Ramsey and Veena Shankaran said, "cancer patients who filed for bankruptcy had a 79 percent higher mortality rate compared to those who had the same cancer and did not file for bankruptcy."

The *American Journal of Medicine* published a sweeping study in 2018 of 9.5 million people who were newly diagnosed with cancer from 2000 to 2012. After only two years, more than 40 percent of them had "depleted their entire life's assets." Average losses exceeded $92,000. Most never dug out of this hole, and more than 38 percent were still insolvent after four years.

More than 90 percent of those 9.5 million people had either Medicare or private insurance. Those best insulated from financial toxicity tended to have private insurance, been married, and suffered the least financial damage from 2008's Great Recession.

Ironically, the fear of being unable to pay for health care causes millions of U.S. consumers to simply reduce or eliminate needed care, including prescription drugs. This, of course, may lead to more severe health problems and care far more costly than the care consumers avoided in the first place.

A second takeaway about dealing with medical debts is offered by medical claims expert Susan Null, and seconded by Bruce McClary, a spokesman for the National Foundation for Credit Counseling (NFCC): tackle medical debts right away, not after they go to a collection agency and can trigger ugly bill-collection efforts, damage to your credit rating, and garnishment of your wages—including reduction in Social Security and other government benefit payments.

Credit-rating agencies don't weigh medical debt as heavily as late or forgone payments on homes, vehicles, and credit cards, McClary noted. Maybe that's because so many people have medical debts—more than 43 million as of a 2014 Consumer Financial Protection Bureau report.

The odds of collecting older medical debt are so low that collection agencies are willing to sell it for pennies on the dollar. Back in 2016, John Oliver, the brilliant host of HBO's *Last Week Tonight*, scooped up millions of medical debt for pennies on the dollar, and then told those who owed the money that he was erasing their debts.

The agency he used to do so—RIP Medical Debt—has since expanded into a favorite place for donors to retire chunks of debt. You cannot petition this site directly to forgive your debt. You can contact the more than 150 medical debt-relief campaigns listed on the site and seek relief there. The site maintains a list of more than thirty pro-consumer organizations that might help.

CROWDFUNDING

Getting strangers to help pay your medical bills is hardly a solid financial plan but sometimes it is the only option. GoFundMe is the eight-hundred-pound leader here. It has attracted others, including wannabees and fraudsters who will use your medical debt woes to make a quick buck. I have not seen evidence-based assessments of these organizations and would limit myself to GoFundMe.

A 2019 *New Yorker* article found that drawing public attention is hard in today's always-on, pay-attention-to-me culture. Compelling stories are a must and are hard to do, spawning a cottage industry of crowdfunding marketing and PR shops.

Donors may be more comfortable with traditional funding platforms. Patient advocacy sites and charities already have credibility and you should certainly work with them to identify sources of possible help paying your medical bills. You may have already been in touch for advice about getting care for your disease or condition, and thus may already have a contact to ask about help repaying treatment expenses. "Contributions through those sites, unlike through most GoFundMe transactions, are also tax deductible," the article noted.

A FEW WORDS ABOUT BANKRUPTCY

If nonrecurring medical bills are crushing you, consider filing for bankruptcy. Most people file under Chapter 7, which erases most debts and can give you breathing room to rebuild your life. Your credit score will be awful for a long time, but then you probably shouldn't be trying to borrow money at such a time.

Chapter 13 is another option. It involves a negotiated, multiyear repayment schedule with creditors. Adhering to Chapter 13 requirements is hard, and many people can't stick with it. Chapter 13 also has higher legal fees than Chapter 7 because it involves ongoing work.

If you think bankruptcy is your best way out, timing is important. You should get an attorney. You will have to pay them up front. Fees depend on local living costs and can be $1,000 and up for Chapter 7 and double that for Chapter 13.

Don't wait until your funds are exhausted or you likely won't find an attorney to handle your filing. On the other hand, if you know you will be incurring more medical debts that you can't pay, try to hold off filing until you're no longer getting hit with new bills.

WHEN ALL ELSE FAILS, THERE'S SHAMING

When appealing in a respectful way to common sense does not carry the day, shaming can be effective.

The recipe for shaming a medical provider requires that you have a compelling story—bad care, egregious pricing, and insensitive responses from the insurer or medical provider making your life miserable.

The next step is to find a sympathetic news outlet. Here, a local outlet often is more effective than trying to get your story on, say, *60 Minutes*.

Sadly, the volume of medical outrage and overbilling stories is so large that they've become a regular staple of leading online news sites. Check out ProPublica, the coverage of emergency room excesses by Vox, and the NPR/*Kaiser Health News* "Bill of the Month" series, among others.

Many hospital lawsuit stories have been so indefensible and embarrassing that hospitals often respond by dropping litigation and promising not to sue patients in the future. Check out Kaiser's "Investigations" tab to see what's happening.

I wrote about Anna Landre in one of my *PBS NewsHour* posts. Then a twenty-year-old student at Georgetown University, she has been profoundly disabled her whole life with spinal muscular atrophy. She requires near-constant care from a health aide and came to me with her story when the insurer in her home state of New Jersey decided that she didn't need 16 hours of daily care and should be able to make do with only 10. Here's an excerpt from that article:

> Landre has been coping with the genetic disorder since birth and relies on extensive on-site help. She has a health aide with her 16 hours a day—10 hours each evening and six hours during the day. She needs help with all daily activities and often requires assistance at night to improve her breathing and move her to a more suitable position in bed. She has been able to live on campus and attend classes, aided by a motorized wheelchair.
>
> Even with on-site help for much of the day, trying to lead a semblance of a normal life is challenging. Her course work had to be rearranged because she can only attend classes when an aide is present. "It would be nice to be able to have someone with me all the time," she said in a phone interview. "God forbid that I could go to the bathroom whenever I want!"

The decline in coverage, she told me, would prevent her from continuing to attend college and was based on outmoded rules and attitudes that regarded people with disabilities as being unable to work outside the home.

Landre immediately went on the offensive to journalists and New Jersey state legislators with influence over state Medicaid rules. Within a week, her story had been told numerous times by national and local media. She pulled in the legislators for a public meeting that included the striking video of her small frame in a wheelchair, sitting at the head of the table surrounded by attentive legislators.

A week later, her hours were renewed with promises they would remain in place during the rest of her college years.

Sarah Kliff, then a reporter for Vox (and now with the *New York Times*), did extraordinary work highlighting medical abuses—outrageous hospital and ER bills, surprise billing horror stories and the like. "I think one of the things we've learned," she said at a 2019 health care meeting, "is one of the best ways to fight a surprise medical bill is to get a reporter to write about your medical bill and then all of a sudden we see them vanish."

Get What's Yours Rx

Never take no for an answer.

Know your rights and fight for them.

Create a paper trail.

Understand how to negotiate for lower prices and debt relief.

Act promptly—waiting to confront problems makes them worse.

Explore experimental treatments and clinical trials.

Learn how to help pay for care via crowdfunding.

Learn how to shame health providers into canceling indefensible bills.

WHEN CONSUMERS
MAKE THE CALL

Rich Berner is part of the seemingly endless flow of entrepreneurs planting their business flags on the terra firma of U.S. health care. They are drawn by money, of course, and there is for sure a lot of that in a country that spends more than $3.6 trillion on health. They also are drawn by an explosion of tech-driven business opportunities.

Berner is part of health care's version of the opening of the American West. Prospectors here are using computer software and artificial intelligence tools to develop on-demand, more affordable care that is often delivered in nontraditional settings. Health care is seen as a consumer brand, not something hidden behind the curtains of a hospital operating room.

This chapter will take you on a selective tour of this landscape. View the stories here as a sampler of models of care. Their shared attributes include being easier and cheaper to use, giving consumers more control, and moving toward on-demand care.

They tend to be built atop powerful informational platforms— reams of clinical data, insurance claims intelligence, and AI—that can empower someone with a smartphone to locate the care they need from on-demand providers. People with health insurance may receive care recommendations that are automatically approved by and consistent with their insurance plans. People without insurance, or who do not want to use it, will still see an expansion of affordable care options.

The emerging world of consumer health care is hardly without risks. It will require people to be responsible for making informed care decisions. Motivated and informed consumers can be winners here. Becoming Jedi Masters of the Internet will be an increasingly valuable skill.

"Although the attractiveness of these products to consumers is clear, direct-to-consumer products bypass the typical filters and safeguards of health-care systems," researchers concluded in a spring 2020 article in the *Lancet*. "The risk is that low value, or even harmful, products will inundate the commercial health-care market."

Traditional medical research leads, albeit slowly, to evidence-based improvements in health care. That model is at risk here. "The ability of the clinician to have a valuable role in guiding the patient," the article said, "is hampered by the continuous and rapid entry of direct-to-consumer digital health products into the market, the pace of which outstrips that of traditional medical drugs and devices."

What medical expert and author Eric Topol calls a "new era of medicine" features digital information with the smartphone as its hub. "We have seen this model already adopted in retail, travel, dining, entertainment, banking, and virtually every other industry," he says. Further, smartphone-enabled health care often is "amazingly frugal"—a phrase seldom association with U.S. medicine.

MILLENNIALS SAY, "OKAY, BOOMER"

Younger consumers prefer online tools and smartphone apps. Millennials, in particular, are drivers of many of the new consumer trends in health care. Born from 1981 to 1996, they comprise the nation's largest generation, with 78 million persons. They are reaching the age where they need more medical care.

Life has been hard on this generation. A late 2019 report, prepared by Moody's Analytics for BlueCross BlueShield, said, "Millennials are seeing their health decline faster than the previous generation as they age."

"One key to the millennial health shock," it posed, "may be behavioral health . . . rapid upticks in conditions like depression, substance abuse, and hyperactivity. Between 2014 and 2017 alone, prevalence of major depression and hyperactivity among millennials was up roughly 30 percent."

Millennials are not fans of traditional health care and widely reject the health care system of their parents, says Joe Harpaz, president of Modernizing Medicine, a health IT company. Many do not have primary care doctors, and are comfortable with walk-in clinics, virtual care, and smartphone health tools.

Millennials expect to access care when they want it, with transparent up-front pricing, he says. Their attitudes are forcing health insurers and care providers to develop on-demand care models that treat medicine as a consumer good.

KaufmanHall & Associates, a Chicago consulting firm, surveyed millennial attitudes toward health care. Its findings help explain why Amazon, Apple, Google, and other big tech companies are major health care prospectors:

As "digital natives," millennials and other young adults have grown up with the dominant tech companies Amazon, Apple, and Google. They are highly familiar with these companies, and are more inclined than older generations to trust big tech to steer their healthcare journey. Three quarters of adults ages 18–44 said they would use a mobile app developed by Amazon, Apple, or Google to help find and select healthcare services, compared to less than half of those ages 45 and older.

The KaufmanHall survey said millennials' top health priorities were "finding cost estimates for their healthcare needs; conducting a video visit with a physician or nurse; finding which providers accept their insurance (and) having the ability to call outside of normal business hours to schedule an appointment."

THE VIRTUAL DOCTOR
WILL SEE YOU NOW

The company Rich Berner headed when we spoke is called MDLIVE, a Florida-based provider of virtual health care that is on its way to becoming the digital doctor to nearly 50 million people in the United States. When I interviewed him in early 2020 (he later left the company), about 43 million employee and insurance plan members had access to the company's national network of 1,300 doctors and other board-certified clinicians in all fifty states. Thirty health systems comprising about 300 hospitals also were clients.

Berner spent twenty-five years working for diverse health firms and came to MDLIVE, he says, because "I saw telehealth as the first real opportunity I came across to disrupt health care."

Lots of people agree with him. A mid-2019 list of telehealth providers contained more than 275 companies; there doubtless are more today, especially following the surge in telehealth use generated by millions of Americans who remotely accessed health care when they were effectively quarantined because of the coronavirus pandemic. Other large telehealth providers include Amwell, Doctor on Demand, HeyDoctor, and Teladoc.

"Consumers do online shopping. Online banking. Online travel. They watch movies online. They listen to music online. . . . So why would anybody not expect to get their health care online?" Berner asked. "You finally can do in health care what you've been doing in every other industry."

His advice to consumers is to use telehealth as an early warning system that can alert them to the need for additional care. "Unless it's an [emergency] situation," he says, "go online first because one of the things our artificial intelligence and doctors do is help you figure out whether or not your condition is appropriate for online care, and if it's not, get you routed to the best location for your condition, and your insurance, and your profile."

MDLIVE's services are offered primarily through employer and patient benefit plans. It does accept cash payments from individuals. Virtual care prices were, as of spring 2020, no more than $75 for primary care appointments, $99 for behavioral counseling, $69 for dermatology, and $259 for an initial psychiatry visit with $99 for additional sessions. People with health insurance generally will pay less.

CONCIERGE MEDICINE COMES TO THE URBAN MASSES

If virtual health care is seen in part as a salvation for medicine-starved rural areas, the density of large urban areas has attracted see-your-doctor-when-you-want start-ups that market themselves as boutique concierge health care for the masses.

With lots of people and lots of health care providers already, these markets provide the financial metrics appealing to venture capital firms looking for the next big thing in health care. One Medical is one such venture; its initial public stock offering was in early 2020.

At the time, it was used by about 400,000 people—employees with health insurance and uninsured individuals. The company charges a $199 annual membership fee that employers generally pay.

One Medical provides virtual care and group wellness sessions along with an app, lots of communications, and an electronic medical record for its members. Additional charges for medical care are billed to employer insurance plans.

It provides on-demand access to primary care physicians. Lack of access to doctors and endless waits for appointments are a sore spot for consumers. The benefits of access to a primary care physician were noted in Chapter Nine.

"According to a 2016 report, 81 percent of consumers are dissatisfied with their healthcare experience," the company said in its stock-offering prospectus, "in part due to limited after-hours and digital access, long wait times for appointments, extended in-office delays, short and impersonal visits, uninviting medical offices in inconvenient locations, constrained access to specialists and a lack of care coordination across clinical settings."

As of early 2020, the company said it has 77 offices spread across ten urban markets—Boston, Chicago, Los Angeles, New York, Phoenix, Portland, San Diego, the San Francisco Bay Area, Seattle, and Washington, D.C. Service in Atlanta and Orange County, California, also is planned.

WHY NOT ON-DEMAND
HEALTH INSURANCE?

At first glance, the idea of on-demand health insurance is a non sequitur. If healthy people can get health coverage whenever they wish, conventional thinking holds, they simply would avoid insurance until they became ill. Insurance companies would not collect premiums from healthy people and would have to rely on payments only from those who need medical care. The result would be that insurers would lose a bundle unless they raised rates sharply on the individuals who need insurance. This would make coverage unaffordable for them, leading to a death spiral of shrinking insurance rolls and ever-rising rates.

A company named Bind is trying to flip that concept. Its story says a lot about the potential to empower consumers to make smarter choices using health care cost and quality information. Whether or not the company succeeds, its approach typifies consumer-driven health solutions.

Bind touts itself as providing on-demand insurance. Its fine print notes that it's not an insurance company but a benefits provider to employers with self-insured health plans. Its CEO, Tony Miller, is a veteran health entrepreneur who sold some of his companies to giant UnitedHealthcare and had worked there before launching Bind (with UHC's financial support).

"We said, let's go look at the data around how people actually use the U.S. health care system," Miller said in a 2020 interview. People don't use health care all the time. They use it in patterns tied to their health needs. Much health care is driven by injuries, diseases, and conditions that require care right away, while other needed care is elective, meaning it can be planned and scheduled at some future date.

Bind's health plans provide comprehensive, ACA-compliant core coverage for preventive health, preexisting conditions, diseases, and prescription drugs. The plans do not cover roughly four dozen types of common elective health procedures and treatments. People with Bind plans who want such care must buy on-demand coverage. To date, Bind customers have not skewed to younger participants.

Bind uses cost and quality information to power online apps showing customers the cost range of care and guiding them to lower-cost providers of high-quality care. Bind members choosing lower-cost solutions for core health services will reduce their employers' health costs; such savings may be shared with employees to lower their expenses.

Here are Bind sample plan member costs—in addition to premiums—for four care scenarios, including details on the covered care specified for each, and how they compare with high-deductible (HD), basic, and preferred provider organization (PPO) plans offered in traditional employer plans. Bind prices consist of co-pays and paycheck contributions: other plans may include deductibles and coinsurance.

Maternity care—a C-section with 15 primary care visits, 20 laboratory tests, one in-patient delivery stay, five prescriptions for a common generic, and one for a branded generic drug.

Bind:	$3,077
HD:	$4,816
Basic:	$5,816
PPO:	$4,252

Breast cancer—two primary care visits, five specialist care visits, two outpatient surgeries, one laboratory test, and one high-tech imaging test.

Bind:	$3,397
HD:	$4,482
Basic:	$4,282
PPO:	$4,252

Diabetes—six primary care visits and 12 prescriptions (covering a year) for a common generic.

Bind:	$1,492
HD:	$2,026
Basic:	$1,966
PPO:	$2,302

Knee replacement—six primary care visits, six specialty care visits, one surgery (outpatient or inpatient), one unit of durable medical equipment, three physical therapy visits, and six prescriptions for a common generic drug.

Bind:	$3,616 (for Bind efficient provider)
	$8,997 (for Bind inefficient provider)
HD:	$4,816
Basic:	$5,816
PPO:	$4,252

The knee replacement is one of Bind's on-demand procedures. To be considered for an on-demand coverage, Miller said, the care must be something a person can plan to have at a later data. This permits the person to make a financial plan to pay the new premium and any related out-of-pocket costs. Typically, these are paid over time via paycheck deductions and not as a worrisome lump sum.

The second requirement is that the care is not a single event. It must lend itself to preparation for the procedure, the care, and subsequent rehabilitative therapy and recovery. This bundled-care approach permits Bind to identify lower-cost providers with the best health outcomes. Bind filters out care determined by clinical standards to be unnecessary and does not offer on-demand coverage for it. (See Appendix 14 for Bind's list of on-demand elective procedures.)

On-demand care often involves low-value procedures, says Bind actuarial expert Trevor Fast, so Bind emphasizes lower-cost alternative treatment options. Its tools emphasize price savings to provide members with incentives to find the highest value, lowest-cost care.

Those incentives can include zero out-of-pocket co-pays for favored procedures, permitting covered employees to have all costs backed out of their paychecks, often over long periods up to twenty-four pay periods. In fact, the absence of annual deductibles allows Bind to look at full episodes of care and not have to reset plan payments at the start of a new year. Disease doesn't recognize the calendar year, the company notes.

Bind is available only through participating employer health plans. Individuals may be offered Bind plans in the future, a spokeswoman said.

A COLOSSUS OF CONSUMER
HEALTH CARE?

CVS Health is in roughly 10,000 retail locations. Seventy percent of the U.S. population lives within three miles of one of them. While you may see your primary care doctor, if you have one, once or twice a year, you are inside your neighborhood pharmacy once or twice a month if not a week.

Other large pharmacy chains have substantial ties to pharmacy benefit managers (PBMs) or health insurers or other providers of health services. None has the breadth of ties, or the scale, of CVS Health. In 2007, it bought Caremark, the big PBM, which is now CVS Caremark. In 2018, it bought Aetna, a top-five health insurer.

"You see the consumer at the nucleus of our strategy," CEO Larry Merlo says, and one of his oft-repeated phrases in public presentations is "We think there's a tremendous unlock here." Consumers may not understand that phrase. Wall Street analysts do.

"Changing consumer behavior, by making health a part of their regular everyday routine, we think is a tremendous opportunity," he told a health conference in 2019. The company's three consumer care imperatives are to be local, to simplify health care for consumers, and to help people create better health outcomes and reduce their health spending.

In-store health clinics also are a focus of Walgreens Boots Alliance. It is investing a billion dollars in Village MD in a five-year program to open between 500 and 700 clinics staffed with physicians within existing Walgreens outlets.

CVS already has more than 1,100 MinuteClinics in its pharmacies. Nurses there offer non-emergency care on site and via video visits that were introduced in late 2019.

The extensive list of MinuteClinic services and prices includes numerous treatments for minor illnesses and injuries, skin conditions, and health screenings. Here is a sampling of other commonly provided care:

Annual physical	$89
Eyelash lengthening consultation	$59
Smoking cessation assessment	$59
TB testing (two tests)	$74
Flu vaccination	$50 to $70
Hepatis for adult	$145
Pneumonia (Prevnar 13)	$226
Shingles	$179

Service at MinuteClinics will be expanded and many will be rebranded as HealthHUBs, with a (pre-pandemic) goal of having 1,500 outlets opened by the end of 2021. In addition to a new physical layout for pharmacies housing HealthHUBs, CVS says the locations will offer:

- Expanded in-store health products, including health devices that sync to a mobile phone, aromatherapy, fitness essentials, durable medical equipment, and sleep apnea products, among others.
- Education and counseling for patients with chronic conditions; pharmacist-led diabetes education counseling and smart device coaching for select blood glucose monitors; smoking cessation plans.

CAN WALMART REMAKE PRIMARY CARE?

In two small northwest Georgia towns, Walmart began in late 2019 to test full-service retail health care outlets that could shake up primary care even more than the company's aggressive employee health care efforts described in Chapter Three. It opened the first center in Dallas in September 2019 and the second in Calhoun in January 2020. As of July 2020, Walmart had opened four clinics and announced plans for a major launch in Florida plus additional units in Georgia and Chicago.

These first Georgia outlets are helping to define the potential and limits of retail health care and, given Walmart's saturation of smaller U.S. markets, the type of care available in rural America.

"Walmart Health is partnering with several on-the-ground health providers to be a first-of-its-kind health center to deliver primary and urgent care, labs, x-ray and diagnostics, counseling, dental, optical and hearing services all in one facility at affordable, transparent pricing regardless of a patient's insurance status," the company said.

The 1,500-square-foot units are adjacent to existing Walmart locations and are open 80 hours a week—7:30 to 7:30 Monday through Saturday and 10 a.m. to 6 p.m. on Sunday.

Marcus Osborne, Walmart's vice president of health transformation, said the company researched public attitudes about health care and came away with three dominant findings:

"It's about cost, it's about convenience, and it's about care," he said in October 2019 at a health industry conference. "The system is just wildly inconvenient. Why can't I get what I want, when I want it, where I want it, how I want it, and the way that I want it? . . . What we see is this: the health care industry just doesn't seem to care. It's designed to be complex, when it should be simple. It's designed to be unsupportive when it should support. It's designed to provide poor service."

Walmart has posted this summary of prices for the Dallas outlet:

Primary Care Basic Price

Office Visit	$40.00
Annual Checkup—Adult	$30.00
Annual Checkup—Youth	$20.00

Primary Care Add-ons

Lipid Test	$10.00
A1C Test	$10.00
Pregnancy Test	$10.00
Flu Test	$20.00
Strep Test	$20.00
Mono Test	$20.00
Stitches & Other	$115.64*

Counseling

Existing Patient (45 minutes)	$45.00
New Patient Therapy Intake	$60.00

Dental

Patient Exam (Including X-Rays)	$25.00
Teeth Cleaning—Adult (Starting at)	$25.00
Teeth Cleaning—Youth (Starting at)	$15.00
Porcelain Crown	$675.00*
Teeth Whitening, in Office	$225.00
Deep Cleaning (Per Quadrant of Mouth)	$75.00
Emergency Treatment	$50.00
Filling	$75.00–$125.00

Optometry

Routine Vision Exam	$45.00
Contact Lens Fitting	$55.00

* Average prices.

"Our challenge is pretty simple," Walmart's Osborne said. "Is it possible to deliver a consumer experience in health care that attempts to fully and unabashedly address the concerns American's have with the health care system? A solution that focuses on lowering costs, improving convenience, and that actually cares. Even crazier, is it possible to deliver an experience that delights in health care?"

The branding and pricing transparency of these retail efforts will engender others, says Cynthia Fisher, the founder of Patient Rights Advocate whom we met in Chapter Thirteen. "It's game changing," she says of the Walmart outlets. "My children could go to Walmart and get access to care. This is affordable. This is something they can do for them and their families."

Consumers will look at these high-visibility efforts, she predicts, and will "start to connect the dots. . . . What about when Walmart competes with Costco and Costco starts doing this? Or Amazon?"

Get What's Yours Rx

Affordable, quality retail care from national brand and brands will be the norm for many consumers.

Doctors, hospitals, and other traditional providers will compete, improving access and prices for everyone.

Insist on complete transparency of prices, quality, and care standards when dealing with retail care outlets.

Telehealth care exploded during the pandemic and is now an affordable, accessible health service.

AFTERWORD

Through the Pandemic Looking Glass

Layering the coronavirus pandemic upon the U.S. health care system produces any number of unknowns, especially for a manuscript submitted months before publication. Are we ready to tackle a reset of the system or will we be so distracted and exhausted that simply finding our bearings in the new normal will be enough?

A few things seem clear enough.

Telehealth has a permanent seat at the table. Convenience and cost will supplant social distancing as reasons for its use. The same factors will drive the rise of on-demand retail health care.

Preventive care showed its worth. Improved wellness practices will endure in proportion to the severity and duration of the pandemic.

Our oldest and most vulnerable citizens were poorly served by nursing homes without the money or staffing to properly care for them. Millions of aging baby boomers who will need nursing care will further overwhelm nursing homes and home-based care agencies.

Caregivers became our new national heroes. They are every bit the soldiers whose service we rightfully celebrate in the military. Getting more of them should be a national priority.

Powerful players—big pharma, insurers, hospitals, and equipment companies—worked to restore their damaged public images. This will boost their effectiveness in fighting expansion of government health coverage.

COVID-19 created spending needs unlikely to disappear. Post-pandemic, the nation's major health crisis once again will be affordability.

Philip Moeller
July 20, 2020

ACKNOWLEDGMENTS

This book's health care hero stories would not be here without the help of the Patient Advocate Foundation and WEGO Health. Thanks to Caitlin Donovan at the PAF and Julie Croner and Kristen Long at WEGO for connecting me with so many amazing people over many months as the book came into focus. WEGO's social media patient advocates include those who shared their insights in Chapter Seven—Ella Balasa, Dana Donofree, Lauren Freedman, Daniel G. Garza, Tracy Greco, Lauri-Anne Hammond, Bree Hogan, and Kristal Kent. Thanks to them and the countless other heroes who fight for themselves, and others who carry patients up medical mountains.

Thanks to the countless experts and communications people who are not mentioned in the book. They shaped it as much as the people, institutions, and research I cite. If the book is helpful, thank them; where it's not, I am to blame. Jerry Strauss, a friend, physician, medical researcher, and former medical school dean, provided invaluable feedback on the manuscript. Others, in no particular order: Ceci Connolly and Tricia Brookes at the Alliance of Community Health Plans; Kelly Rand at Choosing Wisely; April Todd at the Council for Affordable Quality Healthcare; Niall Brennan, Sally Rodriguez, and Sarah Vermeland at the Health Care Cost Institute; Audrey Huang, Marin Hedin, Michael Newman, and Vanessa Wasta for connecting me with so many beautiful medical minds at Johns Hopkins; Chris Lee and Cynthia Cox at the Kaiser Family Foundation; Rabah Kamal at the Peterson-Kaiser Health System Tracker; Katie Bronk at the Joint Commission; Leah Binder, Christine Diven, and Tiggidankay Jalloh at Leapfrog Group; Leslie Bennett at the Washington Health Alliance; Liz Deforest, for Willis Towers Watson and others; Maggie Beckley at MediBid; Bruce Lee and Tracy Watts at Mercer; Viren Prasad Shetty at Narayana Health; Stephanie Miceli at the National Academies of Science; Sarah Anderson at the National Association of Free & Charitable Clinics; Ed Emerman for the Business Group on Health; Olivia Ross at the Pacific Business Group on Health; Alan Balch and Beth Moore at the Patient Advocate Foundation; Linda Bent at PatientRightsAdvocate.org; Sue Ducat at Project Hope; Chris Wing at Scan Health Plan; Tista Ghosh at Grand Rounds, and Jessica Kostner, Forrest G. Burke, John Haben, and Anthony Nguyen at UnitedHealthcare.

This book would not have been possible without health care journalists. Among the sobering lessons of the pandemic is the vital role played by fact-based journalism. In the morning, as I began consuming my outsized daily ration of coffee, I would look at general news outlets—the *New York Times, Wall Street Journal, Washington Post,* and Bloomberg— move on to some of the leading medical news sites—*Modern Healthcare, STAT, Axios,* and *Healthcare Dive,* among others—and then look at that day's new offerings from medical journals—in particular *Health Affairs,* the various *Journals of the American Medical Association* (JAMA), and research that popped up in news feeds. As I reached the end of this caffeine-fueled process, I would visit the home page of *Kaiser Health News* and open its daily summary of health news, which is posted on weekdays around 9 a.m. I would see how many of Kaiser's entries I had already come across, and how many I had missed. As hard as I tried, Kaiser always had links to pieces I had not seen and could not afford to miss.

The errors in this book are solely my responsibility, but I owe an enormous debt to health care journalists and researchers for the accurate informational ground on which I tried to build *Get What's Yours.* It was a privilege to spend so many hours with your work.

As much as health care is changing, the challenges facing book publishing are daunting in their own right. Authors are fortunate to find dedicated people still manning the ramparts. Thanks to Alice Martell, my agent, and to Bob Bender and Johanna Li, my editor and his aide-de-camp at Simon & Schuster.

APPENDIX 1

Health Care Costs: America's Financial Tapeworm

Here are the percentages of income that individuals and families of four (parents and two kids) paid for care, with separate looks depending on whether people were in better, average, or worse health. Totals include the share of taxes spent on government health programs, providing an "all-in" view of what health care costs us. Keep in mind that due to lags in collecting data, the figures you see here are two to three years old. Things today are worse.

Insurance	People*	Income	Health	Spending**	% Inc.
Employer	One	20,000	Better	2,350	12%
			Average	2,550	13%
			Worse	3,550	18%
ACA	One	20,000	Better	2,600	13%
			Average	2,750	14%
			Worse	3,950	20%
Medicaid	One	15,000	Better	700	5%
			Average	850	6%
			Worse	1,100	7%
Employer	One	50,000	Better	5,000	10%
			Average	5,250	11%
			Worse	6,550	13%
ACA	One	50,000	Better	9,550	19%
			Average	10,000	20%
			Worse	13,450	27%
Employer	One	75,000	Better	7,750	10%
			Average	7,950	11%
			Worse	9,500	13%

Insurance	People*	Income	Health	Spending**	% Inc.
Employer	Four	50,000	Better	7,350	15%
			Average	7,450	15%
			Worse	9,250	19%
ACA	Four	50,000	Better	9,400	19%
			Average	9,550	19%
			Worse	13,950	28%
Medicaid	One	30,000	Better	1,150	3%
			Average	1,200	3%
			Worse	1,400	4%
Employer	Four	100,000	Better	12,400	12%
			Average	12,500	13%
			Worse	15,000	15%
ACA	Four	100,000	Better	24,100	24%
			Average	24,300	24%
			Worse	30,400	30%
Employer	Four	150,000	Better	17,800	12%
			Average	17,850	12%
			Worse	20,750	14%

* Individual family of four with parents and two children
** Out-of-pocket spending
Source: Peterson-Kaiser Household Spending Calculator

APPENDIX 2

Walmart Centers of Excellence

Joint replacement

1. Emory Healthcare (Atlanta)
2. Johns Hopkins Medicine (Baltimore)
3. Kaiser Permanente (Irvine, Calif.)
4. Mayo Clinic (Jacksonville, Fla.)
5. Mayo Clinic (Rochester, Minn.)
6. Mercy (Springfield, Mo.)
7. Northeast Baptist Hospital (San Antonio)
8. Ochsner (New Orleans)
9. Scripps Mercy (San Diego)
10. University Hospital (Cleveland)
11. Virginia Mason (Seattle)

Spine

1. Emory Healthcare (Atlanta)
2. Geisinger (Danville, Pa.)
3. Mayo Clinic (Jacksonville, Fla.)
4. Mayo Clinic (Phoenix)
5. Mayo Clinic (Rochester, Minn.)
6. Memorial Hermann (Houston)
7. Mercy (Springfield, Mo.)
8. Virginia Mason (Seattle)
9. Bariatric Clinic (Charlotte, NC)
10. Northeast Baptist Hospital (San Antonio)

11. Northwest Medical Center (Springdale, Ark.)
12. Scripps Mercy (San Diego)
13. University Hospital (Cleveland)

Cancer and transplants

1. Mayo Clinic (Jacksonville, Fla.)
2. Mayo Clinic (Phoenix)
3. Mayo Clinic (Rochester, Minn.)

Cardiac

1. Cleveland Clinic
2. Geisinger (Danville, Pa.)
3. Virginia Mason (Seattle)

APPENDIX 3

State ABLE and Medicaid Home-Value Exemptions

State	ABLE	Home
Alabama	$400,000	$572,000
Alaska	no response	$572,000
Arizona	$486,000	$572,000
Arkansas	$366,000	$572,000
California	$529,000	No Limit on Principal Residence
Colorado	$350,000	$572,000
Connecticut	$300,000	$858,000
Delaware	350,000	$572,000
DC	$500,000	$858,000
Florida	$418,000	$572,000
Georgia	$468,000	$572,000
Hawaii	$305,000	$858,000
Idaho	no response	$858,000
Illinois	$400,000	$572,000
Indiana	$450.00	$572,000
Iowa	$420,000	$572,000
Kansas	$365,000	$572,000
Kentucky	$468,000	$572,000
Louisiana	$500,000	$572,000
Maine	$400,000	$858,000
Maryland	$350,000	$572,000
Massachusetts	$400,000	$858,000

Michigan	$500,000	$572,000
Minnesota	$350,000	$572,000
Mississippi	$235,000	$572,000
Missouri	$468,000	$572,000
Montana	$400,000	$572,000
Nebraska	$400,000	$572,000
Nevada	$370,000	$572,000 - 858,000
New Hampshire	$468,000	$572,000
New Jersey	$305,000	$858,000
New Mexico	$468,000	$572,000
New York	$100,000	$858,000
North Carolina	$420,000	$572,000
North Dakota	$269,000	$572,000
Ohio	$468,000	$572,000
Oklahoma	$468,000	$572,000
Oregon	$400,000	$572,000
Pennsylvania	$511,758	$572,000
Rhode Island	$395,000	$572,000
South Carolina	$462,000	$572,000
South Dakota	$350,000	$572,000
Tennessee	$350,000	$572,000
Texas	$370,000	$572,000
Utah	$416,000	$572,000
Vermont	$468,000	$572,000
Virginia	$500,000	$572,000
Washington	$500,000	$572,000
West Virginia	$468,000	$572,000
Wisconsin	$330,000	$750,000
Wyoming	$464,000	$572,000

SOURCE: Kaiser Family Foundation, 2018

APPENDIX 4

Top-Graded Preventive Care Measures

A Grades

Cervical Cancer: Screening: women aged 21 to 65 years

Colorectal Cancer: Screening: adults aged 50 to 75 years

Folic Acid for the Prevention of Neural Tube Defects: Preventive
Medication: women who are planning or capable of pregnancy

Human Immunodeficiency Virus (HIV) Infection: Screening: pregnant
persons

Human Immunodeficiency Virus (HIV) Infection: Screening: adolescents
and adults aged 15 to 65 years

High Blood Pressure in Adults: Screening: adults aged 18 years or older

Hepatitis B Virus Infection in Pregnant Women: Screening: pregnant
women

Ocular Prophylaxis for Gonococcal Ophthalmia Neonatorum: Preventive
Medication: newborns

Prevention of Human Immunodeficiency Virus (HIV) Infection:
Preexposure Prophylaxis: persons at high risk of HIV acquisition

Rh(D) Incompatibility: Screening: pregnant women, during the first
pregnancy-related care visit

Syphilis Infection in Nonpregnant Adults and Adolescents: Screening:
asymptomatic, nonpregnant adults and adolescents who are at
increased risk for syphilis infection

Syphilis Infection in Pregnant Women: Screening: pregnant women

Tobacco Smoking Cessation in Adults, Including Pregnant Women:
Behavioral and pharmacotherapy interventions

B Grades

Abdominal Aortic Aneurysm: Screening: men aged 65 to 75 years who
 have ever smoked

Abnormal Blood Glucose and Type 2 Diabetes Mellitus: Screening: adults
 aged 40 to 70 years who are overweight or obese

Aspirin Use to Prevent Cardiovascular Disease (CVD) and Colorectal
 Cancer: Preventive Medication: adults aged 50 to 59 years with a ≥10
 percent 10-year CVD risk

Asymptomatic Bacteriuria in Adults: Screening: pregnant persons

BRCA-Related Cancer: Risk Assessment, Genetic Counseling, and
 Genetic Testing: women with a personal or family history of breast,
 ovarian, tubal, or peritoneal cancer or an ancestry associated with
 BRCA1/2 gene mutation

Breast Cancer: Medication Use to Reduce Risk: women at increased risk
 for breast cancer

Breast Cancer: Screening: women aged 50 to 74 years

Breastfeeding: Primary Care Interventions: pregnant women, new
 mothers, and their children

Dental Care in Children from Birth Through Age 5 Years: Screening:
 children from birth through age 5 years

Depression in Adults: Screening: general adult population, including
 pregnant and postpartum women

Depression in Children and Adolescents: Screening: adolescents aged 12
 to 18 years

Falls Prevention in Community-Dwelling Older Adults: Interventions:
 adults 65 years or older

Gestational Diabetes Mellitus, Screening: asymptomatic pregnant
 women, after 24 weeks of gestation

Chlamydia and Gonorrhea: Screening: sexually active women

Healthful Diet and Physical Activity for Cardiovascular Disease
 Prevention in Adults with Cardiovascular Risk Factors: Behavioral
 Counseling: adults who are overweight or obese and have additional
 CVD risk factors

Hepatitis B Virus Infection: Screening, 2014: persons at high risk for
infection

Hepatitis C Virus Infection in Adolescents and Adults: Screening: adults
aged 18 to 79 years

Intimate Partner Violence, Elder Abuse, and Abuse of Vulnerable Adults:
Screening: women of reproductive age

Latent Tuberculosis Infection: Screening: asymptomatic adults at
increased risk for infection

Low-Dose Aspirin Use for the Prevention of Morbidity and Mortality
From Preeclampsia: Preventive Medication: pregnant women who
are at high risk for preeclampsia

Lung Cancer: Screening: adults aged 55–80, with a history of smoking

Obesity in Children and Adolescents: Screening: children and adolescents
6 years and older

Osteoporosis to Prevent Fractures: Screening: postmenopausal women
younger than 65 years at increased risk of osteoporosis

Osteoporosis to Prevent Fractures: Screening: women 65 years and older

Perinatal Depression: Preventive Interventions: pregnant and postpartum
persons

Preeclampsia: Screening: pregnant woman

Prevention and Cessation of Tobacco Use in Children and Adolescents:
Primary Care Interventions: school-aged children and adolescents
who have not started to use tobacco

Rh(D) Incompatibility: Screening: unsensitized rh(d)-negative pregnant
women

Sexually Transmitted Infections: Behavioral Counseling: sexually active
adolescents and adults

Skin Cancer Prevention: Behavioral Counseling: young adults,
adolescents, children, and parents of young children

Statin Use for the Primary Prevention of Cardiovascular Disease (CVD)
in Adults: Preventive Medication: adults aged 40 to 75 years with no
history of CVD, 1 or more CVD risk factors, and a calculated 10-
year CVD event risk of 10 percent or greater

Unhealthy Alcohol Use in Adolescents and Adults: Screening and
    Behavioral Counseling Interventions: adults 18 years or older,
    including pregnant women
Vision in Children Ages 6 Months to 5 Years: Screening: children aged 3
    to 5 years
Weight Loss to Prevent Obesity-Related Morbidity and Mortality in
    Adults: Behavioral Interventions: adults

Source: U.S. Preventive Services Task Force

APPENDIX 5

National Financial Resource Directory

Trying to pick the correct diagnosis and assistance categories from the directory is hard without knowing your options. Here were the categories as of early 2020:

Medical Diagnosis

Cancer

- Abdominal Cancers
- Blood Cancer
- Breast Cancer
- Colorectal Cancer
- Female Reproductive Cancers
- Head and Neck Cancers
- Lung Cancer
- Male Reproductive Cancers
- Nervous System Cancers
- Other Cancers
- Sarcoma
- Skin Cancers

Diabetes

Digestive System Disorder

Genetic Conditions

Heart/Circulatory Condition

Prevention Only—Not Diagnosed

- Hypertension
- Stroke or Vascular Concerns
- Arrhythmia and A-Fib
- Cholesterol and Coronary Heart Disease
- Congenital Heart Defects
- Heart Failure or Heart Attack
- Multiple Conditions Alongside Heart Attack
- Women with Heart Disease
- Heart Valve Disease or Disorders

Hypo or Hyper Disease

Immune System Disease or Disorders

Infectious Disease

Kidney Disease

Lung Disease

Mental Health

Nervous System Conditions

Pediatric Condition

Rare Disease

Transplantation

Assistance Type Needed

Academic Scholarships

Affordable Options for Care

Child Care Resources

Clinical Trial Assistance

Complementary or Holistic Therapy

Credit or Financial Management

Dental Care

Disaster Resources

Disease Information, Research, or Education

Drug Manufacturer Patient Programs

Emotional Support and Community
Employment
Fertility-Related Services
Food and Nutrition
Fund-raising Programs
Genetic and Genomic Testing
Government Services and Programs
Home Health, Respite, or Day Care
Hospice and End-of-Life Services
Housekeeping and Repairs
Housing and Lodging
Insurance Policy Options
Insurance Premium Assistance
Legal or Advocate Services
Medical Bills and General Financial Help
Medical Equipment or Supplies
Other Medication Assistance
Reconstructive Surgery
Rehabilitation Assistance
Resource Directories and Finders
Screening Services
Support for Caregivers
Transportation Assistance
Utilities
Vision Care and Eyeglasses
Wish Fulfillment

APPENDIX 6

Questions to Ask Your Primary Care Physician (PCP)

1. How long have you been a PCP and how much longer do you plan to practice?
2. Does your office provide behavioral health, nutrition advice, physical therapy, or other types of nonclinical help?
3. How many times a year should I see you for a physical and other wellness visits?
4. What tests will you perform as part of your baseline work-up of my health?
5. Can I get my regular vaccinations here? What about blood work? If you think I need scans (MRIs, CTs), where are they provided?
6. Does your office recommend or work closely with any ambulatory surgical centers or emergency clinics?
7. Will you collect my family medical history and is there a form I can fill in for you?
8. Will your practice assemble my electronic health records and how can I get access to them?
9. Do you practice in an accountable care organization? If not, do you and your practice have any financial incentives to keep me healthy?
10. Can you or a staff person answer my questions about drug and treatment costs? Is there someone there who can help me understand how my health insurance works?
11. If I have a problem and want to see you, can I see you the same day?
12. Can you tell me which specialists you recommend for my health issues (list your needs)?

APPENDIX 7

United Hospital Fund Health Quality Rankings Criteria

- Condition-Specific Information
  - Condition- or procedure-specific performance data at the clinician level.
  - Treatment risks and options.

- Clinician-Level Information
  - Reputation (e.g., lists of top providers, professional opinions).
  - Expertise and credentials (e.g., education, training, and board certification).
  - Demographics (e.g., age, gender, ethnicity).
  - Hospital affiliation.
  - History of legal actions.
  - Languages spoken.
  - Photo.
  - Physician statement/video.
  - Patient Experience and Patient-Reported Outcomes
  - Doctors or other health care providers who spend time with me and do not rush.
  - Doctors who listen and show they care about me.
  - Doctors who clearly explain what they are doing and what I need to do later.
  - Someone who treats me with respect.
  - Someone who has compassion.

- Someone who is kind, caring, comforting.
- Someone who involves and shares information with my family members.
- Someone who uses plain language.
- Someone who communicates with me, not over me.
- Someone who presents information to me in a culturally relevant and sensitive way.
- Measures (e.g., functional, quality-of-life indicators) relevant to the patient's condition that can aid treatment decisions.
- Ratings and reviews by patients in similar circumstances.
- Structural and Service Quality Attributes of a Practice
- Health insurance plan participation.
- Access (e.g., scheduling an appointment easily, convenient office hours, minimal wait times).
- Technology capabilities (e.g., online appointments, portal access to medical record information, email/text communication).
- Cleanliness.
- Helpful and friendly office staff.
- Care team members who treat each other with respect.
- Amenities (e.g., parking, access to public transportation).

- Characteristics of the Information Itself
  - Understandable, with visuals to represent data.
  - Simple, clean formatting with limited information on a page.
  - Avoidance of acronyms.
  - Timely information.

APPENDIX 8

The Most Reliable Ratings Sites for Doctors, Hospitals, and Nursing Homes

Physicians

Healthgrades
U.S. News & World Report
WebMD
Zocdoc

Hospitals

CAHPS Adult Hospital Survey
Healthgrades
IBM/Watson Health 100 Top Hospitals
Leapfrog Group
U.S. News & World Report

Nursing Homes

Long Term Care Community Coalition
Long-Term Care Ombudsman Program
National Association of Area Agencies on Aging

CMS "Compare" Tools

Physician Compare
Hospital Compare
Nursing Home Compare

Hospice Compare
Inpatient Rehabilitation Facility Compare
Dialysis Facility Compare
Home Health Compare
Long-Term Care Hospital Compare

deficiency, or **dual-energy x-ray absorptiometry** (DEXA) screening for osteoporosis in women younger than 65 or men younger than 70 with no risk factors.

- You should avoid **screening for colorectal cancer** if you're 50 or older and **coronary angiography** unless you have cardiac symptoms and other high-risk markers.
- Women should avoid unnecessary cervical cancer screening (**Pap smear and HPV** test) if you've had adequate prior screening and are not otherwise at high risk for cervical cancer.
- Men should never have **PSA-based screening** for prostate cancer, regardless of age.

Source: Virginia Center on Health Innovation

APPENDIX 9

The ABCs of "Don't"

Some of these entries are in "medspeak"; Google as needed.

Common Treatments

- Don't take **antibiotics** for adenoviral conjunctivitis (pink eye).
- If your doctor prescribes oral **antibiotics** for upper ear infections, including uncomplicated acute tympanostomy tube otorrhea (infections related to ear tubes in children), you should decline.
- If you have children under four years of age, they should not be taking **cough and cold medicines**.

Diagnostic Testing

- If you have **low back pain,** you shouldn't get MRIs or other image tests within the first six weeks, unless the condition get much worse.
- **Headaches** don't require brain scans. Or **electroencephalography** (EEG).
- **Brain imaging** studies (CT or MRI) are not recommended if you've fainted (simple syncope) or as part of a normal neurological examination. Ditto on imaging of your **carotid arteries** without other neurologic symptoms.
- If your doctor says you need a **computed tomography** (CT) scan for sudden hearing loss, say no loud enough to make sure they hear you. If your doctor says your child (17 years

of age or younger) needs a head CT, decline unless a specific and serious health condition has been identified. They're not recommended as part of an emergency room work-up for severe dizziness, either.

- **Postcoital tests** (PCT) for the evaluation of infertility are an inconvenient and possibly embarrassing waste of money.
- If you're having infertility problems, say "No" to **advanced sperm function** testing, such as sperm penetration or hemizona assays, as part of your initial evaluation.
- If you don't have cardiac symptoms or other high-risk markers, you shouldn't have stress **cardiac imaging** or advanced non-invasive imaging as part of an initial evaluation.
- If your doctor recommends **diagnostic tests** to evaluate an allergy, ask if the tests have proven diagnostic value. Some, including immunoglobulin G (IgG) testing or a battery of immunoglobulin E (IgE) tests, do not.
- If you have a child younger than twenty-four months with their first urinary tract infection, they should not be routinely prescribed a **voiding cystourethrogram** (VCUG).
- If you or your child have **chronic urticaria** (skin allergy), decline a diagnostic test.
- Routine imaging tests are not recommended for uncomplicated **acute rhinosinusitis** (sinus infection) or for the eyes where there are no symptoms or signs of significant eye disease.
- **Coronary artery** calcium scoring is not recommended, even if you have coronary artery disease (including stents and bypass grafts).

Disease Approach

- Unless you're in physical distress, don't schedule ele non-medically indicated inductions of labor or **Cesa deliveries** before thirty-nine weeks of pregnancy.
- If you have knee osteoarthritis, **arthroscopic knee su** not recommended.
- Computed tomography (CT) scans are not recommen the routine evaluation of abdominal pain.
- If you have one or more osteoporotic vertebral fracture **vertebroplasty** treatment is not recommended.
- **Antidepressants** should not be the only treatment (kno monotherapy) if you have bipolar 1 disorder.
- Be very careful about taking NSAIDS and usually avoid th if you have hypertension or heart failure or chronic kidney disease (CKD) of all causes, including diabetes.

Preoperative Evaluation

- Expensive imaging scans and baseline blood panels are not recommended for low- or moderate-risk surgeries unless you have serious underlying health issues.

Routine Joint MRIs

- Say "no thanks" to MRIs to routinely monitor inflammatory arthritis.

Screening Tests

- Many screening tests are not called for in the absence of documented health issues. This includes annual electrocardiograms (**EKGs**) or any other cardiac screening, **population-based screening** for 25-OH-vitamin D

APPENDIX 9

The ABCs of "Don't"

Some of these entries are in "medspeak"; Google as needed.

Common Treatments

- Don't take **antibiotics** for adenoviral conjunctivitis (pink eye).
- If your doctor prescribes oral **antibiotics** for upper ear infections, including uncomplicated acute tympanostomy tube otorrhea (infections related to ear tubes in children), you should decline.
- If you have children under four years of age, they should not be taking **cough and cold medicines**.

Diagnostic Testing

- If you have **low back pain,** you shouldn't get MRIs or other image tests within the first six weeks, unless the condition get much worse.
- **Headaches** don't require brain scans. Or **electroencephalography** (EEG).
- **Brain imaging** studies (CT or MRI) are not recommended if you've fainted (simple syncope) or as part of a normal neurological examination. Ditto on imaging of your **carotid arteries** without other neurologic symptoms.
- If your doctor says you need a **computed tomography** (CT) scan for sudden hearing loss, say no loud enough to make sure they hear you. If your doctor says your child (17 years

of age or younger) needs a head CT, decline unless a specific and serious health condition has been identified. They're not recommended as part of an emergency room work-up for severe dizziness, either.

- **Postcoital tests** (PCT) for the evaluation of infertility are an inconvenient and possibly embarrassing waste of money.
- If you're having infertility problems, say "No" to **advanced sperm function** testing, such as sperm penetration or hemizona assays, as part of your initial evaluation.
- If you don't have cardiac symptoms or other high-risk markers, you shouldn't have stress **cardiac imaging** or advanced non-invasive imaging as part of an initial evaluation.
- If your doctor recommends **diagnostic tests** to evaluate an allergy, ask if the tests have proven diagnostic value. Some, including immunoglobulin G (IgG) testing or a battery of immunoglobulin E (IgE) tests, do not.
- If you have a child younger than twenty-four months with their first urinary tract infection, they should not be routinely prescribed a **voiding cystourethrogram** (VCUG).
- If you or your child have **chronic urticaria** (skin allergy), decline a diagnostic test.
- Routine imaging tests are not recommended for uncomplicated **acute rhinosinusitis** (sinus infection) or for the eyes where there are no symptoms or signs of significant eye disease.
- **Coronary artery** calcium scoring is not recommended, even if you have coronary artery disease (including stents and bypass grafts).

Disease Approach

- Unless you're in physical distress, don't schedule elective, non-medically indicated inductions of labor or **Cesarean deliveries** before thirty-nine weeks of pregnancy.
- If you have knee osteoarthritis, **arthroscopic knee surgery** is not recommended.
- Computed tomography (CT) scans are not recommended for the routine evaluation of abdominal pain.
- If you have one or more osteoporotic vertebral fractures, **vertebroplasty** treatment is not recommended.
- **Antidepressants** should not be the only treatment (known as monotherapy) if you have bipolar 1 disorder.
- Be very careful about taking NSAIDS and usually avoid them if you have hypertension or heart failure or chronic kidney disease (CKD) of all causes, including diabetes.

Preoperative Evaluation

- Expensive imaging scans and baseline blood panels are not recommended for low- or moderate-risk surgeries unless you have serious underlying health issues.

Routine Joint MRIs

- Say "no thanks" to MRIs to routinely monitor inflammatory arthritis.

Screening Tests

- Many screening tests are not called for in the absence of documented health issues. This includes annual electrocardiograms (**EKGs**) or any other cardiac screening, **population-based screening** for 25-OH-vitamin D deficiency, or **dual-energy x-ray absorptiometry** (DEXA) screening for osteoporosis in women younger than 65 or men younger than 70 with no risk factors.

- You should avoid **screening for colorectal cancer** if you're 50 or older and **coronary angiography** unless you have cardiac symptoms and other high-risk markers.

- Women should avoid unnecessary cervical cancer screening (**Pap smear and HPV** test) if you've had adequate prior screening and are not otherwise at high risk for cervical cancer.

- Men should never have **PSA-based screening** for prostate cancer, regardless of age.

Source: Virginia Center on Health Innovation

APPENDIX 10

Checklist for Getting the Right Care

Tell Your Story Well

- Be Clear. Think about when your symptoms started, what made them better or worse, and if they were related to taking medications, eating a meal, exercising, or a certain time of day.
- Be Complete. Try to remember important information about your illness. Make notes and bring them with you. A family member may be able to help you with this.
- Be Accurate and Consistent. Sometimes you may see multiple clinicians during a medical appointment. Make sure your clinicians hear the same story regarding your illness.

Be a Good Historian

- Remember what treatments you have tried in the past, if they helped, and what, if any, side effects you experienced.
- Think about how your illness has progressed.
- Think about your family's medical history and if you may be at risk for similar illnesses.

Keep Good Records

- Keep your own records of test results, referrals, and hospital admissions.
- Keep an accurate list of your medications.
- Bring your medication list with you when you see your clinician or pharmacist.

Be an Informed Consumer

- Learn about your illness by looking at reliable sources on the Internet or visiting a local library.
- Learn about the tests or procedures you are having done.
- Learn about your medications:
    - Know the names of your medications (generic and brand names).
    - Know what the medication is for.
    - Know the amount (dose) you need to take.
    - Know the time(s) you need to take it during the day.
    - Know the side effects to watch for and report to your clinician.
    - Know if the medication interacts with any food or drugs.

Take Charge of Managing Your Health

- When meeting with your clinician, ask these main questions:
    - What is my main problem?
    - What do I need to do?
    - Why is it important for me to do this?
- And, as needed, these related questions:
    - What could be causing my problem?
    - What else could it be?
    - When will I get my test results, and what should I do to follow up?
- If you have more than one clinician, make sure each doctor knows what their peers are doing.
- Make sure each clinician knows all of your test results, medications, or other treatments.

Know Your Test Results

- Make sure you and your clinician get the results from any tests that are done.
- Don't assume that no news is good news; call and check on your test results.
- Ask what the test results mean and what needs to be done next.

Follow Up

- Ask when you need to make another appointment (follow up) with your clinician once you start treatment.
- Ask what to expect from the treatment or what it will do for you.
- Ask what you need to do if you get new symptoms or start to feel worse.

Make Sure It Is the Right Diagnosis

- Sometimes your diagnosis is the "likely" thing that is wrong. It may not be the "right" diagnosis.
- Don't be afraid to ask "What else could this be?"
- Encourage your clinicians to think about other possible reasons for your illness.

Excerpt from Medical Journal Article
Coauthored by Cynthia Buness

She was diagnosed with blastocystis hominis and treated with ciprofloxacin and metronidazole (for 10 days), and later with nitazoxanide (for 4 days). Her symptoms improved while on the ciprofloxacin/metronidazole, but returned when the treatment was completed. She was admitted to the hospital 3 months later with erythema nodosum which resolved without treatment. She discontinued the doxycycline treatment just prior to her hospitalization. Her labs showed slight elevations in alanine aminotransferase (ALT), alkaline phosphatase (ALP), and perinuclear anti-neutrophil cytoplasmic antibodies were positive at 113.9 EU/mL. The patient was diagnosed by colonoscopy with moderate chronic active ulcerative pancolitis and was started on mesalamine, which she did not tolerate and had worsening bloody diarrhea and abdominal pain. She was transitioned to 9 mg of budesonide and later also to 6,750 mg/day balsalazide, the latter which also caused worsening diarrhea. The patient elected to stop all medication and started herbal remedies for 6 months: VSL#3 probiotic, curcumin, and Nopalea (cactus juice; Trivita in Scottsdale, AZ, USA). The patient continued to experience diarrhea up to 4–5 times a day and azathioprine was initiated. Screening blood tests for azathioprine therapy in August 2012 revealed increased liver enzymes. Quantitative immunoglobulin G (IgG) was normal and screening for hepatic autoimmune antibodies (anti-nuclear antibodies, and anti-liver/kidney microsomal antibodies) was negative. The IgG subclasses panel showed normal IgG4. A magnetic resonance cholangiopancreatography (MRCP) showed localized common hepatic duct prominence measuring 7 mm proximally at the porta hepatis of uncertain significance with no changes of PSC. A liver biopsy showed mild portal lymphocytic infiltrates with focal infiltration of bile duct epithelium. Several small and medium-size bile ducts were surrounded by concentric fibrosis with mild bile ductular proliferation. There was no significant fibrosis. Findings were consistent with small-duct PSC.

APPENDIX 12

Maryland Knee Replacements (2015–2016 procedures)

Hospital	Total Cost	PAC Rate*	Readmit Rate (%)
Northwest Hospital	$33,162	Worse	3.80%
Sinai Hospital of Baltimore	$32,192	Average	17.60%
Medstar Harbor Hospital	$31,636	Average	2.80%
Medstar Southern Maryland Hospital Center	$31,030	Average	3.30%
Peninsula Regional Medical Center	$30,932	Worse	13.60%
UM Rehab & Ortho	$30,786	Worse	1.70%
Medstar Good Samaritan Hospital	$29,759	Average	12.50%
Johns Hopkins Bayview Medical Center	$29,714	Average	0.00%
Medstar Union Memorial Hospital	$27,805	Average	3.90%
Adventist Healthcare Shady Grove Medical Center	$27,787	Average	3.40%
Greater Baltimore Medical Center	$27,642	Average	2.00%
Holy Cross Hospital	$27,233	Better	2.10%
Doctors Community Hospital	$26,959	Worse	4.00%
Medstar Franklin Square Medical Center	$26,474	Average	6.90%
Medstar Montgomery Medical Center	$26,311	Worse	0.00%
UM Baltimore	$26,292	Worse	2.90%
Howard County General Hospital	$26,180	Average	2.10%
Carroll Hospital Center	$25,636	Better	0.00%
Western Maryland Regional Medical Center	$25,100	Average	0.00%
Frederick Memorial Hospital	$24,321	Average	3.00%
Upper Chesapeake	$24,226	Average	0.00%

University of Maryland St. Joseph Medical Center	$24,034	Average	1.60%
Saint Agnes Hospital	$24,019	Average	4.70%
Anne Arundel Medical Center	$23,751	Average	2.40%
Mercy Medical Center	$23,151	Average	2.60%
Meritus Medical Center	$23,064	Average	2.50%
Suburban Hospital	$22,970	Average	0.60%
UM Easton	$21,839	Average	2.50%

* PAC = potentially avoidable complications

APPENDIX 13

*Ardon List of Specialty Drugs with
Patient Assistance Programs*

Asthma and Allergy

Dupixent®–Dupixent My Way
Nucala®–My Nucala
Xolair®–Xolair Co-pay Program

Blood Cell Deficiency

Neulasta®–Amgen Assist 360Uden
Promacta®–Promacta4U
Udenyca™–Coherus Complete
Zarxio™–Sandoz One Source

Oncology

Afinitor®–Novartis Universal Co-pay Card
Alecensa®–Genentech Access Solutions
Gleevec® (imatinib)–Novartis Universal Co-pay Card
Kisqali®–Novartis Universal Co-pay Card
Lupron Depot®–Lupron Depot Savings Card
Sprycel®–Sprycel Assist One Card
Tarceva®–Genentech Access Solutions
Zytiga™(abiraterone)–Janssen Care Path

Cystic Fibrosis

Bethkis®*–Chiesi Care Direct
Pulmozyme®*–Genentech Access Solutions

Endocrine Disorders

Lupaneta Pack™–Lupaneta Pack Savings Card
Lupron Depot-Ped®–Lupron Depot Ped Savings Care
Somatuline Depot®–Ipsen Cares

Growth Deficiency

Genotropin®–Pfizer Bridge Program
Humatrope®–Humatrope Co-pay Program
Norditropin®–NordiSure

Hemophilia

Advate®–Takeda's Co-pay Programeloct
Eloctate™–Eloctate Co-pay Program

Hepatitis C

Epclusa®–Support Path
Mavyret™–Mavyret Savings Card

Idiopathic Pulmonary Fibrosis

Esbriet™–The Esbriet $5 Support Program

Inflammatory Conditions

Actemra®–Actemra Co-pay Card Program
Cimzia®–Cimplicity
Cosentyx™–$0 Co-pay Offer
Enbrel®–Enbrel Support
Humira®–Humira Costelaramplete

Olumiant®–Olumiant Together
Orencia®–Orencia Co-pay Program
Skyrizi™–Skyrizi Complete
Stelara™–Janssen Care Path

Miscellaneous Specialty Conditions

Austedo®–Shared Solutionsbotox
Botox®–Botox Savings Program
Makena™ (hydroxyprogesterone caproate)–Makena Care
  Connection
Vivitrol®–Vivitrol Co-pay Savings Program

Multiple Sclerosis

Aubagio®–MS One to One
Avonex®–Above MS
Copaxone®–Copaxone Co-pay Solutions
Ocrevus™–Ocrevus Co-pay Program
Tecfidera™–$0 Co-pay Program

Osteoporosis

Forteo®–Forteo Connect
Prolia™–Prolia Support

Bind On-Demand Elective Procedures

Cardiovascular (Heart Health)

- Cardiac Ablation
- Carotid Endarterectomy and Stents
- Coronary Artery Bypass Graft Surgery
- Coronary Catheterization and Percutaneous Coronary Interventions
- Pacemakers and Defibrillators
- Valve Replacement

ENT (Ears, Nose, and Throat)

- Ear Tubes
- Sinus and Nasal Septum Surgery
- Tonsillectomy and Adenoidectomy

Gastrointestinal (Digestive System)

- Bariatric Surgery
- Gallbladder Removal Surgery (Cholecystectomy)
- Hernia Repair
- Reflux and Hiatal Hernia Surgery
- Upper GI Endoscopy

Musculoskeletal (Muscles, Joints, etc.)

- Ankle and Foot Bone Fusion
- Ankle Arthroscopy and Ligament Repair

- Ankle Replacement and Revision
- Bunionectomy and Hammertoe Surgery
- Carpal Tunnel Surgery
- Cervical Spine Disc Decompression
- Cervical Spine Fusion
- Elbow Arthroscopy and Tenotomy
- Elbow Replacement and Revision
- Ganglion Cyst Surgery
- Hip Arthroscopy and Repair
- Hip Replacement and Revision
- Knee Arthroscopy and Repair
- Knee Replacement and Revision
- Lumbar Spine Disc Decompression
- Lumbar Spine Fusion
- Morton's Neuroma Surgery
- Plantar Fasciitis Surgery
- Shoulder Arthroscopy and Repair
- Shoulder Replacement and Revision
- Spinal Ablation and Neurostimulators
- Wrist and Hand Joint Replacement
- Wrist Arthroscopy and Repair

Other

- Breast Reduction Surgery
- Cataract Surgery
- Fibroid Removal (Myomectomy)
- Hysterectomy
- Hysteroscopy and Endometrial Ablation
- Kidney Stone Ablation and Removal (Lithotripsy)
- Prostate Removal Surgery
- Sling Surgery for Female Urinary Incontinence

NOTES

Chapter 1: Game On

3   *a story:* "To Save Money, American Patients and Surgeons Meet in Cancun," *Kaiser Health News*, August 12, 2019, https://khn.org/news/to-save-money-american-patients-and-surgeons-meet-in-cancun/.

3   *Ashley Furniture Industries:* https://www.ashleyfurnitureindustriesinc.com/.

5   *A study:* "Telehealth: A quarter-trillion-dollar post-COVID-19 reality?," McKinsey & Company, https://www.mckinsey.com/~/media/McKinsey/Industries/Healthcare%20Systems%20and%20Services/Our%20Insights/Telehealth%20A%20quarter%20trillion%20dollar%20post%20COVID%2019%20reality/Telehealth-A-quarter-trilliondollar-post-COVID-19-reality.ashx.

6   *Healthcare Bluebook:* https://www.healthcarebluebook.com/.

8   *Organisation for Economic Co-operation and Development:* Organisation for Economic Co-operation and Development (OECD), Frequently Requested Health Data, November, 2019, http://www.oecd.org/health/OECD-Health-Statistics-2019-Frequently-Requested-Data.xls.

13   *recent:* Health, United States, 2018, National Center for Health Statistics, Hyattsville, Maryland, 2019, https://www.cdc.gov/nchs/data/hus/hus18.pdf.

Chapter 2: Health Insurance: Friend and Foe

15   *subject of a book I wrote:* Philip Moeller, *Get What's Yours for Medicare: Maximize Your Coverage, Minimize Your Costs* (New York: Simon & Schuster, 2016), https://www.amazon.com/Get-Whats-Yours-Medicare-Maximize/dp/1501124005/.

15   *primary reason for its invention:* Peter L. Bernstein, *Against the Gods: The Remarkable Story of Risk* (New York: Wiley, 1998), https://www.amazon.com/Against-Gods-Remarkable-Story-Risk/dp/0471295639/.

17 *Patient Protection and Affordable Care Act:* Patient Protection and Affordable Care Act, HealthCare.gov, U.S. Centers for Medicare & Medicaid Services, https://www.healthcare.gov/where-can-i-read -the-affordable-care-act/.

20 *employers need to follow:* Federal rules on high-deductible health plans, HealthCare.gov, U.S. Centers for Medicare & Medicaid Services, https://www.healthcare.gov/glossary/high-deductible-health-plan/.

21 *IRS Publication 969:* "Health Savings Accounts and Other Tax-Favored Health Plans," IRS Publication 969, https://www.irs.gov /pub/irs-pdf/p969.pdf.

22 *23andme:* https://www.23andme.com/.

22 *IRS Publication 502:* "Medical and Dental Expenses," IRS Publication 502, https://www.irs.gov/pub/irs-pdf/p502.pdf.

24 *More than one-third:* "Health Care Administrative Costs in the United States and Canada, 2017," *Annals of Internal Medicine*, January 21, 2020, https://annals.org/aim/article-abstract/2758511/health -care-administrative-costs-united-states-canada-2017.

24 *Dignity Health:* https://www.dignityhealth.org/.

25 *posted a story:* "How One Employer Stuck a New Mom with an $898,984 Bill for Her Premature Baby," ProPublica, November 4, 2019, https://www.propublica.org/article/how-one-employer-stuck -a-new-mom-with-a-bill-for-her-premature-baby.

26 *how Medicare covers something:* "What Medicare Covers," Medicare .gov, U.S. Centers for Medicare & Medicaid Services, https://www. medicare.gov/what-medicare-covers.

Chapter 3: Employers Get to Work on Health Care

34 *article:* "How Employers Are Fixing Health Care," *Harvard Business Review*, March 2019, https://hbr.org/cover-story/2019/03/how -employers-are-fixing-health-care.

34 *Health Affairs:* "Self-Insured Employers Are Using Price Transparency to Improve Contracting with Health Care Providers: The Indiana Experience," *Health Affairs*, October 7, 2019, https://www .healthaffairs.org/do/10.1377/hblog20191003.778513/full/.

35 Rosen Hotels & Resorts: https://www.rosenhotels.com/.

35   *RosenCare:* https://www.rosencare.com/.

35   *employer insurance premiums:* "Average Annual Single Premium per Enrolled Employee for Employer-Based Health Insurance," Kaiser Family Foundation, 2018, https://www.kff.org/other/state-indicator /single-coverage/.

36   *was updated:* Paul Starr, *The Social Transformation of American Medicine: The Rise of a Sovereign Profession and the Making of a Vast Industry,* 2nd ed. (New York: Basic Books, 2017), https://www.amazon.com/Social -Transformation-American-Medicine-Profession/dp/0465093027/.

37   *Haven:* https://havenhealthcare.com/.

37   *Lisa Woods:* "The Future of Healthcare with Lisa Woods, US Strategy and Design for Walmart," Thrive Global, February 18, 2020, https://thriveglobal.com/stories/the-future-of-healthcare-with-lisa -woods-senior-director-of-strategy-and-design-for-u-s-benefits-at -walmart/.

37   *her and company CEO Doug McMillon:* "World's 50 Greatest Leaders," *Fortune,* 2019, https://fortune.com/worlds-greatest-leaders/2019 /doug-mcmillon-lisa-woods/.

38   *Covera Health:* https://www.coverahealth.com/.

38   *Grand Rounds:* https://grandrounds.com/.

40   *wrote in early 2020:* "Self-Insured Companies Do No Better on Cost Control," *Axios,* January 27, 2020, https://www.axios.com/ employers-health-care-insurance-costs-57f06e79-dbb8-4233-898d -f5fd7664d201.html.

42   *Crossover Health:* https://crossoverhealth.com/.

44   *annual outlook:* "National Business Group on Health Identifies Six Open Enrollment Trends for 2020," Business Group on Health, September 25, 2019, https://www.businessgrouphealth.org/who-we-are /newsroom/press-releases/identifies-six-open-enrollment-trends-for -2020.

44   *sixteen Walmart COE providers:* "The 16 Health Systems to Which Walmart Sends Employees for Care," *Becker's Hospital Review,* May 21, 2019, https://www.beckershospitalreview.com/strategy/the-16 -health-systems-where-walmart-sends-employees-for-care.html.

44   *Optum:* https://www.optum.com/.

45 *Rally:* https://health.werally.com/partner/optum/optum_360/register/.

46 *are booming:* "2019: The Year We Learned to Love Instability," Mercer, January 7, 2020, https://www.mercer.us/our-thinking/healthcare/2019-the-year-we-learned-to-love-instability.html.

46 *Anthem's:* "Say Hi to Sydney, Anthem's Mobile App," Anthem, November 25, 2019, https://www.anthem.com/ca/blog/member-news/sydney-app-anthem-ca/.

46 *Aetna's:* "Health is the Real Win," Aetna, https://www.attainbyaetna.com/.

46 *digital health care:* "Health on Demand," U.S. Report, Mercer, February 2020, https://www.mercer.us/our-thinking/health/mercer-marsh-benefits-health-on-demand.html.

49 *Motion:* https://www.unitedhealthcaremotion.com/.

49 *Healthcare Bluebook:* https://www.healthcarebluebook.com/.

49 *Health Care Cost Institute:* https://www.healthcostinstitute.org/.

Chapter 4: The Affordable Care Act and Other Health Plans

51 *Kaiser Family Foundation's:* Featured Affordable Care Act Resources, Kaiser Family Foundation, https://www.kff.org/tag/affordable-care-act/.

51 *2020 ACA primer:* "Explaining Health Care Reform: Questions About Health Insurance Subsidies," Kaiser Family Foundation, January 16, 2020, https://www.kff.org/health-reform/issue-brief/explaining-health-care-reform-questions-about-health/.

51 *certain circumstances:* "Dates and Deadlines for 2020 Health Insurance," HealthCare.gov, U.S. Centers for Medicare & Medicaid Services, https://www.healthcare.gov/quick-guide/dates-and-deadlines/.

51 *Preventive health services:* "Preventive health services," HealthCare.gov, U.S. Centers for Medicare & Medicaid Services, https://www.healthcare.gov/coverage/preventive-care-benefits/.

51 *Coverage for preexisting conditions:* "Coverage for pre-existing conditions," HealthCare.gov, U.S. Centers for Medicare & Medicaid Services, https://www.healthcare.gov/coverage/pre-existing-conditions/.

52 *Dental coverage in the marketplace:* "Dental Coverage in the Marketplace," HealthCare.gov, U.S. Centers for Medicare & Medicaid Services, https://www.healthcare.gov/coverage/dental-coverage/.

52   *Birth control benefits:* "Birth Control Benefits," HealthCare.gov, U.S. Centers for Medicare & Medicaid Services, https://www.healthcare .gov/coverage/birth-control-benefits/.

52   *Breastfeeding benefits:* "Breastfeeding Benefits," HealthCare.gov, U.S. Centers for Medicare & Medicaid Services, https://www.healthcare .gov/coverage/breast-feeding-benefits/.

52   *Mental health and substance abuse coverage:* "Mental Health & Substance Abuse Coverage," HealthCare.gov, U.S. Centers for Medicare & Medicaid Services, https://www.healthcare.gov/coverage/mental -health-substance-abuse-coverage/.

52   *Emergency services:* "Emergency Services," HealthCare.gov, U.S. Centers for Medicare & Medicaid Services, https://www.healthcare .gov/using-marketplace-coverage/getting-emergency-care/.

52   *Pregnancy, maternity, and newborn care:* "Pregnancy, Maternity, and Newborn Care," HealthCare.gov, U.S. Centers for Medicare & Medicaid Services, https://www.healthcare.gov/what-if-im-pregnant -or-plan-to-get-pregnant/.

52   *Mental health and substance use disorder services:* "Mental Health and Substance Use Disorder Services," HealthCare.gov, U.S. Centers for Medicare & Medicaid Services, https://www.healthcare.gov/coverage /mental-health-substance-abuse-coverage/.

52   *Preventive and wellness services:* "Preventive and Wellness Services," HealthCare.gov, U.S. Centers for Medicare & Medicaid Services, https://www.healthcare.gov/coverage/preventive-care-benefits/.

53   *Federal Poverty Level guidelines:* "HHS Poverty Guidelines for 2020," U.S. Department of Health and Human Services, https://aspe.hhs .gov/poverty-guidelines.

53   *a flowchart:* "Premium Tax Credit Flow Chart: Are You Eligible?" IRS, https://www.irs.gov/affordable-care-act/individuals-and-families /premium-tax-credit-flow-chart-are-you-eligible.

53   *Publication 5187:* "Affordable Care Act: What You and Your Family Need to Know," Publication 5187, IRS, https://www.irs.gov/pub/irs -pdf/p5187.pdf.

53   *Instructions for Form 8962:* "Instructions for Form 8962," IRS, https:// www.irs.gov/pub/irs-pdf/i8962.pdf.

53 *Form 8962:* "Premium Tax Credit (PTC)," Form 8962, IRS, https:// www.irs.gov/pub/irs-pdf/f8962.pdf.

53 *summary page:* "About Form 8962, Premium Tax Credit," IRS, https://www.irs.gov/forms-pubs/about-form-8962.

54 *ACA navigator:* Find Local Help," HealthCare.gov, U.S. Centers for Medicare & Medicaid Services, https://localhelp.healthcare.gov/#/.

54 *ACA calculator:* Health Insurance Marketplace Calculator, Kaiser Family Foundation, https://www.kff.org/interactive/subsidy-calculator/.

54 *an online tool:* Income levels and ACA savings, HealthCare.gov, U.S. Centers for Medicare & Medicaid Services, https://www.healthcare .gov/lower-costs/.

54 *an online map:* "Insurer Participation on ACA Marketplaces, 2014– 2020," Kaiser Family Foundation, https://www.kff.org/private -insurance/issue-brief/insurer-participation-on-aca-marketplaces -2014-2020/.

55 *homeless:* "How to Claim an Exemption if You Were Homeless," HealthCare.gov, U.S. Centers for Medicare & Medicaid Services, https://www.healthcare.gov/exemptions-tool/#/results/2018/details/ homeless.

55 *eviction or foreclosure:* "How to Claim an Exemption Because You Experienced Eviction or Foreclosure," HealthCare.gov, U.S. Centers for Medicare & Medicaid Services, https://www.healthcare.gov /exemptions-tool/#/results/2018/details/eviction.

55 *utility shut-off notice:* "How to Claim an Exemption Due to a Utility Shut-off," HealthCare.gov, U.S. Centers for Medicare & Medicaid Services, https://www.healthcare.gov/exemptions-tool/#/results/2018 /details/utilities-shut-off.

55 *domestic violence:* "How to Claim an Exemption if You Experienced Domestic Violence," HealthCare.gov, U.S. Centers for Medicare & Medicaid Services, https://www.healthcare.gov/exemptions-tool/# /results/2018/details/domestic-violence.

55 *a death in the family:* "How to Claim an Exemption Due to the Death of a Close Family Member," HealthCare.gov, U.S. Centers for Medicare & Medicaid Services, https://www.healthcare.gov/exemptions -tool/#/results/2018/details/death-in-family.

55   *a natural disaster:* "How to Claim an Exemption Due to Fire, Flood, or Other Disaster," HealthCare.gov, U.S. Centers for Medicare & Medicaid Services, https://www.healthcare.gov/exemptions-tool/#/results /2018/details/disaster.

55   *bankruptcy:* "How to Claim an Exemption if You Filed for Bankruptcy," HealthCare.gov, U.S. Centers for Medicare & Medicaid Services, https://www.healthcare.gov/exemptions-tool/#/results /2018/details/bankruptcy.

55   *medical expenses:* "How to Claim an Exemption for Unpaid Medical Expenses," HealthCare.gov, U.S. Centers for Medicare & Medicaid Services, https://www.healthcare.gov/exemptions-tool/#/results /2018/details/owe-medical-expenses.

55   *caregiver expenses:* "How to Claim an Exemption Due to Increased Expenses Caring for a Family Member," HealthCare.gov, U.S. Centers for Medicare & Medicaid Services, https://www.healthcare.gov /exemptions-tool/#/results/2018/details/care-for-family.

55   *child medical support:* "How to Claim an Exemption for a Child Who's Medically Supported by Another Party and Not Eligible for Medicaid or CHIP," HealthCare.gov, U.S. Centers for Medicare & Medicaid Services, https://www.healthcare.gov/exemptions-tool/#/results /2018/details/medicaid-chip-denied.

55   *eligibility appeals:* "How to Claim an Exemption if You Were Uncovered While Waiting for a Successful Appeal," HealthCare.gov, U.S. Centers for Medicare & Medicaid Services, https://www.health-care.gov/exemptions-tool/#/results/2018/details/eligible-based-on -appeal.

55   *ineligible for Medicaid:* "How to Claim an Exemption if You Would Have Qualified for Medicaid if Your State Had Expanded Coverage," HealthCare.gov, U.S. Centers for Medicare & Medicaid Services, https://www.healthcare.gov/exemptions-tool/#/results/2018 /details/secretary-hardship.

56   Healthcare.gov: "Out-of-Pocket Maximum/Limit," on ACA-covered health expenses, HealthCare.gov, U.S. Centers for Medicare & Medicaid Services, https://www.healthcare.gov/glossary/out-of-pocket -maximum-limit/.

56 *struck down:* "Obamacare Insurance Mandate Is Struck Down by Federal Appeals Court," *New York Times,* December 18, 2019, https://www.nytimes.com/2019/12/18/health/obamacare-mandate.html.

56 *3 million people*: "Short-term Plans Enrolled 3 Million People, House Committee Finds," *Modern Healthcare*, June 26, 2020, https://www.modernhealthcare.com/insurance/short-term-plans-enrolled-3-million-people-house-committee-finds.

57 *a guide:* "The Expansion of Short-Term Limited-Duration Policies and Implications for Patients," Milliman, https://milliman-cdn.azureedge.net/-/media/milliman/pdfs/articles/patient-implications-brief-20200224.ashx.

58 *a million people:* "New York State Investigates Christian Health Cost-Sharing Affiliate," *New York Times,* January 8, 2020, https://www.nytimes.com/2020/01/08/health/christian-health-insurance-subpoena.html.

59 *studies regularly find:* "VA Health System Generally Delivers Higher-Quality Care Than Other Health Providers," RAND Corporation, April 26, 2018, https://www.rand.org/news/press/2018/04/26.html.

59 Wounds of War: Suzanne Gordon, *Wounds of War: How the VA Delivers Health, Healing, and Hope to the Nation's Veterans* (Ithaca, NY: Cornell University Press, 2018), https://www.amazon.com/Wounds-War-Delivers-Veterans-Politics-ebook/dp/B07BTCBP64/ref.

60 *extensive survey:* "2018 Survey of Veteran Enrollees' Health and Use of Health Care," Advanced Survey Design, January 9, 2019, https://www.va.gov/HEALTHPOLICYPLANNING/SOE2018/2018EnrolleeDataFindingsReport_9January2019Final508Compliant.pdf.

61 *preferred generic drugs:* "2020 Tier 1 Copay Medication List," Veterans Health Administration, https://www.pbm.va.gov/PBM/Tiered_Copay/Tier_1_CO-PAY_MEDICATION_LIST.pdf.

Heroes II: The Insurance Claims Expert Marsha Meytlis

63 *developmental delay:* "Developmental Delay," Michigan Medicine, University of Michigan, http://www.med.umich.edu/yourchild/topics/devdel.htm.

64 *Applied Behavior Analysis:* "Applied Behavior Analysis," *Psychology Today*, https://www.psychologytoday.com/us/therapy-types/applied -behavior-analysis.

66 *FaxZero.com:* https://faxzero.com/.

Chapter 5: Medicare Coverage, Costs, and Concerns

68 *Medicare book:* Philip Moeller, *Get What's Yours for Medicare: Maximize Your Coverage, Minimize Your Costs* (New York: Simon & Schuster, 2016), https://www.amazon.com/Get-Whats-Yours-Medicare -Maximize/dp/1501124005/.

68 *Get What's Yours:* http://getwhatsyours.org/medicare/.

69 *current enrollee costs:* "Medicare Costs at a Glance," Medicare.gov, U.S. Centers for Medicare & Medicaid Services, https://www .medicare.gov/your-medicare-costs/medicare-costs-at-a-glance.

69 *provides broad coverage:* "What Medicare Covers," Medicare.gov, U.S. Centers for Medicare & Medicaid Services, https://www.medicare .gov/what-medicare-covers.

69 *guide to Medigap: Choosing a Medigap Policy: A Guide to Health Insurance for People with Medicare*, Medicare.gov, U.S. Centers for Medicare & Medicaid Services, https://www.medicare.gov/pubs/pdf /02110-medicare-medigap-guide.pdf.

71 *link to current rates:* "Medicare Costs at a Glance," Medicare.gov, U.S. Centers for Medicare & Medicaid Services, https://www.medicare .gov/your-medicare-costs/medicare-costs-at-a-glance.

75 *MA plans can include:* "Medicare Advantage Plans Cover All Medicare Services," Medicare.gov, U.S. Centers for Medicare & Medicaid Services, https://www.medicare.gov/what-medicare-covers/what -medicare-health-plans-cover/medicare-advantage-plans-cover-all -medicare-services.

75 *four savings programs:* "Medicare Savings Programs," Medicare.gov, U.S. Centers for Medicare & Medicaid Services, https://www .medicare.gov/your-medicare-costs/help-paying-costs/medicare -savings-program/medicare-savings-programs.html.

76 *projects: The Budget and Economic Outlook: 2020 to 2030*, Congressional Budget Office, January 2020, https://www.cbo.gov/publication/56073.

77   *MedPAC's reports*: "Medicare and the Health Care Delivery System," Medicare Payment Advisory Commission Report to the Congress, June 2020, http://www.medpac.gov/docs/default-source/reports/jun20_reporttocongress_sec.pdf?sfvrsn=0.

77   *MACPAC*: Medicaid and CHIP Payment and Access Commission, https://www.macpac.gov/.

78   *annual maximum deductibles*: "Yearly Deductible for Drug Plans," Medicare.gov, U.S. Centers for Medicare & Medicaid Services, https://www.medicare.gov/drug-coverage-part-d/costs-for-medicare-drug-coverage/yearly-deductible-for-drug-plans.

78   *current rules*: "Costs for Medicare Drug Coverage," Medicare.gov, U.S. Centers for Medicare & Medicaid Services, https://www.medicare.gov/drug-coverage-part-d/costs-for-medicare-drug-coverage.

80   *complete this Extra Help application*: "Extra Help with Medicare Prescription Drug Plan Costs," U.S. Social Security Administration, https://secure.ssa.gov/i1020/start.

81   *Plan Finder*: "Find a Medicare Plan," Medicare.gov, U.S. Centers for Medicare & Medicaid Services, https://www.medicare.gov/find-a-plan/questions/home.aspx.

82   *useful rundown*: "Medigap Enrollment and Consumer Protections Vary Across States," Kaiser Family Foundation, July 2018, http://files.kff.org/attachment/Issue-Brief-Medigap-Enrollment-and-Consumer-Protections-Vary-Across-States.

82   *Medigap Finder*: "Find a Medigap Policy That Works for You," Medicare.gov, U.S. Centers for Medicare & Medicaid Services, https://www.medicare.gov/medigap-supplemental-insurance-plans/.

83   *set by rules*: "IRMAA Sliding Scale Tables," Program Operations Manual System (POMS), U.S. Social Security Administration, https://secure.ssa.gov/poms.nsf/lnx/0601101020.

84   *TurboTax*: "What Is the Difference Between AGI and MAGI on Your Taxes?" Intuit TurboTax, https://turbotax.intuit.com/tax-tips/irs-tax-return/what-is-the-difference-between-agi-and-magi-on-your-taxes/L7kHckNS3.

85 *COBRA:* "Continuation of Health Coverage (COBRA)," U.S. Department of Labor, https://www.dol.gov/general/topic/health-plans/cobra.

Chapter 6: Medicaid: A Program Everyone May Need

87 *split about 60–40:* "Medicaid Financing: The Basics," Kaiser Family Foundation, https://www.kff.org/medicaid/issue-brief/medicaid-financing-the-basics/.

87 *Nearly 70 percent: Acceptance of New Patients with Public and Private Insurance by Office-Based Physicians: United States, 2013,* National Center on Disease Statistics, Centers for Disease Control and Prevention, U.S. Department of Health and Human Services, https://www.cdc.gov/nchs/products/databriefs/db195.htm.

88 *research finds:* "Data Note: Three Findings about Access to Care and Health Outcomes in Medicaid," Kaiser Family Foundation, March 23, 2017, https://www.kff.org/medicaid/issue-brief/data-note-three-findings-about-access-to-care-and-health-outcomes-in-medicaid/.

88 *2020 report: Medicaid and CHIP Eligibility, Enrollment, and Cost Sharing Policies as of January 2020: Findings from a 50-State Survey,* Kaiser Family Foundation, March 2020, http://files.kff.org/attachment/Report-Medicaid-and-CHIP-Eligibility,-Enrollment-and-Cost-Sharing-Policies-as-of-January-2020.pdf.

89 *averaged thirty months: Medicaid Home and Community-Based Services Enrollment and Spending,* Kaiser Family Foundation, https://www.kff.org/medicaid/issue-brief/medicaid-home-and-community-based-services-enrollment-and-spending/.

90 *online national locator:* "Find Aging Resources in Your Area," National Association of Area Agencies on Aging, https://www.n4a.org/.

90 *same functional eligibility: Key State Policy Choices About Medicaid Home and Community-Based Services,* Kaiser Family Foundation, http://files.kff.org/attachment/Issue-Brief-Key-State-Policy-Choices-About-Medicaid-Home-and-Community-Based-Services.

90 *ADvancing States:* http://www.advancingstates.org/.

94 *according to:* "Medicaid's Treatment of the Home," Martindale, December 19. 2019, https://www.martindale.com/legal-news/article_levene-gouldin-thompson-llp_2522603.htm.

94 *Medicare Savings Programs:* Medicare Savings Programs, Medicare .gov, U.S. Centers for Medicare & Medicaid Services, https://www .medicare.gov/your-medicare-costs/get-help-paying-costs/medicare -savings-programs.

94 *Extra Help:* "Find Your Level of Extra Help (Part D)," Medicare .gov, U.S. Centers for Medicare & Medicaid Services, https:// www.medicare.gov/your-medicare-costs/get-help-paying-costs/find -your-level-of-extra-help-part-d.

94 *State Health Insurance Assistance Program:* State Health Insurance Assistance Programs, https://www.shiptacenter.org//.

95 *directory of state programs:* "Directory of State ABLE Account Programs," Academy of Special Needs Planners, https://specialneeds answers.com/able-accounts.

Chapter 7: Your Personal Health Plan

105 *Research done a few years ago:* "The Association Between Income and Life Expectancy in the United States, 2001–2014," *Journal of the American Medical Association (JAMA)*, April 26, 2016, https://jama network.com/journals/jama/fullarticle/2513561.

106 *a deep dive:* "Knowing Is Not Enough—Act on Your Family Health History," Centers for Disease Control and Prevention, U.S. Department of Health and Human Services, https://www.cdc.gov/genomics /famhistory/knowing_not_enough.htm.

106 *online family history form:* "My Family Health Portrait," Centers for Disease Control and Prevention, U.S. Department of Health and Human Services, https://phgkb.cdc.gov/FHH/html/index.html.

107 *genomics information:* "Genomics and Health Resources (A–Z)," Centers for Disease Control and Prevention, U.S. Department of Health and Human Services, https://phgkb.cdc.gov/PHGKB/phgHome .action?action=a2z.

107 *23andMe:* https://www.23andme.com/

108   *expanding array of reports:* "Reports Included in All Services,"
       23andMe, https://www.23andme.com/dna-reports-list/.

108   *a directory:* "Find a Genetic Counselor," National Society of Genetic
       Counselors, https://www.nsgc.org/page/find-a-genetic-counselor.

109   *Nebula Genetics:* https://nebula.org/anonymous-sequencing.

109   *preventive health tool:* "What Is Preventive Health on Facebook?"
       Facebook,   https://www.facebook.com/help/279392126259317?ref
       =preventive_health_microsite.

109   *Federally Qualified Health Centers:* "Federally Qualified Health Cen-
       ters," Health Resources & Services Administration, U.S. Department
       of Health and Human Services, https://www.hrsa.gov/opa/eligibility
       -and-registration/health-centers/fqhc/index.html.

111   *U.S. Preventive Services Task Force:* https://www.uspreventiveservices
       taskforce.org/.

111   *Advisory Committee on Immunization Practices:* Advisory Committee
       on Immunization Practices, Centers for Disease Control and Pre-
       vention, U.S. Department of Health and Human Services, https://
       www.cdc.gov/vaccines/acip/index.html.

111   *American Academy of Pediatrics:* https://www.aap.org/en-us/Pages
       /Default.aspx.

111   *Health Resources and Services Administration:* https://www.hrsa.gov/.

112   *top-graded preventive care measures:* "USPSTF A and B Recom-
       mendations," U.S. Preventive Services Task Force, https://www
       .uspreventiveservicestaskforce.org/Page/Name/uspstf-a-and-b-rec
       ommendations/.

112   *a 2018 study:* "Few Americans Receive All High-Priority, Appropriate
       Clinical Preventive Services," *Health Affairs,* June 2018, https://www
       .healthaffairs.org/doi/10.1377/hlthaff.2017.1248.

Chapter 8: Your Personal Care Team

115   *Health care:* Trudy Lieberman, *Consumer Reports Complete Guide to
       Health Services for Seniors* (New York: Three Rivers Press, 2000),
       https://www.amazon.com/Consumer-Reports-Complete-Services
       -Seniors/dp/0812931475/.

115 *read it online:* "Health Care Journalist Struggles to Navigate Her Own Health Crisis," Tarbell, February 25, 2019, https://tarbell.org/2019/02 /health-care-journalist-struggles-to-navigates-her-own-health-crisis/.

119 *free patient access:* "UpToDate Subscriptions for Patients and Caregivers," Wolters Kluwer, https://www.uptodate.com/home/uptodate -subscription-options-patients.

120 *PatientsLikeMe:* https://www.patientslikeme.com/.

120 The Patient Will See You Now: Eric Topol, MD, *The Patient Will See You Now: The Future of Medicine Is in Your Hands* (New York: Basic Books, 2016), https://www.amazon.com/Patient-Will-See-You-Now /dp/0465040020/.

120 *WEGO Health:* https://www.wegohealth.com/.

121 *community standards:* "Community Standards," Facebook, https:// www.facebook.com/communitystandards/introduction.

122 *National Finance Resource Directory:* "National Finance Resource Directory," Patient Advocate Foundation, https://www.patientadvocate .org/explore-our-resources/national-financial-resource-directory/.

123 *Center for Improving Value in Health Care:* https://www.civhc.org/.

124 *a 2018 study:* "Assessment of US Hospital Compliance with Regulations for Patients' Requests for Medical Records," *Journal of the American Medical Association (JAMA),* October 5, 2018, https://jama network.com/journals/jamanetworkopen/fullarticle/2705850.

125 *Prepare for Your Care:* https://prepareforyourcare.org/welcome.

125 *downloaded for your state:* "Downloading Your State's Advance Directive," National Hospice and Palliative Care Organization, https://www .nhpco.org/patients-and-caregivers/advance-care-planning/advance -directives/downloading-your-states-advance-directive/.

126 *Social Security:* "Form SSA-1696—Appointment of Representative," U.S. Social Security Administration, https://www.ssa.gov/forms/ssa -1696.html.

126 *Medicare:* "Appointment of Representative," U.S. Centers for Medicare & Medicaid Services, https://www.cms.gov/Medicare/CMS -Forms/CMS-Forms/downloads/cms1696.pdf.

127 *state directory:* "Click a state for more information," National POLST Paradigm, https://polst.org/programs-in-your-state/.

Heroes IV: The Social Media Maven Julie Croner

129 *avascular necrosis:* "What Is Avascular Necrosis?" Johns Hopkins Medicine, https://www.hopkinsmedicine.org/health/conditions-and -diseases/avascular-necrosis.

131 *Regenexx:* https://regenexx.com/.

131 *Centeno-Schultz Clinic:* https://centenoschultz.com/.

Chapter 9: Your Professional Care Team

133 *live longer and healthier:* "Interpersonal Continuity of Care and Care Outcomes: A Critical Review," *Annals of Family Medicine,* March 2005, https://www.annfammed.org/content/3/2/159.

133 *Dr. Jennifer DeVoe:* https://www.ohsu.edu/providers/jennifer-e-devoe -md.

133 *Oregon Health & Science University:* https://www.ohsu.edu/.

134 *Knoema:* "US Population by Age and Generation in 2020," Knoema, April 16, 2020, https://knoema.com/infographics/egyydzc/us-popu lation-by-age-and-generation.

134 *Accenture: Accenture 2019 Digital Health Consumer Survey,* Accenture, March 2020, https://www.accenture.com/_acnmedia/pdf-94 /accenture-2019-digital-health-consumer-survey.pdf.

134 *sobering report: The Economic Consequences of Millennial Health,* Moody's Analytics and Blue Cross Blue Shield Association, November 6, 2019, https://www.bcbs.com/the-health-of-america/reports/how-millennials -current-and-future-health-could-affect-our-economy.

135 *emotional retelling:* "Dad's Last Week," *Annals of Family Medicine,* May 2016, http://www.annfammed.org/content/14/3/273.full.pdf+html.

135 *ranked 27th out of 36:* "Doctors," OECD Data, https://data.oecd.org /healthres/doctors.htm.

136 *predicts:* "New Findings Confirm Predictions on Physician Shortage," Association of American Medical Colleges, April 23, 2019, https:// www.aamc.org/news-insights/press-releases/new-findings-confirm -predictions-physician-shortage.

136 *reported:* "Geisinger's Med School to Provide Free Tuition for Primary-Care Students," *Modern Healthcare,* November 6, 2019,

https://www.modernhealthcare.com/physicians/geisingers-med
-school-provide-free-tuition-primary-care-students.

137 *UpToDate:* https://www.uptodate.com/home.

138 *Beth Bortz:* "Meet Our Team," Virginia Center for Health Innovation, https://www.vahealthinnovation.org/our-team/.

138 *direct primary care:* "Direct Primary Care Gains Ground as Employer Strategy," Mercer, July 9. 2020, https://www.mercer.us/our
-thinking/healthcare/direct-primary-care-as-a-strategy-to-manage
-cost.html.

139 *concierge medicine:* "What to Know About Concierge Medicine,"
AARP, April 25, 2019, https://www.aarp.org/health/conditions
-treatments/info-2019/what-to-know-about-concierge-medicine
.html.

139 *Accountable care organizations:* "Accountable Care Organizations
(ACOs): General Information," U.S. Centers for Medicare & Medicaid Services, https://innovation.cms.gov/initiatives/ACO/.

140 *Ambulatory Surgical Center:* "ASC Quality Reporting," U.S. Centers
for Medicare & Medicaid Services, https://www.cms.gov/Medicare
/Quality-Initiatives-Patient-Assessment-Instruments/ASC-Quality
-Reporting/index.html.

141 *Affordability concerns:* "Health Insurance Affordability Concerns and
Health Care Avoidance Among US Adults Approaching Retirement," *Journal of the American Medical Association (JAMA)*, February 7,
2020, https://jamanetwork.com/journals/jamanetworkopen/fullarticle
/2760437.

142 *formally asked:* "Implementation of Financial Education Curriculum
for Medical Students and Physicians in Training," American Medical
Association, October 2019, https://www.ama-assn.org/system/files
/2019-10/i19-refcomm-c-addendum.pdf.

142 *Dr. Caroline Sloan:* https://medicine.duke.edu/faculty/caroline-sloan
-md.

142 *The 7 Habits of Highly Effective Cost-of-Care Conversations:* "The 7
Habits of Highly Effective Cost-of-Care Conversations," *Annals
of Internal Medicine*, May 7, 2019, https://annals.org/aim/fullarticle
/2732826/7-habits-highly-effective-cost-care-conversations.

144 *surging growth:* "Implications of the Rapid Growth of the Nurse Practitioner Workforce in the US," *Health Affairs*, February 2020, https://www.healthaffairs.org/doi/full/10.1377/hlthaff.2019.00686.

145 *National Association of Free & Charitable Clinics:* http://www.nafcclinics.org/.

145 *searchable directory:* "Find Free/Low-Cost/Sliding Scale Clinics," NeedyMeds, https://www.needymeds.org/free-clinics-branch.

Chapter 10: What Quality Looks Like

148 *a 2019 survey: 2019 Healthcare Consumer Insight & Digital Engagement Survey,* Binary Fountain, September 2019, https://go.binaryfountain.com/2019-healthcare-consumer-insights-survey.html.

148 *Consumer Assessment of Healthcare Providers and Systems:* https://www.ahrq.gov/cahps/index.html.

149 *Healthgrades:* https://www.healthgrades.com/.

149 *RateMDs:* https://www.ratemds.com/.

149 *U.S. News & World Report:* https://health.usnews.com/doctors.

149 *ShareCare:* https://www.sharecare.com/.

149 *WebMD:* https://doctor.webmd.com/.

149 *Zocdoc:* https://www.zocdoc.com/.

149 *Vital Signs:* Vital Signs, ProPublica, https://projects.propublica.org/vital-signs/.

149 *state-by-state details:* "Your Doctor Might Have a Disciplinary Record. Here's How to Find Out," ProPublica, updated December 11, 2019, https://projects.propublica.org/graphics/investigating-doctors.

150 *recommends:* "Using Physician Rating Websites," Center for Advancing Health, GW Cancer Institute, 2016, https://www.guroo.com/#!insights/Quality/quality-using-physician-rating-websites.

150 *a thorough review: Empowering New Yorkers with Quality Measures That Matter to Them,* United Hospital Fund, December 2017, https://nyshealthfoundation.org/wp-content/uploads/2017/12/empowering-new-yorkers-with-quality-measures-dec-2017.pdf.

150 *Agency for Healthcare Research and Quality:* "Get to know the AHRQ Quality Indicators," Agency for Healthcare Research and Quality, https://www.qualityindicators.ahrq.gov/.

151 *recommended telehealth care:* "Virtual Visits", United HealthCare, https://www.uhc.com/individual-and-family/member-resources /health-care-tools/virtual-visits.

151 *the telehealth transition:* "Positioning Virtual Care to Transform Health Benefits," Mercer, June 4, 2020, https://www.mercer.us/our-thinking /healthcare/positioning-virtual-care-to-transform-health-benefits.html.

151 *do not have a primary care physician:* "One-Fourth Of Adults and Nearly Half of Adults Under 30 Don't Have a Primary Care Doctor," Kaiser Family Foundation, February 8, 2019, https://www .kff.org/other/slide/one-fourth-of-adults-and-nearly-half-of-adults -under-30-dont-have-a-primary-care-doctor/.

152 *American Telehealth Association:* https://www.americantelemed.org/.

153 *American Board of Medical Specialties:* https://www.abms.org/.

153 *Certification Matters:* https://www.certificationmatters.org/.

153 *Centers for Medicare & Medicaid Services:* https://www.cms.gov/.

154 *HHS.gov:* https://www.hhs.gov/.

154 *Physician Compare:* "Physician Compare," Medicare.gov, U.S. Centers for Medicare & Medicaid Services, https://www.medicare.gov/physi ciancompare/.

154 *Hospital Compare:* "Hospital Compare," Medicare.gov, U.S. Centers for Medicare & Medicaid Services, https://www.medicare.gov/hospi talcompare/search.html?.

154 *Nursing Home Compare:* "Nursing Home Compare," Medicare.gov, U.S. Centers for Medicare & Medicaid Services, https://www.medi care.gov/nursinghomecompare/search.html?.

154 *Hospice Compare:* "Hospice Compare," Medicare.gov, U.S. Centers for Medicare & Medicaid Services, https://www.medicare.gov/hospice compare/.

154 *Inpatient Rehabilitation Facility Compare:* "Inpatient Rehabilitation Facility Compare," Medicare.gov, U.S. Centers for Medicare & Medicaid Services, https://www.medicare.gov/inpatientrehabilita tionfacilitycompare/.

154 *Dialysis Facility Compare:* "Dialysis Facility Compare," Medicare.gov, U.S. Centers for Medicare & Medicaid Services, https://www.medi care.gov/dialysisfacilitycompare/.

154 *Home Health Compare:* "Home Health Compare," Medicare.gov, U.S. Centers for Medicare & Medicaid Services, https://www.medicare .gov/homehealthcompare/search.html.

154 *Long-Term Care Hospital Compare:* "Long-Term Care Hospital Compare," Medicare.gov, U.S. Centers for Medicare & Medicaid Services, https://www.medicare.gov/longtermcarehospitalcom pare/.

156 *Agency for Healthcare Research and Quality:* "Major Hospital Quality Measurement Sets," Agency for Healthcare Research and Quality, https://www.ahrq.gov/talkingquality/measures/setting/hospitals /measurement-sets.html.

156 *National Quality Forum:* http://www.qualityforum.org/About_NQF/.

157 *AHRQ Quality Indicators:* https://www.qualityindicators.ahrq.gov/.

157 *National Hospital Quality Measures:* "Measures," Joint Commission, https://www.jointcommission.org/measurement/measures/.

157 *CAHPS Hospital Survey:* "CAHPS Adult Hospital Survey," Agency for Healthcare Research and Quality, https://www.ahrq.gov/cahps /surveys-guidance/hospital/about/adult_hp_survey.html.

157 *ORYX:* "ORYX Performance Measurement Reporting," Joint Commission, https://www.jointcommission.org/measurement/reporting /accreditation-oryx/.

157 *The Leapfrog Group:* http://www.leapfroggroup.org/.

157 *The Advisory Board:* https://www.advisory.com/.

157 *series of briefs:* "How Hospital Quality Ratings Work," Advisory Board, February 2020, https://www.advisory.com/research/physician -executive-council/resources/2017/metrics-used-in-hospital-quality -rating-programs#CMSstar.

157 *evaluated:* "Rating the Raters: An Evaluation of Publicly Reported Hospital Quality Rating Systems," *New England Journal of Medicine*, August 14, 2019, https://catalyst.nejm.org/doi/full/10.1056 /CAT.19.0629.

157 *conflicting ratings:* "National Hospital Ratings Systems Share Few Common Scores and May Generate Confusion Instead of Clarity," *Health Affairs*, March 2015, https://www.healthaffairs.org/doi/full /10.1377/hlthaff.2014.0201.

158 *conflicting information for patients:* "Consumers' Interest in Provider Ratings Grows, and Improved Report Cards and Other Steps Could Accelerate Their Use," *Health Affairs*, April 2016, https://www.healthaffairs.org/doi/10.1377/hlthaff.2015.1654.

158 *IBM/Watson Health:* "IBM Watson Health Recognizes Top -Performing U.S. Hospitals and Health Systems," IBM, June 20, 2020, https://www.prnewswire.com/news-releases/ibm-watson -health-recognizes-top-performing-us-hospitals-and-health-systems -301085296.html.

159 *assessed Nursing Home Compare:* "Does Nursing Home Compare Reflect Patient Safety in Nursing Homes?" *Health Affairs*, November 2018, https://www.healthaffairs.org/doi/full/10.1377/hlthaff.2018.0721.

159 *provides details:* "Nursing Home Staffing 2019 Q3," Long Term Care Community Coalition, https://nursinghome411.org/category/nursing -home-information/staffing/.

159 *who has reviewed:* "How Are Nursing Homes Doing When It Comes to Staffing? This Tool Helps You Find Out," Association of Health Care Journalists, January 3, 2020, https://healthjournalism.org/blog /2020/01/how-are-nursing-homes-doing-when-it-comes-to-staffing -this-tool-helps-you-find-out/.

160 *of her program:* "How to Find a Long-Term Care Ombudsman Program," National Consumer Voice for Quality Long-Term Care, https://theconsumervoice.org/get_help.

160 *National Association of Area Agencies on Aging:* https://www.n4a.org/.

160 *find one near you:* "PACEFinder: Find a PACE Program in Your Neighborhood," National PACE Association, https://www.npaonline .org/pace-you/pacefinder-find-pace-program-your-neighborhood.

160 *rules adopted in 2019:* "Medicare and Medicaid Programs; Revision of Requirements for Long-Term Care Facilities: Arbitration Agreements," *Federal Register*, July 18. 2019, https://www.federalregister .gov/documents/2019/07/18/2019-14945/medicare-and-medicaid -programs-revision-of-requirements-for-long-term-care-facilities -arbitration.

161 *lack the fact-based comparative rankings:* "Quality Measurement Lags in the Outpatient Surgery Arena," *Modern Healthcare*, April 6, 2019,

https://www.modernhealthcare.com/safety-quality/quality-measure
ment-lags-outpatient-surgery-arena.

161 *performance information*: "Quality Measures Developed and Tested
by the ASC Quality Collaboration," ASC Quality Collabora-
tion, https://higherlogicdownload.s3.amazonaws.com/ASCACON
NECT/1b34f1a1-0180-4005-9507-902fdf8f242e/UploadedImages
/ASC_Quality_Collaboration/Documents/2019-Summary-ASC-QC
-Measures.pdf.

Chapter 11: Unneeded and Misdiagnosed Care

170 *research found*: "Surgery for Blocked Arteries Is Often Unwarranted,
Researchers Find," *New York Times*, November 16, 2019, https://
www.nytimes.com/2019/11/16/health/heart-disease-stents-bypass
.html.

170 *American Board of Internal Medicine:* https://www.abim.org/.

170 *Choosing Wisely:* https://www.choosingwisely.org/.

171 *MedInsight Waste Calculator:* "MedInsight Health Waste Calculator,"
Milliman, https://milliman-cdn.azureedge.net/-/media/medinsight
/pdfs/medinsight-health-waste-calculator.ashx.

171 *A study found:* "Is Great Information Good Enough? Evidence from
Physicians as Patients," National Bureau of Economic Research,
https://www.nber.org/papers/w26038.

171 *The authors of the study:* "Do as the Doctor Says, Not as He or She
Does," *STAT*, July 22, 2019, https://www.statnews.com/2019/07/22
/doctors-information-personal-health-decisions/.

172 *2017 study:* "Treating, Fast and Slow: Americans' Understanding
of and Responses to Low-Value Care," *Milbank Quarterly*, March
2017, https://www.milbank.org/quarterly/articles/treating-fast-slow
-americans-understanding-responses-low-value-care/.

172 *Virginia Center on Health Innovation:* https://www.vahealthinnovation
.org/.

173 *A research study:* "Cascades of Care After Incidental Findings in a US
National Survey of Physicians," *Journal of the American Medical Association (JAMA)*, October 16, 2019, https://jamanetwork.com/journals
/jamanetworkopen/fullarticle/2752991.

173 *comprehensive study:* "Waste in the US Health Care System: Estimated Costs and Potential for Savings," *Journal of the American Medical Association (JAMA)*, October 7, 2019, https://jamanetwork.com /journals/jama/fullarticle/2752664.

175 *study: 2017 Statewide Low Value Services Report*, Virginia Center on Health Information, April 2917, http://www.vahealthinnovation.org /wp-content/uploads/2019/04/2017-Statewide-and-Regional-Low -Value-Service-Reports-Final.pdf.

175 *2018 analysis: Medicare and the Health Care Delivery System*, Medicare Payment Advisory Commission, June 2018, http://www.medpac.gov /docs/default-source/reports/jun18_medpacreporttocongress_rev _nov2019_note_sec.pdf?sfvrsn=0.

176 *Connecticut collaboration:* "Leveraging Choosing Wisely as a Tool for Achieving Health Equity," Connecticut Choosing Wisely Collaborative, July 2017, http://nebula.wsimg.com/dab11e19782c2936871939 6db04d1d01?AccessKeyId=EE1E8CCBEA1024792D71&dispositio n=0&alloworigin=1.

177 *four-page checklist:* "Improving Diagnosis in Health Care: Improving Resources for Patients, Families, and Health Care Professionals," Institute of Medicine, National Academy of Sciences, https://www.nap .edu/resource/21794/DiagnosticError_Toolkit.pdf.

177 *National Patient Safety Foundation:* https://npsf.digitellinc.com/npsf/.

177 *Society to Improve Diagnosis in Medicine:* https://www.improvediagno sis.org/.

177 *document never got presented:* "The Missing Pathology Report." Society to Improve Diagnosis in Medicine, https://www.improvediag nosis.org/stories_posts/the-missing-pathology-report/.

178 *Consumers Advancing Patient Safety:* https://www.patientsafety.org/.

178 *Patient-Centered Outcomes Research Center:* https://www.pcori.org/.

178 *Idaho Supreme Court:* "SHERIDAN v. John J. Jambura, M.D., David B. Bettis, M.D. and John Does I-V, Defendants," Supreme Court of Idaho, May 22, 2001, https://caselaw.findlaw.com/id-supreme-court /1364599.html.

179 *estimates made twenty years ago:* "Patient Safety 15 Years After To Err Is Human—NAM Symposium," National Academy of Medicine,

December 10, 2015, https://www8.nationalacademies.org/onpinews /newsitem.aspx?RecordID=12072015a.

179 *2014 study:* "The Frequency of Diagnostic Errors in Outpatient Care: Estimations from Three Large Observational Studies Involving US Adult Populations," *BMJ (British Medical Journal),* 2014, https://qualitysafety.bmj.com/content/23/9/727.

180 *acid reflux or GERD:* "Gastroesophageal Reflux Disease (GERD)," Mayo Clinic, https://www.mayoclinic.org/diseases-conditions/gerd /symptoms-causes/syc-20361940.

180 *Resource Directory:* https://www.patientadvocate.org/explore-our -resources/national-financial-resource-directory/.

181 *patient toolkit:* "Patient's Toolkit for Diagnosis," Society to Improve Diagnosis in Medicine, https://www.improvediagnosis.org/patients -toolkit/.

182 *a 2019 study:* "Diagnosis Errors Account for One-Third of Severe Harm Malpractice Claims," *Modern Healthcare,* July 11, 2019, https:// www.modernhealthcare.com/safety-quality/diagnosis-errors-account -one-third-severe-harm-malpractice-claims.

Chapter 12: When You're in Control, and When You're Not

185 *2017 research:* "One in Five Inpatient Emergency Department Cases May Lead to Surprise Bills," *Health Affairs,* January 2017, https:// www.healthaffairs.org/doi/full/10.1377/hlthaff.2016.0970?

185 *American College of Emergency Physicians:* "EMTALA Fact Sheet," American College of Emergency Physicians, https://www.acep.org /life-as-a-physician/ethics--legal/emtala/emtala-fact-sheet/.

186 *are charged more:* "Per Visit Emergency Department Expenditures by Insurance Type, 1996–2015," *Health Affairs,* July 2018, https://www .healthaffairs.org/doi/pdf/10.1377/hlthaff.2018.0083.

186 *2019 research:* "The High Cost of Avoidable Hospital Emergency Department Visits," UnitedHealth Group, July 22, 2019, https:// www.unitedhealthgroup.com/newsroom/posts/2019-07-22-high -cost-emergency-department-visits.html.

187 *ER Inspector:* "Be Prepared: Find the ER You Want to Go to Before an Emergency Happens," ProPublica, September 19, 2019, https://

www.propublica.org/article/prepared-find-the-er-you-want-to-go-to
-before-an-emergency-happens.

189 *American Ambulance Association:* https://ambulance.org/.

190 *Urgent Care Association (UCA):* https://www.ucaoa.org/.

191 *A 2017 study:* "Comparing Utilization and Costs of Care in Free-standing Emergency Departments, Hospital Emergency Departments, and Urgent Care Centers," *Annals of Emergency Medicine,* February 15, 2017, https://www.annemergmed.com/article/S0196
-0644(16)31522-0/abstract.

195 *enhanced recovery after surgery:* "Enhanced Recovery after Surgery," American Association of Nurse Anesthetists, https://www.aana.com
/practice/clinical-practice-resources/enhanced-recovery-after-surgery.

195 *an online checklist:* "Which Facility Is Best for My Outpatient Procedure?" Medicare.gov, U.S. Centers for Medicare & Medicaid Services, https://www.medicare.gov/what-medicare-covers/outpatient
-facility-checklist.

196 *Top 10 ASC Outpatient Procedures:* "Top Outpatient Procedures at Hospitals vs Surgery Centers," Definitive Healthcare, July 2019, https://blog.definitivehc.com/top-outpatient-procedures-at-hospitals
-versus-ascs.

197 *Healthcare Bluebook:* https://www.healthcarebluebook.com/.

198 *Patients Beyond Borders:* https://www.patientsbeyondborders.com/.

198 *Joint Commission:* https://www.jointcommission.org/.

198 *glossary:* "Glossary of Terms," Joint Commission, https://www.quality
check.org/glossary/.

198 *QualityCheck.org:* https://www.qualitycheck.org/.

198 *WorldHospitalSearch.org:* https://www.worldhospitalsearch.org/.

198 *specific procedures:* "Benefits of JCI Accreditation and Certification," worldhospitalsearch.org, Joint Commission International, https://
www.worldhospitalsearch.org/the-value-of-jci-accreditation/benefits
-of-jci-accreditation-and-certification/.

199 *price comparisons:* "International Medical Treatment Prices," Medical Tourism Association, https://www.medicaltourism.com/compare
-prices.

200 *Narayana Health:* https://www.narayanahealth.org/.

200 *The story:* "The World's Cheapest Hospital Has to Get Even Cheaper," *Bloomberg Businessweek,* March 26, 2019, https://www.bloomberg.com/news/features/2019-03-26/the-world-s-cheapest-hospital-has-to-get-even-cheaper.

200 *coronary thromboendarterectomy:* "Pulmonary Thromboendarterectomy," Cleveland Clinic, https://my.clevelandclinic.org/health/treatments/21024-pulmonary-thromboendarterectomy-surgery.

200 *MediBid.com:* https://www.medibid.com/.

200 *cost calculator:* https://www.medibid.com/cost-calculator/.

Heroes VI: The Warrior Mother Cynthia Buness

201 *published a piece:* "Oral Vancomycin Therapy in a Child with Primary Sclerosing Cholangitis and Severe Ulcerative Colitis," *pghn (Pediatric Gastroenterology, Hepatology & Nutrition),* September 2016, https://pghn.org/search.php?where=aview&id=10.5223/pghn.2016.19.3.210&code=1121PGHN&vmode=FULL.

Chapter 13: Shopping for Health Care

207 *controversial health insurance substitutes:* "'Sham' Sharing Ministries Test Faith of Patients and Insurance Regulators," *Kaiser Health News,* May 17, 2019, https://khn.org/news/sham-sharing-ministries-test-faith-of-patients-and-insurance-regulators/.

207 *cost calculator:* https://www.medibid.com/cost-calculator/.

208 *Patient Rights Advocates:* https://www.patientrightsadvocate.org/.

208 *Cynthia Fisher:* "A Powerful Lobbying Tool in the Trump Era: the President's Ear," *Wall Street Journal,* April 17, 2019, https://www.wsj.com/articles/a-powerful-lobbying-tool-in-the-trump-era-the-presidents-ear-11555493400.

208 *New Choice Health:* https://www.newchoicehealth.com/.

208 *ClearHealthCosts:* https://clearhealthcosts.com/.

208 *Surgery Center of Oklahoma:* https://surgerycenterok.com/.

208 *KISx Card:* https://getkisx.com/.

209 *downloads of its chargemaster:* "Hospital Standard Charges" (Excel spreadsheet), University of Utah Health, https://healthcare.utah.edu/bill/pdfs/standard-charges-to-publish.xlsx.

210 *2,900-item chargemaster:* "Intermountain Medical Center Charge-master" (Excel spreadsheet), Intermountain Healthcare, https://intermountainhealthcare.org/-/media/files/chargemasters/2019-cm/intermountain-medical-center---chargemaster.xlsx?la=en.

211 *report from Altarun:* "Revealing the Truth about Healthcare Price Transparency," Altarun, June 2018, https://www.healthcarevaluehub.org/advocate-resources/publications/revealing-truth-about-health care-price-transparency.

211 *later study by Altarum:* "Consumer-Centric Evaluation of Health-care Price and Quality Transparency Tools," Altarum, April 19, 2019, https://altarum.org/publications/consumer-centric-evaluation-healthcare-price-and-quality-transparency-tools.

213 *popularized by Malcolm Gladwell:* Malcolm Gladwell, "Complexity and the Ten-Thousand-Hour Rule," *New Yorker*, August 21, 2013, https://www.newyorker.com/sports/sporting-scene/complexity-and-the-ten-thousand-hour-rule.

216 *"Find a Fair Price":* "Find Your Fair Price," Healthcare Bluebook, https://www.healthcarebluebook.com/ui/consumerfront.

217 *Health Care Cost Institute:* https://www.healthcostinstitute.org/.

217 *Healthy Marketplace Index:* https://www.healthcostinstitute.org/research/hmi.

218 *Guroo.com:* https://www.guroo.com/#!

219 *FAIR Health:* https://www.fairhealthconsumer.org/.

219 *Healthcare Common Procedural Coding System:* "HCPCS—General Information," CMS.gov, U.S. Centers for Medicare & Medicaid Services, https://www.cms.gov/Medicare/Coding/MedHCPCSGenInfo/index.

219 *Procedure Price Lookup Tool:* https://www.medicare.gov/procedure-price-lookup/.

220 *keeps track:* "Interactive State Report Map," All-Payer Claims Database (APCD) Council, https://www.apcdcouncil.org/state/map.

221 *Maryland Health Care Commission:* http://mhcc.maryland.gov/.

221 *Center for Improving Value in Health Care:* https://www.civhc.org/.

222 *Illinois Hospital Report Card:* http://www.healthcarereportcard.illinois.gov/.

222 *Compare Maine:* https://www.comparemaine.org/.

222 *MNHealthScores:* http://www.mnhealthscores.org/.

222 *NH HealthCost:* https://nhhealthcost.nh.gov/.

222 *Oregon Hospital Guide:* https://oregonhospitalguide.org/.

222 *Hospital Report Cards:* "Review and Compare Hospitals Using Hospital Report Cards (2020)," Vermont Department of Health, https://www.healthvermont.gov/health-statistics-vital-records/health-care-systems-reporting/hospital-report-cards.

222 *Healthcare Pricing Transparency Report:* "Healthcare Pricing Transparency," Virginia Health Information, https://www.vhi.org/Healthcare Pricing/default.asp.

222 *Washington State MONAHRQ:* http://www.wamonahrq.net/.

222 *My Health Wisconsin:* http://wisconsinhealthinfo.org/.

223 *ViaCord:* https://www.viacord.com/.

Chapter 14: Getting and Paying for Drugs

225 *NeedyMeds:* https://www.needymeds.org/.

226 *insulin availability and pricing crisis:* "The Blame Game: Everyone and No One Is Raising Insulin Prices," *Kaiser Health News,* April 10, 2019, https://khn.org/news/the-blame-game-everyone-and-no-one-is-raising-insulin-prices/.

229 *Ardon Health:* http://ardonhealth.com/.

230 *Stelara:* https://www.stelarainfo.com/.

230 *FundFinder:* https://fundfinder.panfoundation.org/.

230 *pharmaceutical assistance programs:* "Find a Pharmaceutical Assistance Program for the Drugs You Take," Medicare.gov, U.S. Centers for Medicare & Medicaid Services, https://www.medicare.gov/pharmaceutical-assistance-program/.

230 *RxAssist:* https://www.rxassist.org/patients.

230 *National Financial Resource Directory:* https://www.patientadvocate.org/explore-our-resources/national-financial-resource-directory/.

231 *Several federal prosecutions:* "Fourth Foundation Resolves Allegations That It Conspired with Pharmaceutical Companies to Pay Kickbacks to Medicare Patients," U.S. Attorney's Office, District of Massachusetts, https://www.justice.gov/usao-ma/pr/fourth-foundation-resolves-allegations-it-conspired-pharmaceutical-companies-pay.

231 *GoodRx:* https://www.goodrx.com/.

233 *Blink Health:* https://www.blinkhealth.com/.

233 *FamilyWize:* https://familywize.org/.

233 *WeRx:* https://werx.org/.

233 *HealthWarehouse:* https://www.healthwarehouse.com/.

234 *drug shopping test:* "Shop Around for Lower Drug Prices," *Consumer Reports*, April 5, 2018, https://www.consumerreports.org/drug-prices/shop-around-for-better-drug-prices/.

235 *PharmacyChecker.com:* https://www.pharmacychecker.com/.

235 *in a story:* "Shopping Abroad for Cheaper Medication? Here's What You Need to Know," *Kaiser Health News*, August 22, 2019, https://khn.org/news/shopping-abroad-for-cheaper-medication-heres-what-you-need-to-know/.

235 *Valisure:* https://www.valisure.com/.

235 *cipa.com:* http://www.cipa.com/.

Heroes VII: The Warrior Daughter Areta Buness

238 *erythema nodosum:* "Erythema Nodosum," Web MD, https://www.webmd.com/skin-problems-and-treatments/erythema-nodosum.

240 *autobiographical story:* "My Story of Perseverance: Indomitable Spirit," Stanford University Athletics, Stanford University, https://gostanford.com/feature/indomitablespirit.

Chapter 15: How to Fight Back

243 *2019 study:* "Claims Denials and Appeals in ACA Marketplace Plans," Kaiser Family Foundation, February 25, 2019, https://www.kff.org/report-section/claims-denials-and-appeals-in-aca-marketplace-plans-issue-brief/.

244 An American Sickness: Elisabeth Rosenthal, *An American Sickness: How Healthcare Became Big Business and How You Can Take It Back* (New York: Penguin Books, 2017), https://www.amazon.com/dp/B01IOHQ9LO/.

244 *Paying Till It Hurts:* "Paying Till It Hurts," *New York Times*, https://www.nytimes.com/interactive/2014/health/paying-till-it-hurts.html.

244 *a 2017 piece:* "Those Indecipherable Medical Bills? They're One Reason Health Care Costs So Much," *New York Times Magazine*, March 29, 2017, https://www.nytimes.com/2017/03/29/magazine /those-indecipherable-medical-bills-theyre-one-reason-health-care -costs-so-much.html.

245 *Alliance of Claims Assistance Professionals:* https://www.claims.org/.

247 *Medicare's prices for outpatient surgeries:* "Procedure Price Lookup," Medicare.gov, U.S. Centers for Medicare & Medicaid Services, https://www.medicare.gov/procedure-price-lookup/.

249 *ClinicalTrials.gov:* ClinicalTrials.gov, U.S. National Library of Medicine, U.S. National Institutes of Health, U.S. Department of Health and Human Services, https://clinicaltrials.gov/ct2/home.

250 *related educational materials:* "Learn About Clinical Studies," Clinical Trials.gov, U.S. National Library of Medicine, U.S. National Institutes of Health, U.S. Department of Health and Human Services, https://clinicaltrials.gov/ct2/about-studies/learn.

250 *Project Patient Voice:* U.S. Food and Drug Administration, https:// www.fda.gov/about-fda/oncology-center-excellence/project-patient -voice.

250 *reported:* "FDA and NIH Let Clinical Trial Sponsors Keep Results Secret and Break the Law," *Science*, January 13, 2020, https://www. sciencemag.org/news/2020/01/fda-and-nih-let-clinical-trial-spon sors-keep-results-secret-and-break-law.

250 *National Financial Resource Directory:* https://www.patientadvocate.org /explore-our-resources/national-financial-resource-directory/.

250 *AllTrials.net:* https://www.alltrials.net/.

250 *a website:* "Who's Sharing Their Clinical Trial Results?" FDAAA Trials Tracker, https://fdaaa.trialstracker.net/.

251 *cancer patients who filed for bankruptcy:* "Financial Insolvency as a Risk Factor for Early Mortality Among Patients with Cancer," *Journal of Clinical Oncology*, 2016, https://www.ncbi.nlm.nih.gov/pmc/articles /PMC4933128/.

251 *sweeping study:* "Death or Debt? National Estimates of Financial Toxicity in Persons with Newly-Diagnosed Cancer," *American Journal*

of Medicine, June 12, 2018, https://www.amjmed.com/article/S0002
-9343(18)30509-6/pdf.

252   *National Foundation for Credit Counseling:* https://www.nfcc.org/.

252   *RIP Medical Debt:* https://ripmedicaldebt.org/.

252   *a list:* "Debt Resources," RIP Medical Debt, https://ripmedicaldebt
.org/debt-resources/.

253   *GoFundMe:* https://www.gofundme.com/.

253   New Yorker *article:* "The Hidden Cost of GoFundMe Health Care,"
New Yorker, July 1, 2019, https://www.newyorker.com/magazine
/2019/07/01/the-perverse-logic-of-gofundme-health-care.

254   *ProPublica:* "Health Care," ProPublica, https://www.propublica.org
/topics/healthcare.

254   *by Vox:* "Hospitals Kept ER Fees Secret. We Uncovered Them,"
Vox, https://www.vox.com/2018/2/27/16936638/er-bills-emergency
-room-hospital-fees-health-care-costs.

254   *"Bill of the Month":* "Bill of The Month," *Kaiser Health News*, https://
khn.org/news/tag/bill-of-the-month/.

254   *"Investigations":* "Investigations," *Kaiser Health News*, https://khn.org
/news/tag/investigation/.

255   *that article:* "Column: A 20-Year-Old Fights Back Against Her Health
Insurer," *PBS NewsHour*, https://www.pbs.org/newshour/health/col
umn-a-20-year-old-fights-back-against-her-health-insurer.

Chapter 16: When Consumers Make the Call

258   *spring 2020 article:* "Direct-to-Consumer Digital Health," *Lancet*, April
2020,   https://www.thelancet.com/journals/landig/article/PIIS2589
-7500(20)30057-1/fulltext.

258   *author Eric Topol:* Eric Topol, MD, *The Patient Will See You Now:
The Future of Medicine Is in Your Hands* (New York: Basic Books,
2016),   https://www.amazon.com/Patient-Will-See-You-Now/dp
/0465040020/.

258   *late 2019 report:* The Economic Consequences of Millennial Health, Moody's
Analytics for the Blue Cross Blue Shield Association, September 2019,
https://www.bcbs.com/sites/default/files/file-attachments/health-of
-america-report/HOA-Moodys-Millennial-10-30.pdf.

259   *Modernizing Medicine:* https://www.modmed.com/.

259   *Its findings:* "How Millennials Are Reshaping Healthcare's Future," KaufmanHall, 2019, https://www.kaufmanhall.com/ideas-resources /ebook/how-millennials-are-reshaping-healthcares-future.

260   *MDLIVE:* https://www.mdlive.com/.

260   *mid-2019 list of telehealth providers:* "275+ Telehealth Companies to Know | 2019," *Becker's Hospital Review,* June 28, 2019, https://www .beckershospitalreview.com/lists/275-telehealth-companies-to-know -2019.html.

260   *Amwell:* https://business.amwell.com/.

260   *Doctor on Demand:* https://www.doctorondemand.com/.

260   *HeyDoctor:* https://www.heydoctor.com/.

260   *Teladoc:* https://www.teladoc.com/.

261   *One Medical:* https://www.onemedical.com/.

262   *Bind:* https://www.yourbind.com/.

266   *investing a billion dollars*: "Walgreens to Open Doctors' Offices at Its U.S. Stores," *Wall Street Journal,* July 8, 2020, https://www.wsj .com/articles/walgreens-to-open-doctors-offices-at-its-u-s-stores -11594209601.

266   *extensive list:* "Services," Minute Clinic, CVS Pharmacy, CVS, https:// www.cvs.com/minuteclinic/services.

268   *summary of prices:* "Summarized Pricing List for Dallas, GA Store #3403," https://corporate.walmart.com/media-library/document/walmart -health-center-summarized-pricing-list/_proxyDocument?id=0000016d -26f0-da5a-ab7d-26fb9d760000.

270   *Patient Rights Advocate:* https://www.patientrightsadvocate.org/.

INDEX

Page numbers in *italics* refer to tables and charts.